The Lure of Neptune

Studies in Maritime History

William N. Still, Jr.
General Editor

The Lure of Neptune

German-Soviet Naval Collaboration and Ambitions, 1919–1941

Tobias R. Philbin III

University of South Carolina Press

Copyright © 1994 University of South Carolina
Published in Columbia, South Carolina, by the
University of South Carolina Press
Manufactured in the United States of America

Library of Congress Cataloging-in-Publication Data

Philbin, Tobias R.
The lure of Neptune : German-Soviet naval collaboration and
ambitions, 1919–1941 / by Tobias R. Philbin, III.
p.   cm. — (Studies in maritime history)
Includes bibliographical references and index.
Contents: Background and context: Soviet-German relations — The
national canvas for naval issues — Navy to navy: coexistence and
interface — Navy to navy: competition — Nazi-Soviet naval
relations — The naval dimension of the Hitler-Stalin pact —
Operations — Basis nord — Cruiser "L": from Germany with reticence
— Submarines and merchant cruisers — Conclusion.
ISBN 0–87249–992–8
1. Sea-power—Germany.   2. Sea-power—Soviet Union.   3. Germany—
Military relations—Soviet Union.   4. Soviet Union—Military
relations—Germany.   5. World War, 1939–1945—Naval operations,
German.   6. World War, 1939–1945—Naval operations, Soviet.
I. Title.   II. Series.
VA513.P45   1994
359'.00943'09041—dc20   94–3207

The Dream of World Empire

Their strength lay in the greatness of their navy,
and by that and that alone they gained their empire.
—Alcibiades of the Athenians
415 B.C.

To Mary Baker-Philbin and Joan Linda Philbin—
the most important people, after all.

Contents

Illustrations

Preface

Germany is again united, with the blessing of its old enemies. In July 1990 the Soviet journal *International Affairs* published the first documents from the Soviet side on "Soviet-German Military Cooperation, 1920–1930." These, and others from the Ministry of Defense, the Soviet navy, and the Ministry of Shipbuilding, have helped significantly in clarifying some points in this book, especially in chapter 1.[1]

The writing of history after World War I has focused on the record of the war itself, not on interwar events. Also, the cold war has driven historians on both sides to focus *away* from events that might be politically difficult. Developments following World War II—the establishment of the North Atlantic Treaty Organization (NATO) and the creation of the Federal Republic of Germany (FRG) and the Bundeswehr—caused German postwar historians and former officers of the German navy to downplay cooperation with the Soviets and to emphasize the anti-Communist position of the navy from 1918. From 1919 to 1933 the historiography is mixed. The memoirs emerging from that time tend to be true apologia, and the overarching works tend to adhere to either Left or Right interpretations of a war, which was, after all, disastrous for the navy. Later interpretations of the period followed the wakes of their respective intellectual schools. Regarding the period 1933–45, Adolf Hitler was charged with Germany's military and diplomatic failures. On the other hand, the Soviets chose to avoid any discussion of their naval collaboration with Fascist Germany. Only recently have they been willing to provide details and interpretations of Stalin's errors in foreign and military policies.

This study investigates German and Soviet naval activities in the interwar period and is intended to illuminate Soviet and German naval intentions and interface vis-à-vis their defense policies and political systems. In particular, Stalin's ambitions for naval power and his strategy for building Soviet military power and his evaluation of Hitler and German policies during the period 1933–41 can be appreciated from a new perspective. The analysis presented here represents a bridge between the disciplines of

German and Soviet/Russian naval and military history as contained in the pioneering works of Jost Dülffer, Michael Salewski, and Gerhard Schreiber for the Germans and John Erickson and Robert W. Herrick for the Soviets.[2] It is possible that the study of Soviet/Russian naval history will be to the twenty-first century what the 1970s and 1980s were to German naval history. Post–cold war German naval historiography may also provide new interpretations and perhaps a new biography or two of key naval policymakers.

Also, there needs to be further investigation into the strategic mission of Stalin's fleet and his plan for a navy that exceeded the German 1939 "Z" plan. Both Hitler and Stalin were obsessed by the battleship. Further examination of British views of Soviet-German relations might yield new insights into British military and diplomatic activities during this period. The synergy between German planning and actions and Soviet naval policy in the 1920s and 1930s, in particular the Soviet appreciation of lessons learned from the German naval experience, clearly emerges as a lesson from this study.

The Soviet-German naval agreements in 1939 and 1940 were important for German naval operations. The oil provided by the Soviets essentially fueled German naval operations in 1939–40, and German naval technology ultimately contributed to Stalin's knowledge of German strengths and weaknesses. The Soviets provided a base (Basis Nord) to support German U-boat and commerce raiding during this period, and this base was an important, if transitory, symbol of German-Soviet naval cooperation. The relationship was not critical to Germany's successful Norwegian campaign or operations in northern waters. It demonstrated, however, salient issues in the Soviets' handling of foreigners and the complexity of the Stalin/Soviet state.

In writing this book, significant developments in the scholarship of this period seem potentially congruent; the post-1970 interpretations of the development of German sea power in the twentieth century and the analysis of Soviet naval power, which was delayed by World War II, finally occurred with the post–World War II Soviet blue-water navy.

The relationship between the former enemies has returned to that of "valued economic partner" in a "common European home." It is very probable that Germany will play an extremely significant role in the reconstruction of Russia's post-Communist economy. There can also be no doubt that military relationships are a subset of the political economic relations. In the final analysis the Soviet-German naval relationship was *not* as warm or extensive as that between the Reichswehr and the Red Army from 1919 to 1933, even during the height of the Hitler-Stalin Pact, from 1939 to 1941.

The course of Soviet-German naval relations from 1919 to 1941 mirrored the political climate in both countries and the diplomatic relations between them. The time covered falls into three periods. In the first period the Soviets and the Germans faced common isolation. In the second, 1933 to 1939, Hitler did his best to isolate the USSR. Finally, the third, 1939–41, saw an uneasy detente between Hitler and Stalin and their regimes. Both states suffered political isolation of one degree or another for two decades after the World War I. The rise of Hitler to power made conflict between Soviet Russia and Germany inevitable. Events were to demonstrate Hitler's consistency in his views and plans for Russia from as far back as the early 1920s. "The present rulers of Russia have no idea of honorably entering into an alliance, let alone observing one . . . and you do not make pacts with anyone whose sole interest is the destruction of his partner. . . . In Russian bolshevism we must see the attempt undertaken to achieve world domination."[3]

Stalin believed he could manage Hitler's visceral hatred; moreover, he desired greater knowledge and power, which the more advanced technology of Germany promised for his own war machine. At the Eighteenth Party Congress in 1939 held just prior to the signing of the pact, Stalin approved a vast expansion of the Soviet military as a whole and the navy in particular. Stalin directed the navy to view the world as one in which the democracies were plotting to involve the Soviet Union in a war with Germany which would exhaust both nations. Nevertheless, Stalin's own troops, who were not prepared for the Molotov-Ribbentrop Pact of 23 August 1939, were less sanguine and thought "the Pact would lead to No Good and in the end Hitler would cheat Stalin."[4]

The specific political documents describing the ultimate mission of Stalin's high seas fleet have not yet surfaced. However, the complete reprioritization of resources inside the former Soviet Union has now shown that the Russians believe that attempting to build a fleet for global naval supremacy was a mistake, and the whole policy and its origins are now areas of legitimate historical inquiry. The September 1988 issue of *Morskoy sbornik* was the first publication to open this path of intellectual inquiry in the last years of the former Soviet Union. A second edition of the authoritative *Sovetskaya voyennaya entsiklopediya* was to be issued from 1991 to 1996. According to the new head of the Soviet navy's editorial commission, Vice Admiral A. Sarkisov:

> Many important matters did not receive proper elucidation in the first edition. For instance, in my opinion, insufficient attention was devoted to the problem of a balanced build-up of the Soviet armed forces, in particular, the Navy. Neither is there a

basis for hiding miscalculations made at the time. At the 18th
Party Congress in Spring 1939 Stalin publically underlined the
necessity of building an oceangoing fleet. Even then it had become clear that the USSR navy was substantially inferior to
the naval forces of National Socialist Germany and its allies.
But instead of a scientific approach to the matter of further
development of the Soviet fleet, the administrative style pre-
vailed. Large resources and funds were invested in building
several battleships which they did not have time to finish before the start of the war.[5]

The Soviets have subsequently specified the exact numbers of battleships begun (four), but the numbers planned (fifteen battleships and fifteen
battle cruisers) exceeded the German Z Plan of some dozen or so very
powerful battleships. Hitler and Stalin's dreams of world dominion both
entailed large navies. Hitler needed Soviet raw materials and fuel for his
navy, cut off as he assumed he would be in the first stage of his Continental war.[6]

Hitler's dreams have been known in outline and detail for decades, but
it was the pioneering work of Gerhard Schreiber in 1978 which placed
them in appropriate naval political context. Schreiber's work *Revisionismus
und Weltmachtstreben* not only clearly documented the continuity of the
Imperial Navy's ambitions for a Weltflotte (Global Fleet) but revealed
the navy's "affinity for fascism," which facilitated its accommodation, or
Gleichschaltung (coordination), with Hitler and the Nazi state.[7] Schreiber's
further analysis of the German navy's *Seemacht* (Seapower) doctrine paral-
lels the ambitions of Stalin and the Soviets for a navy second to none
and an instrument of national power capable of projecting power on a
global basis.[8]

On the German side of this issue additional insight into the complexity
of Soviet-German military and naval relations has emerged. Among other
things, current revisionist scholarship has begun to provide a distinctly
less benign picture of German navy commander in chief, Grand Admiral
Erich Raeder. In the 1930s we have a clearly Russophile, anti-Communist,
navalist building his big-ship navy for his führer.[9] In postwar defeat Raeder
emerges as a man who may have cooperated to some extent to enhance his
position with his Soviet captors. Time may yet provide the records of
Raeder's extensive interrogations by the Soviets after World War II.
Raeder may have been led to believe that he would find his Russian captors
more genial than the Western allies. The Western allies had felt the sting
of his naval war machine and were aware of his duplicity regarding treaties.
He may have thought that the Russians would be more receptive because

of his knowledge of Russian and his extensive research and publications on Russian naval history. With an eye to the future Raeder probably also believed his known opposition to *Barbarossa*, which he carefully documented in the naval war diary, might endear him to the Soviets.

Nevertheless, Raeder was as surprised by the temporary accommodation with the Soviets in 1939 as was his service. Indeed, Hitler had a section of *Mein Kampf* dedicated to the naval issue[10] and had grasped the technical truism that ships had to be built which were individually more powerful than *any* English counterpart. Nevertheless, political expediency had caused the führer to depart from his doctrine on occasion. Hitler's naval policy was a repudiation of the "cost-effective" building policies of Grand Admiral von Tirpitz, whose legacy was a lost naval war. Hitler did not intend to lose his struggle for world power and up until the Polish campaign had given the navy primacy of place in capital expenditures.[11] Indeed, the German navy was never at ease with either the political or military relationship engineered by Ribbentrop nor convinced that the relationship would last. The early historiography on the German navy of the Hitler era indicates that the Germans wished to present a picture of an apolitical navy, a navy that would, therefore, be at some distance from national socialism. It was such an image that German historians and naval officers wished to foster in the immediate postwar period.[12]

The Soviets, for their part, did not wish to deal with the issues either, even in the period of de-Stalinization. In his memoirs (1964 version and to a lesser degree the 1966 version) former commander in chief of the Soviet navy, Fleet Admiral N. G. Kuznetzov, does not treat in detail the German-Soviet naval cooperation. Kuznetzov attempted to diminish the German-Soviet naval relationship by characterizing the German naval attaché to Moscow as a "has-been," implying that the Soviets, at least, regarded his efforts as dismissive. There is, however, another version, published in 1990, which includes a comprehensive treatment of many sensitive issues, except the subject of this work. It is part of a general trend which shows up in the many other new Soviet articles. Brezhnev-era Soviet authors, however, who were stridently advocating the virtues of World War II victory, and busily justifying their Soviet Weltflotte again, did not want to admit any political cooperation with a Germany commonly believed to aspire to world dominion or any dependence on German military technology. They certainly could not comfortably admit that a period of "ideological detente" had occurred with Nazi Germany. To do so would have implied the Soviet political apparat and the Soviet military had collaborated in some way with the Nazis.

Specifically, Fleet Admiral S. G. Gorshkov's *Sea Power of the State*, often cited public justification of the Brezhnev-era Soviet high-seas fleet, its intellectual successor *The Navy*, and N. G. Kuznetzov's serialized memoirs *Before the War*, which appeared in the last gasp of the Khrushchev-era thaw, all dealt with the issue of German naval activity in a somewhat oblique way.[13] *Before the War*, the serialized English-language version of *Nakanune*, deals only indirectly with the major developments in the German navy and limits itself to the dismissive evaluation of the German naval attaché. Kuznetzov does describe the Soviet naval buildup in some detail. Gorshkov's two volumes establish a historical record that includes some assessment of German naval developments. The Gorshkov works were designed to support (*Sea Power of the State*) and preserve (*The Navy*) the massive resource allocations that resulted in the massive growth of the Soviet fleet of the mid-1980s. Neither addresses the 1939–41 Soviet-German naval relationship.

To his credit Admiral Kuznetzov harbored no illusions about the Germans or their navy. In August 1940 he suspected the German fleet was to be the enemy, noting "our defenses in the Gulf of Finland were patterned on those of World War I, but we had a weak spot—a point on which the mine position [defensive minefields] was pivoted in World War I belonged to Finland . . . it became obvious in the event of war with Germany, Finland would side with her." This view, of course, reflected the military concerns about Finland held by the Soviet high command which may have led to the Winter War as much as any ideological concerns. More important, though, Kuznetzov was reflecting a suspicion of German naval motives which dated back to 1928: "We should be particularly cautious in naval matters, sabotaging cooperation with them and reducing it in the main to sending our people here, securing blueprints and so on. Under no circumstances should we admit their specialists to our naval system for a long time. The only thing we may offer them is our waters for submarine training and tests in their ships manned in part by us."[14] With little modification this was the policy the Soviets followed in dealing with the German navy until 22 June 1941. It explains much of the behavior that is chronicled here.

In the West, scholarship has placed Soviet-German naval relations in the context of German and Soviet domestic and foreign policies that found their expression in the Molotov-Ribbentrop Pact. Soviet-German military relations in their naval subset play yet more light on Stalin's persona. The record of the 1939–40 Soviet-German negotiations shows that Stalin was technically knowledgeable on naval issues. Soviet-German naval relations represent (1919–41) an opportunity to fill in the blanks between the wars and to answer some questions about the Soviet-German naval race of the 1930s. Finally, intellectual revisionism has begun on both sides to reexamine the political, military, and naval aspects of the Soviet-German relationship.

This work is arranged in three parts. The first covers the period from 1919 to 1939 and its many technical and political developments, which affected the two navies and their respective countries. The purpose is to provide political, military, and naval context for what follows. It also addresses ambitions, delusions, and realities that beset both navies prior to World War II. The second part deals with the record of what the Soviets and the Germans expected of each other in the political and military agreements of 1939–41 as well as the navy-to-navy relationship. Both sides were unrealistic about what they might derive from the relationship. The third part covers events arising from the agreements laid out in the previous part. It is a chronicle of the reality of the relationship. It includes a detailed discussion of the German floating base on the Kola Peninsula outside Murmansk (including the latest published view from the Soviet side), the transfer of the heavy cruiser *Lützow* to the Soviet Union, and an account of other naval operations such as the use of the northern sea route from Scandinavia to the Pacific.

This is a case study of how a hostile geopolitical environment may drive two powers together despite mutually hostile doctrines and interests. The Soviets delivered hundreds of millions of dollars worth of raw materials to the German war machine. The Germans, for their part, provided much naval technology in return for fuel and raw materials.[15] They also served Soviet interests by damaging Western and particularly British capitalism.

Analysis and examination of archival sources indicate that the Germans could not have carried on their campaigns against Western Europe and the naval campaign against Britain in 1939 and early 1940 without the Soviet fuel and material support. The 900,000 tons of fuel oil supplied to Germany represented the approximate total German naval usage during 1939–40.[16] Other significant aspects of the relationship include the transfer of a heavy cruiser, plans for the *Bismarck*, heavy naval gun designs, and finally the probable delivery of large-caliber guns for Stalin's battle cruisers.

Establishing a base to support U-boat and pocket battleship operations from outside the normal German naval locus of the Baltic Sea indicates the degree to which Stalin was willing to sacrifice long-term Soviet interests for short-term tactical gains and, as a by-product, advance German war aims. Much to Stalin's regret, those war aims expanded rapidly with the unexpected German military success early in the war. The Soviets were very surprised and discomfited by the German success in Norway and later France. This success made a U-boat base in Russia tactically and strategically redundant. That redundancy made the base politically useless for Stalin.

It also eliminated the base as a strategic solution to a long German debate on how they would break out of the North Sea—Adolf Hitler solved the problem by providing the German navy with its French and Norwegian bases and eliminated the need for a Soviet operational base. Nevertheless, despite the fact that the base at Zapadnaya Litza on the Kola Peninsula was not used to any great extent, the Soviets appear to have intended to live up to their obligations, as the new Soviet material in chapter 3 and chapter 5 indicates. Further, they did clear the heavy cruiser *Hipper* twice for fueling from the base, though the ship did not have to avail itself of the facility. One area that clearly suggests itself to further study is the view the British took of this warming relationship and its operational implications for them.

The Russo-Finnish War came very close to involving the British against the Soviet Union. It also severely strained the German commitment to the Soviets. Italy supported the Finns and, for a while, was in common cause with the British. The whole diplomatic fallout from the pact and its naval codicils adversely affected German-Italian relations because of the Finnish issue. Nevertheless, Hitler and Ribbentrop were determined that Finnish interests could be sacrificed for the short-term gains that detente with the USSR provided. The Soviet-German naval relationship supported political objectives while providing some positive benefits for the Germans. Hitler wanted to exclude French and British influence in the USSR; he wanted to fight the USSR on his own terms and in a one-front campaign. The relationship, however, logistically supported the Germans' pursuit of the war against France and England from 1939 to 1941. In turn, success in the West allowed the Germans to conduct a one-front land war against the USSR from 1941 to 1944, at terrible cost. Again glasnost has shown the West that the Soviet/Russian military has become aware of the costs that the pact extracted and that it now has a more balanced view of many of Stalin's deeds.

There are illustrations of the contradictory and complex relationship in the chapters that follow. Relations came about frequently as a subset of Soviet-German military relations. They were multifaceted and included base rights, technology transfer, and strategic gamesmanship. It was a relationship between two countries with differing social systems, antagonistic ideologies, and only unstable and fleeting common interests. The relationship might serve as a model for national behavior under circumstances in which external and internal factors dictated a foreign policy not very much to the liking of German or Russian leadership. The relationship between the two naval establishments is of interest because it underlines the limits of naval confraternity, or the concept that, since both institutions faced the power of a hostile politicostrategic environment and thousands of years of seafaring values, other larger issues ultimately decide the fate of any such confraternal relationship.

In the context of civil-military relations navies are representative national institutions and subject to political direction and performance criteria in totalitarian dictatorships as well as in democracies. Navies are highly visible entities that can constitute windows on the intentions of their states.

There is no doubt that the political and naval leadership of Russia and Germany were equally tempted by the lure of Neptune and his trident.

Acknowledgments

This book and its author owe much to many scholars and colleagues. Professors Bruce Watson, Joseph Gordon, William F. Scott, and Harriet Fast Scott provided initial inspiration and guidance for the original work, which was written in the last decade of the cold war. Professors Kenneth J. Hagan of the United States Naval Academy, William C. Green of Boston University, and Keith W. Bird of New Hampshire provided inspiration, assistance, and encouragement to see this through a succession of rewrites and revision. Professors Bird and Green were of great assistance in expanding the scope of the original work in an attempt to bridge German and Soviet naval history. Both made numerous suggestions and corrections. The University of South Carolina Press's thorough readers have also helped. The fine maps and graphics are the work of GEOGRAFIK Design Group Inc. of Alexandria, Virginia. I would also like to express thanks to Ms. Pat Lanzara, whose brilliant decryption abilities enabled her to produce consistently superior manuscripts. Any faults the work may have are the author's.

The Lure of Neptune

Part One

Background and Context
Soviet-German Relations, 1917–1939

Chapter One

The National Canvas for Naval Issues

Germany and Russia

Russian relations with Germany have always been characterized by a high degree of contradiction. As Ronald Hingley says, they "probably cut deeper than those with any other European power." Russo-German naval relations are interesting in that they reveal to some extent the national caricatures and display the contrasts that Lord Curzon once described as "the overwhelming antithesis between German and Russian character, the one diligent, uncompromising, stiff, precise, the other sleeps [sic], nonchalant, wasteful and lax."[1] Further, every now and then, from the time Alexander Nevsky defeated the Teutonic Knights on Lake Peipus to the days of the Warsaw Pact, Germany has been branded as enemy Par Excellence.[2]

The themes of this work follow a common military context between the Germans and the Soviets. There is no question German-Russian relations remain central to the Russo-Western relations today. The record of "naval relations" exists in a political and ideological context. Sources include records of the German naval attaché to Moscow and World War II analysis done by the German naval staff and later, by former German officers, for the Allied powers after Germany's defeat in World War II. Not surprisingly, the postwar analysis by former German officers does not cover in any depth the earlier political-military context.[3] The postwar analysis is an appreciation of what the Germans thought as well as a chronicle. It supports Walter Laqueur's assertion that: "What Russians and Germans thought about each other, their civilization, ways of life and political systems mattered much more than all the diplomatic reports."[4]

Rapallo, the Reichswehr, the Navy, and Soviet Internal Policies

The noted Russian military scholar John Erikson's view that "the German Navy was at least as willing as the Army to find ways to circumvent the [Versailles] treaty" was and is valid.[5] Soviet concerns were driven by the larger German-Soviet military relationship, which had its origins in the outcome of the kaiser's eastern front war. Three important factors were Germany's stillborn victory and "iron peace" imposed by the Treaty of Brest Litovsk in March 1918 and, specifically, its slightly less onerous protocol of 29 August 1918. Having sent Lenin into Russia to bring down the provisional government, the German military dictatorship of 1917–18 exercised the antithesis of enlightened self-interest in inflicting a treaty that deprived Russia of more than a third of its territory, populace, industry, food sources, and almost everything else of value. Ironically, the Allied intervention of 1918 gave the Soviets common cause, albeit transitory, with the hated German imperialists. As a recently published Soviet perspective notes, "prior to the conclusion of the Soviet-German Treaty in Rapallo on 16 April 1922 Soviet Russia and Germany were in a comparable international situation." Both countries found themselves in foreign political isolation and were outside the Great Powers "club" for a time. The Soviets had several reasons to end the isolation, as did the Germans. The Soviets credit General Hans von Seeckt, commander in chief of the Reichswehr, and Leon Trotsky, while he was still chairman of the Soviet Revolutionary Council (RMC), as responsible for the military aspects of the Rapallo Treaty. This treaty provided the political chapeau for military intercourse with foreign nations which developed in the following decade.

It now appears that both the Soviets and the Germans were more interested in ground and aviation cooperation than naval operations or lessons. Soviet policy was driven by: (1) military necessity that land forces get priority in their first five-year program; (2) the deep distrust driven from the discussions by the early postwar relationship between Soviet Russia and Germany; and (3) a distrust of German naval objectives.

Germany had only the Communist menace to play to the Allies in the confused months of late 1918 and early 1919. The Paris Peace Conference at Versailles showed how limited this approach was, however, and left Germany with an army of only 100,000 people without tanks, aircraft, or heavy artillery and a minuscule navy of obsolete warships, with no submarines and no aircraft.[6]

The military and naval relationship between the USSR and Germany had its origins in conflict: the Germans were deep in Russian territory. Fifty-eight divisions and thirteen brigades were fully prepared to advance to Petersburg. At the point of these bayonets the Soviets signed the Brest-Litovsk Accords of 3 March 1918.[7] Soviet difficulties in trusting any German authority had their origin in this paradigm shift. Soviet appeals to the Allies proved unfruitful, thus dealing the new revolutionaries a harsh lesson in realpolitik, of which many more were to be administered in the course of the Russian Civil War. The Imperial German Navy hoped to acquire by guile or force of arms such Russian ships that were of any combat value. The Germans, in fact, actually took over the *Imperatsiya Maria* dreadnought in the Black Sea, renaming it *Volga*. The German acquisitions were inconsequential to the balance of naval power for the Central Powers with the Allies. Ironically, the first and most successful Soviet naval movement after the October Revolution was the movement of ships of the Baltic fleet from Helsingfors to the naval base in Kronstadt. Subsequent Soviet Baltic naval operations were aimed, after the German armistice in 1918, against British naval operations in the Baltic. In the Black Sea the Russian units were largely scuttled in an attempt at preventing the aforementioned German takeovers. The 27 August 1918 Protocol to Brest Litovsk, negotiated by Bolshevik foreign minister Chicherin, took the German disasters on the western front into account. Any possible collaboration between the German naval authorities and the embryonic Soviet fleet in the immediate postarmistice period was doomed by military anarchy in both old imperial services.

In 1919 military anarchy in both countries was supplanted by a combination of German revanchism and naval revolt in Russia. This was manifest in the abortive Kapp Putsch in Germany and in the Kronstadt rebellion in Russia.[8] The consequences for the Red Navy were severe. The Baltic Sea fleet Russian sailors who had led the October Revolution for Lenin rebelled against what they saw as a betrayal of the Soviet ideal by Lenin and his followers. The rebellion retarded the reconstruction of the Soviet Baltic fleet because of its political reliability as well as technical difficulties until the mid-1920s.[9] The Reichswehr indirectly assisted the Russians in the 1920 battles around Warsaw, through benevolent neutrality.[10] Throughout the 1919–20 period the Reichswehr ground force and its various associated illegal auxiliaries were still faced with serious difficulties in guaranteeing the integrity of the old German-Russian frontier.[11] In fact, General von Seeckt, whose appointment as head of the Reichswehr was judged by E. H. Carr as a victory for those who believed in the traditional German-Russian alliance, believed the situation could be salvaged by an agreement with, rather than destruction of, the Communists. Seeckt also thought by late July 1920 that Soviet victory in Poland was likely. The German foreign office was also acting in the context of the series of diplomatic exchanges between Berlin and Moscow toward the repatriation of German and Russian prisoners of war (POWs). Ultimately, however, there appears to have been no collusion between Germans and Soviets in a German "war of revenge" on Poland, although Poland figured prominently in the military planning of both powers.[12] At its earliest stages the Soviet-German military relationship was, to say the least, fluid.

At this stage Soviet-German military cooperation was appropriate from a Bolshevik point of view: the existence of wartime conditions were favorable to revolution in Germany. Indeed, in Eastern and Central Europe the traditional order had all but collapsed; the Communists believed Germany showed "brilliant revolutionary prospects."[13] The British and French made demarches to the Soviets on their expansion of naval military operations to areas in the undefined border areas between Russia and Germany. The victorious Allied Powers considered those areas Polish and were willing to provide the Germans increased military flexibility in any confrontation with the Bolshevik menace. The Germans were willing to deal with the new Soviet/Russian state and its armies for foreign policy reasons, as it gave them some negotiating flexibility with the Allies. Ironically, there was danger from Poland to both Germany and Russia, and this motivated the early German-Soviet military condominion in the early 1920s.

German domestic politics, however, were about to endure the abortive Kapp Putsch in March 1920. This seizure of power in March 1920 by several right-wing political elements was led by Wolfgang Kapp, a senior east Prussian official and General Walter von Lüttwitz, commander of Army Group Command I and "de facto commander of all field forces in Germany." It also included the 15,000-man naval Erhardt Brigade, which was unwilling to disband in accordance with the terms of the Versailles Treaty. The government of Friedrich Ebert and Gustav Bauer fled first to Munich and then to Stuttgart. When Vice-Chancellor Schiffer could not negotiate a solution with Kapp and Erhardt's troops, the Republican government called a general strike, and Kapp occupied only empty buildings. The Reichswehr and its leadership were as neutral in support of the putsch as they were in support of the government. As Wallace Lewis puts it, "There was one small group that immediately joined the *putsch*. That was the small struggling *Reichsmarine*."[14] This resulted in disgrace and dismissal for right-wing former imperial military and naval elements, including Admiral Adolph von Trotha, navy commander in chief, who were prominently involved. Trotha's chief of staff, then Captain Erich Raeder, is alleged to have been the real *spiritus rector* in the admiralty support of the Kapp Putsch.[15] Thus, the German naval officer corps was ironically in similar political straits to the revolutionaries at Kronstadt who also suffered defeat. Fortunately for the German navy's future, the leaders of the Weimar Republic were considerably less brutal than the *Cheka*. Both navies were thus the targets of political opprobrium.

By the end of 1920 the Soviet-German relationship was founded on a political dictum from Lenin that it was vital for the new Soviet state to come a working understanding with the German bourgeoisie.[16] Even so, "the Soviets continued to see Germany through a haze of ideological preconceptions . . . as the European country most ripe for revolution."[17] The

Soviets manifested Lenin's policy in the ratification of the prisoner of war exchanges in May 1920.

Having been cut off by the strictures of Versailles from a westward-looking foreign policy, Germany's desire to look east was obvious. Moscow and Berlin, regardless of the lack of native German Bolshevik success in the stillborn revolution of 1918, had to look to common interests, especially after the Soviet defeat in Poland in 1920: "the lessons of the Soviet-Polish war were not forgotten in either Moscow or Berlin and cleared the way which eventually led to the treaty of Rapallo."[18]

On 16 April 1922 Germany and the Soviet Union signed the Treaty of Rapallo. Article 1 vacated any and all claims by either side regarding losses sustained because of World War I, thus negating the effect of article 116 of the Versailles Treaty, which had been designed to resolve such issues completely in Russia's favor. Articles 3 and 5 restored diplomatic relations and provided a structure to reconstruct economic relations between the two countries.[19] The Versailles ring was broken. Between 1922 and 1926 several events bearing on the relationship transpired, both inside Germany and the Soviet Union.

Despite political accommodation elements of distrust persisted, including suspicion of German naval objectives in the Baltic, German interests in Finland, the Soviet perception of a pro-British orientation of the Reichsmarine and the implication for global power position in the future which such a positive relationship would imply. Indeed, the German navy and Erich Raeder, its principal post–World War I architect, were not only anti-Communist; they were also latently possessed of elements of Nazi ideology which pointed clearly to world dominion. Ultimately, there was no room for allies in Hitler's pantheon or that of his navy.

Despite conflicting ideologies, a determined effort was made by Bolshevik and German socialist factions to place Soviet-German relations successfully in economic and political accommodation.[20] Even in this period of politically warm Soviet-German relations the German navy saw the Communists as an ideological enemy and generally did not participate as much as the army in the otherwise significant military trafficking with Soviet Russia. They never supported the national policy of accommodation with Soviet Russia.

The German Navy between Rapallo and Hitler

In Germany the navy was undergoing the trauma of having to defend itself against the Rightist politicians, who accused it of being the source of revolution and the events that caused the collapse of 1918 as well as its unfulfilled promises in war. At the same time the Left were hostile to the navy. Its members noted its failure to the republic and its support for the Kapp Putsch. They were very suspicious of an unrepentant imperialist naval officer corps that longed for a national return to enthusiasm for seapower. The navy's remnants had terrible internal morale problems, funding problems, and a stigma of defeat and surrender. Events seem to have demonstrated that the navy's prewar political and military justifications were involved. Germany's national strategy should have dictated that the bulk of defense monies go to the ground forces. The situation was even more pressing in the 1920s, when defense was severely limited. The navy was left with a single squadron of eight obsolete pre-dreadnought battleships, a squadron of hopelessly outdated cruisers, and two flotillas of destroyers. The navy was denied submarines or aircraft by the Versailles Treaty. It was barely able to promise, much less provide, defense of the German North Sea and Baltic Sea frontiers. Of the ships allowed to the German navy of 1920–26 only about 60 percent operated at any one time, and only the light cruiser *Emden*, laid down in 1921, joined the fleet in 1925 as a badly needed replacement.

The behavior of the German naval officer corps in the 1920s did not serve to endear itself to the German political center, much less with the German left wing. In addition to Kapp Putsch the German navy made significant overt and clandestine efforts to blame the mutinies of 1917 and 1918 on the German socialist parties and, of course, the Communists. After the war German naval-political strategy concentrated on a corpswide effort to resell the navy as a vitally needed instrument of German national power—*Seegeltung* (Sea Power). Beyond this the characterizations of the German sea service as "Weimar's virulently reactionary Navy appear justified."[21] Indeed, the question that arises is how, if the German naval political attitudes were so far from the Soviets, was any cooperation at all possible?

The answer has at least three dimensions. The first is the congruence of interest between the Soviets and the Germans in avoiding international isolation for political, strategic, and economic reasons; the second is the subordination of the German navy to General Hans von Seeckt's War Ministry; and the third is the desire of the navy itself to somehow circumvent the Versailles restrictions. If the Soviets were willing to help, so much the better.

Chapter Two

Navy to Navy
Coexistence and Interface, 1920–1933

Defining Coexistence and Interface

It is an irony of history that two navies that were so ideologically incompatible coexisted and even worked together for a time. Between 1920 and 1933 the relationship between the two navies was driven by a different, slightly more benign political paradigm than the period 1933–39, and yet a third set of circumstances obtained from 1939 to 1941. Domestic political concerns and national strategies of Germany and Russia drove both services toward similar objectives from 1929 to 1933. There was political "coventry" for both—national reconstruction and international political isolation. The modern term *interface* is used because it captures juxtaposition, opposition, and communication, which in the author's view describes what actually happened.

The Soviet Navy of the 1920s:
Ambitions and Reality

The Soviet navy during this period was in worse condition than the Reichsmarine. Most of the czarist ships had either been sunk by their own crews or rendered ineffective by neglect. The czarist crews were scattered throughout Soviet service, dead, or imprisoned. The Soviet navy itself was under the political cloud of mutiny at Kronstadt in March 1921. Like its German cousin, the Soviet navy found itself in trouble over a mutiny and its loyalty to its government questioned—but for totally different reasons: the Russian navy's part in the 1917 revolution was unquestioned and critical, the German navy's part in the German revolution was stillborn and indeed blameworthy and suspect by the right wing in Germany; at the same time, the postwar German navy was held in contempt by the Left because of its refusal to admit military defeat and its continued adherence to an outdated monarchist ideology.

From an operational standpoint it took until the summer of 1923 for the Soviet navy to obtain enough supplies to make repairs and conduct training exercises in the Baltic Sea. According to Soviet sources, the Frunze Military Reforms of 1924 included provisions "for the regular supply of the military forces as well as an orderly, if exceedingly modest program of replacing military equipment including ships."[1] The Soviets actually had one battleship, eight destroyers, and a small number of submarines authorized for service in the Baltic. These were backed up by extensive mine fields and new batteries of heavy guns ashore. The Soviets realistically understood the limits on national resources for a navy whose nation had been devastated by seven years of war and its initial associated economic mismanagement, characterized by the early Bolsheviks as "war communism." The Soviet defense commissar Klement V. Voroshilov, following Trotsky's lead, threw cold water on any schemes of large-scale shipbuilding which would satisfy the "old-school strategy still in vogue in Soviet naval war colleges in the 1920s."[2] When the first approaches were made to the Soviet navy by a German navy dragooned into the German general staff dealings in 1926, the Soviet navy was being given, according to its commissar, "only that which is essential to defend our country from surprise attack."[3]

Early Soviet-German Naval Interface

Indeed, the same was true of the German fleet in 1926. Admiral Paul Behncke, who had commanded the leading Third Battle Squadron in *SMS König* at Jutland, assumed command of the German navy after Admiral von Trotha's resignation in the aftermath of the Kapp Putsch. He succeeded in organizing the few ships left for the Germans and under the army/navy bill of 1921 subsequently managed to get the German navy to sea again——as Raeder notes, "German naval ships were making foreign cruises again."[4] Behncke was replaced by Admiral Karl Adolf Zenker, who had a superb combat record commanding the battle cruiser *von der Tann* during World War I. The evolution of the German navy from draftee to an all-volunteer force under the Versailles Treaty allowed a thorough purge of left-wing elements as well as attracted some very talented people.

Despite the political background and attendant institutional hostilities, German naval records do contain records of certain "transactions of interest to the German and Soviet Navy."[5] Among the more interesting appear to have been meetings between Soviet representatives on the one hand and the German Communist Karl Radek, functioning as a "friend in court" for the Bolsheviks, and Colonel Max Bauer,[6] late of the Oberste Heeres Leitung (OHL [German Army High Command]), Operations Department II, in 1917 and 1918, and a key figure among the more reactionary elements of the German military ("We always have our machine guns!"). Bauer was also a Ludendorff partisan and an early and effective advocate of unrestricted U-boat warfare. He was later involved heavily in Germany's abortive Scheer Program, which supported the last-ditch, massive U-boat building program in World War I. The other German representative was Rear Admiral Paul von Hintze, former German naval attaché to Moscow. He was a longtime naval diplomat, noted for his ability, and had even been suggested by the kaiser's Chef der Marinekabinett (chief of Naval Cabinet) as a potential interim chancellor instead of the "inexperienced" Max von Baden.[7] Thus, a cross-section of the German politicomilitary spectrum favored dealing with the Soviets for the same reason: to circumvent the Versailles Treaty. A subsequent meeting took place between Radek, Seeckt, and a possible naval emissary, probably Admiral Paul Behncke, and probably Freiderich Wilhelm von Bülow, manager of the Berlin office of Krupp.[8] The Soviets had a need for ordnance research and development information and may have been aware that the Soviets were interested in German military research. Indeed, the Germans were concentrating on cannon design rather than on production in the early 1920s. Krupp patents filed publicly in the early 1920s included twenty-six for artillery control devices, eighteen for electrical fire control, nine for fuses and shells, seventeen for field guns, and one for heavy cannon, which could only be used by rail.[9] The evidence, however, of the precise degree of naval involvement is less clear at this early stage. What is known is that the Soviets were very pleased by the production of new 320-mm (12.4-in.) guns by the Putilov works, which were emplaced in coastal defenses and later mounted in the reconditioned Soviet dreadnoughts. The presence of, or contributions by, German engineers and designers during their manufacturing process of the guns cannot be confirmed. The Soviets assert that they had to "start from scratch" designing new very large caliber guns for battleships, because the largest they had experience with were 356-mm (14-in.) guns for the Izmail-class czarist battleships.[10]

The meeting between Seeckt, Radek, and the others reportedly led to the presence of Krupp representatives to oversee the manufacture of projectiles at Soviet assembly lines in the Urals and at the famous Putilov works outside Leningrad. The quid pro quo was provision by Moscow of "tracts of land for the Germans who used it to test heavy artillery and instruct young fighter pilots."[11] Gustav Krupp's finest designers were working in clandestine quarters in Berlin during the 1920s, when most of this occurred.

Soviet-German Secret Naval Conference 1926

From 1924 onward the German economy was stabilized under the Dawes Plan, and Germany's situation improved politically with the signing of the Locarno Pact in 1925, which secured the western borders. By 1926 British and American occupation troops had gone home, although French troops did not withdraw from parts of the Rhineland until 1930. The Soviet ambassador to Germany, Nikolay Krestinskiy, believed it was time to review the status of the military and naval contacts between the USSR and Germany. To this end he believed a conference between senior Soviet and German military and political leaders was needed. The conference was held in March 1926, when the relationship was still relatively secret. Krestinskiy received the approval of Soviet foreign minister Chicherin as well as commissars Litvinov and Stalin. The meeting was held in Berlin, and the Soviet delegation was headed by Iosif Unshlikht, deputy chairman of the union Revolutionary Military Committee (RMC). General von Seeckt, head of the Reichswehr, headed the German delegation. The principal points of contact were identified as Herr Leith-Thomsenn on the German side (head of the Reichswehr Ministry Office in Moscow) and Commissar Luniev, military attaché at the Soviet Embassy, Berlin.

Based on previous Soviet requests for assistance and an initially positive German response, the German naval high command submitted to the Soviet naval command "a detailed questionnaire on submarine operations, on the administration of a submarine fleet, and on all matters ranging from crew selection to points of . . . naval doctrine."[12] This is consistent with Soviet submarine construction plans. The Soviet reaction recognized that the Germans could not support Soviet-German joint ventures at the Nikolayev shipyards because the Germans simply did not have the money. Beyond this the Soviets were convinced that, at least in 1926, the Germans wanted an effective submarine force because of the threat such a force would pose to Britain—and the lessons the Germans might glean from Soviet developments. This was because the Germans offered detailed technical information on U-boat construction, including blueprints, specifications, patents, and inventions. The Germans also offered naval expertise and postwar research from official and industrial sources. The offer was made in principle, and the Soviets, being equally short of cash, pressed the Germans for gratis provision of all information promised. In turn, the Germans also promised to see what could be done to meet the Soviet requests.

Subsequently, on 25 March 1926, six German officers, including the submarine construction expert and World War I U-boat commander Rear Admiral Arno Spindler, met with two Soviets in Berlin to discuss German assistance for Soviet naval projects. The Soviets planned to build large and small submarines, as well as torpedo boats, in the Black Sea yards. At the time the Soviets asserted that they did not intend to pursue shipbuilding in the Baltic because of "danger from neighboring countries." The Soviets desired the Germans to review blueprints they had drawn up and to make the appropriate modifications "to take advantage of German experience."[13] Despite it being the principal German interest during the talks, the Soviets, according to the German records of the conference, were unwilling to build submarines in Russia for the Germans as that would be a clear violation of the Versailles Treaty. This, of course, represents the actual focus of German avoidance of Versailles strictures on U-boat construction as being Holland, not the Soviet Union, and the German effort began in 1922. The German effort to circumvent the treaty had been underway for four years prior to the Spindler Conference with the Soviet navy. The truth was that the Germans did not have any money. The Soviets wanted to be able to build everything necessary for the construction of submarines, including engines, guns, and torpedoes, in the USSR.

The Germans were apparently reasonably well informed on the state of the Soviet navy from Soviet sources. Everything the Soviets wanted, however, did not involve treaty violations such as would have resulted by their building submarines for Germany. The Soviets desired German participation in the Soviet Scientific-Technical Committee of the Naval Administration and participation by German officers on temporary duty at their Naval War College, either as instructors or to work on projects of certain mutual interest with the Soviets. In return they wanted to send officers to Germany to learn about gunnery, torpedoes, mines, and shipbuilding. They proposed something like an internship at Kiel's Deutsche Werke. It was decided to postpone consideration of detailed cooperation and have one officer, Rear Admiral Arno Spindler, go to the USSR. The head of the Soviet delegation visiting Berlin agreed to the visit *ad referendum* to Moscow, and Moscow subsequently approved.

Exploiting the opening to the Soviet Union provided by the 1926 conference, and the 25 March 1926 meeting in Berlin, Admiral Spindler, accompanied by another officer who was probably a representative of naval intelligence,[14] visited the Soviet Union from 2 to 18 June 1926. While there he met with Commissar I. S. Unshlikht and Admiral V. I. Zof, commander in chief of the Soviet navy, purportedly the two most important men in the naval administration at the time. Unshlikht was a professional revolutionary from old Russian Poland and had been a participant in the events of 1917 and subsequently on the Bolshevik western front, had several commands in the Polish campaign, and was a graduate of the OGPU (the Unified State Political Administration, or Soviet secret police, predecessor to the Commisariat for Internal Affairs [NKVD]) from Belorussia. Trotsky described him as an "ambitious but talented intriguer." In 1923 he had been sent by Stalin and Lenin to organize the "Red Hundreds" in the abortive Communist takeover of Germany. Zof had been the first, or senior, naval commissar (political officer) until December 1922, when he assumed the formal leadership of the navy. In 1927 he took over the Soviet merchant marine and later was first deputy commissar for inland waterway transport. He reportedly died in 1940. Zof's career was basically as a political "enforcer" involved with naval affairs.[15]

Ultimately, it was *not* the USSR but, rather, Holland, Finland, Japan, and Spain that provided the Germans their first opportunities to resume the submarine building trade in 1920 and 1922.

Lohman did perform some useful service in Russia, arranging for the return of certain captured German merchant ships from Russia, using clandestine methods, according to *Russo-German Naval Relations.*[16]

The Russian activity related to the Spindler mission, regarding German assistance in Soviet submarine construction, resulted in a Soviet visit to the Dutch branch of the secret German U-boat building effort. On 2 April 1926 representatives of the USSR visited the offices of the Ingenieur Kantoor voor Scheepsbouw (IVS) in the Hague, where they were to be shown a design for a 600-ton submarine.

Further, on 8 April 1926, a Soviet official was shown aboard the new cruiser *Emden* and the old predreadnought battleship *Elsass* at Kiel.[17] During his time in Moscow, Admiral Spindler met with Commissar Unshlikht on 5–8 June, while the latter held the post of deputy chairman of the Revolutionary Military Committee. The Germans' principal meeting took place on 7 June, during which they pressed the Soviets for a visit to a battleship and a submarine. Commissar V. I. Zof was not accommodating, asserting that nothing thus far had really come of Soviet-German naval relations and that the submarine design they had been shown promised nothing more than that performance level reached in 1916 by the Germans. The Italians had been much more forthcoming, according to Commissar Zof. Soviet policy on submarine construction was identical to that on heavy cruisers: to design and build the best in the world. They had many initiatives underway. Other than having some impact on Soviet submarine designs and early cruiser studies, the results of the 1920s interface does not appear to have been significant for the Soviet fleet.[18]

The ability of native designers to produce first-class ships and of Soviet yards to build them supports the assessment that the policy of naval dealings with Germany was intended to determine German weaknesses.

A final note of mistrust surfaced at the Spindler meetings when Chief Naval Commissar Zof also hinted that the Soviets were suspicious about

German submarine construction in Turkey and the activities of German officers in that country. The Germans concluded that the Soviets really wanted German technical knowledge as cheaply as possible and that they should not be trusted. The Soviets specifically asked if the German navy would arrange for them to have a look at the Turkish submarine plans, which were based on some of the most recent wartime German submarine plans; they requested German advice on the types of submarines that should be built for the Soviet navy and German naval backing in ordering parts for its submarines from German manufacturers. Even the manufacture of such parts violated the Versailles Treaty. The Germans, for their part, asked for the Soviet naval budget for 1926 and an organizational chart of the Russian navy; both were promised, "providing they are not secret."[19]

Admiral Spindler, whose expertise on submarine operations included authorship of the German World War I U-boat war official history, recommended against acceding to Soviet requests with regards to Turkish submarine designs. Concerning World War I German U-boat plans, Spindler proposed that they should be provided in sufficient detail to satisfy the client. Finally, a technical delegation should accompany delivery of any plans. Spindler believed the Soviets would be more likely to accommodate German submarine construction ambitions if the latter were forthcoming. He recommended that the high command provide a memorandum to the Soviets immediately on what types of submarines should be built and supported the Soviet desire for German navy support with German firms if orders for parts were placed, but he was uncertain about whether three submarine experts could be provided until the scope of future cooperation could be decided.[20]

Reflecting its established anti-Communist outlook, the German naval high command opposed any significant follow-through on Spindler's recommendations. Lieutenant Commander Wilhelm Canaris (later admiral and chief of the Abwehr) opposed giving the Soviets anything at all. The German naval staff, section A II, also noted that dealings with the Soviets were extremely dangerous.[21] Indeed, it is now confirmed that all Soviet-German exchanges were under the control of Commissar Yan Berzin, chief of the Intelligence Directorate of the Red Army from 1924 to 1935. German intelligence had previous detailed knowledge of the visit by Soviet naval representative "Oras" and Admiral Spindler to Kiel and Wilhelmshaven in March 1926 and also of the German visit to Moscow. The Germans decided to provide the Soviets by courier with a selection of the plans of submarines which had already been surrendered to the entente. The Soviets subsequently dismissed the drawings as too dated and reflecting only German state of the art as of 1918. They also asserted that the plans were no longer relevant and that they had decided not to construct submarines. The Soviets, of course, continued their own submarine design program. More important, we now know that the Soviets recognized the pluses and minuses of the German relationship. In January 1926 a memorandum compiled at the Soviet embassy in Berlin indicated a significant degree of circumspection:

> Turning to the German's likely approach to using our aid, mention should be made of the difference in their approach to ground and naval forces. In the case of ground forces, they are not interested in our weakening and indeed have a direct stake in our strengthening (we have no common frontier for the time being, and so they can stay neutral in any conflict). As for naval forces, their attitude is entirely different. A stronger Soviet navy would mean going beyond the Gulf of Finland and hence making it necessary for them to make a definite stand in the event of our clashing with a third country (to say nothing of anglophile tendencies in their navy).[22]

The head of the German navy, Admiral Karl Zenker, and his successor, Erich Raeder, succeeded in fending off any meaningful contacts with the Soviets from 1926 to 1929. Although it was the policy of the German army leadership (Heeresleitung) to try to get the navy interested in contacts with the Soviets, the navy bridled at the suggestions. Although the secret U-boat-related program of Captain Lohman ultimately required the resignation of defense minister Otto Gessler and of Admiral Zenker, the German army managed to continue its clandestine relationship with the Soviets for several years, until 1933, when contact was cut off at political direction.[23]

The covert German program had well-documented problems, including the handling of certain "black" funds, which were placed in the hands of one Captain Günther Lohman, who invested them in enterprises to make money for other than what were clearly German national interests. A subsequent scandal forced the chief of the naval staff, Admiral Zenker, from his post and saw him replaced by Admiral Raeder.[24]

In 1929 the Soviets again tried to establish contacts between the two navies. On the instruction of the 1929 defense minister, General Wilhelm Groener, the German military representative in Moscow, Oscar von Neidermeyer, raised the issue of the possibility of improved navy-to-navy relations with Soviet commisar for War Kliment Voroshilov. The Soviets responded positively, probably because observers were allowed to be present at military maneuvers on a reciprocal basis, Red Army commanders had undertaken fieldwork at the German Military Academy, and intelligence on certain topics was being exchanged regularly.[25] Moreover, they anticipated a friendly reception of Red Fleet visitors at Swinemünde. Despite his own reservations, interservice rivalry, resentment over army meddling in the navy's chain of command, and the attitudes prevalent in his service, navy chief Raeder submitted a plan to send Rear Admiral Friedrich Brutzer, head of the Command Division of the German naval staff and one other officer to Moscow. The German naval officers presented three questions to their Soviet hosts: What was the state of the Soviet navy? Did the Soviet Union intend to develop it for offensive or defensive purposes? And whom did Russia consider to be its enemy in the east (China or Japan)?[26] It is noteworthy that the navy did not wish to raise the issue of Western enemies. Whatever the discussions in Moscow, Raeder complained about Groener's tendency to bypass him in matters relating to his department chiefs. Groener, the Reichswehr, and its Soviet affairs offices pushed Raeder and the navy to maintain contact with the Soviets, and the navy participated in a 20 February 1930 visit by high-level Soviet naval officers.

The 1930 Conference and International Naval Negotiations

In late February and early March a Soviet delegation also visited German naval installations, where they were permitted to inspect "Panzerschiff A" (the new pocket battleship *Deutschland*) and other naval installations and ships at Kiel, Hamburg, and Wilhelmshaven.[27] According to the German record, the Soviet participants included Admiral V. M. Orlov, then commander of the Black Sea fleet (later navy commander in chief); P. A. Smirnov, purportedly commander of a destroyer flotilla; Commissar A. Berg, president of the Naval Section of the Military-Scientific Committee; "Oras" (deputy to Berg); and "Leonov," chief of the Artillery Section of the Military-Scientific Committee. The Germans included Admiral Brutzer, flag officer in charge of the fleet section, Marineleitung (Naval High Command); Korvetten Kapitän Otto Hormel of the A II Admiralty Staff Section; and Korvetten Kapitän R. von Bonin, who served as translator along with the Soviet military attaché Commissar Vikovt K. Putna.[28]

The Germans prefaced their remarks to the Soviets at the Berlin conference by requesting that the Soviets treat everything they had seen as confidential, especially since no other foreign attachés or missions had been shown the new pocket battleship. Admiral Orlov posed a series of questions, which the Germans answered as best they could:

> Orlov: What are the principal duties of the German navy within the framework of overall policy?

Admiral Brutzer:
>   (1) The Fleet is an instrument of power for the State.
>   (2) If the German Fleet were disbanded, the 15,000 men per-
>   mitted as naval personnel under the Treaty of Versailles
>   would also have to be dismissed and cannot be transferred to
>   the army.
>   (3) A decision not to build any large ships but merely main-
>   tain small craft and coastal defense would entail the passing
>   of the navy.
>   (4) Although only small, the German Fleet is a modern in-
>   strument of power and most certainly of value to any ally.

Orlov's question was an important, if obvious, one, and the answer was quite revealing of German naval attitudes of the time. The Soviets have since published that they believe the failure of the German navy in the World War I was directly attributable to the lack of mutual support provided the German submarine forces by naval surface and air forces as well as a lack of coordination with land arms.[29] The conventional wisdom has been that the German navy could have done much more to work with its military counterparts, but its own chain of command as well as the imperial grand headquarters were too diffuse to have this happen on a day-to-day basis.[30] Brutzer's last point is of interest as it resurfaces Tirpitz's argument about the international political, or strategic "alliance," value to Germany of a "fleet in being." It almost begs the question that Germany should have a navy at all—which in 1930 was a matter of great concern to the German navy. Indeed, the "*existenzfrage*" (existence question) had been widely debated in German political and military circles since World War I; his third point puts the German navy and Raeder squarely in the "old school."[31] The German navy's policy was to advocate a fleet built to fight *any* other fleet. The Germans, like the Soviets, were busy planning a larger fleet at that time.[32] The meeting continued:

> Orlov: Am I correct in assuming that the transfer of the fleet com-
> mand to Kiel represents a simplification, a kind of rationalization?
> Admiral Brutzer: That is correct. In this way fleet, activities will also
> be more centralized. Before the war, the Fleet command was also in
> Kiel for these same reasons.

Brutzer was being somewhat disingenuous, because the German navy considered the immediate/near-term principal threat to be from the USSR and Poland in the Baltic, with a possible French threat from the West. The official position of Raeder and the naval command was that a naval war with Britain was hopeless, especially in the early 1930s; war with France was only marginally less so.[33]

The Germans, when asked what plans they had for their fleet, asserted that they had lost the critical archives at the end of World War I, that the German navy's mission was one of creating a trained cadre for the future, and that no actual war plans had been developed.[34]

The canard of all prewar operations orders being destroyed is admitted to be untrue by the Germans themselves in the memorandum from which this record is taken; it had been often used as a convenient excuse to keep foreign and domestic critics of World War I German naval activities at bay. The records of the high-seas fleet and the admiralty staff were, in fact, safe in the German archives. The Germans had only four operational battleships in 1930, all pre–World War I era; Panzerschiff A was still under construction. Finally, to say there was no war plan stretches credulity: Gemzell documents the operational planning process as a "wave of new ideas" in the 1930s, and, according to Gemzell, the Germans assumed France and possibly Poland as principal enemies during this period.

According to Orlov, the inspection of the German fleet proved highly satisfactory to the Soviet representatives. The Soviets did ask for Admiral Brutzer's vision of further cooperation and strengthening of the ties now existing and his thoughts regarding reciprocation of the Soviet visit. He responded:

> We would like to visit Sevastopol and Leningrad with several other representatives to get an impression of the Soviet fleet. If I may be quite frank, I am less interested in the development of weapons in Russia since I believe we are ahead in this field. I should prefer to be able to have naval aviators trained in Russia as combat pilots in bombers and torpedo planes, that is in tactics prohibited for us under the Versailles Treaty. However no steps can be taken until a personal impression of the feasibility of this project has been obtained.

Brutzer's response to the Soviets about their technical inferiority was a professional high point in the conference; the German desire to get real-time training and experience in aircraft for naval air pilots was genuine. This is something the army had already accomplished and something that the Germans desperately needed if they were to lay the foundations for a naval air arm. Admiral Orlov concluded that he hoped liaison would improve between the two services and that a German delegation could visit the Russian fleet in the near future. In his report to Commissar Voroshilov, Orlov suggested that the contact àlready established should soon be followed up in order to prepare for the systematic continuation of relations.

There was no reason Orlov and his entourage should have been disappointed in the German visit; they were apparently shown much of what the German navy had, including the new Panzerschiffe, thus far unseen by any other foreigners. And there was a reciprocal visit. Brutzer's cover memorandum to the other department heads of the Marineleitung indicated that the Germans wanted to get a feel for how competent the Soviet service was; technical issues were purely secondary. Vice Admiral Brutzer headed the German delegation, which included Korvetten Kapitän (Lieutenant Commander) Max Seeburg, a member of the secret naval air section and a technical expert. They left 26 July and returned 13 August 1930. The delegation visited Leningrad first, where they were shown the naval academy and where they met Professor Mikhail A. Petrov, noted advocate of the old school of battle fleets at sea, whose advocacy of classic seapower theories later cost him his life.[35]

The Germans also inspected the school for special courses and the naval training establishment. On 2 August they embarked on the destroyer *Uritskiy*, sailing down the Neva to Kronstadt, where they were met by the destroyer *Karl Liebknecht*[36] (the destroyer was named after the German revolutionary killed in the fighting in Berlin during the aborted revolution). The symbolism should not have been lost on the German visitors. In Moscow the Germans were received by R. A. Muklevich, who had taken over effective command of the navy from Zof. Like his predecessor, Muklevich was a political officer. In the 1930s he played a key role in applying Stalin's social policies and totalitarian methods to naval construction; he was shot in the 1937 purge.[37] B. M. Shaposhnikov, who the Germans thought to be commander of the Moscow military district, was in fact chief of the Soviet general staff.[38] The delegation soon headed south for Sevastopol and the Soviet Black Sea fleet. There they inspected a cruiser at Yalta—this may have been the *Chervona Ukraina*—a ship commanded about this time by Captain (later admiral of the fleet of the Soviet Union) N. G. Kuznetsov, about whom more will be said later.[39] With Germans on board a torpedo boat column proceeded to sea for antisubmarine exercises. In Sevastopol they were shown the arsenal, ammunition depot, torpedo factory, aviation school, and naval air squadron. They also had a chance to take part in the crew's off-duty evening entertainment. The Germans rated the average quality of the Soviet naval officer as "not any higher than our old *Deckoffiziere*." Further, Vice Admiral Brutzer believed that "no improvement was likely from the new officers coming from the naval academies."

A short description of living conditions, party roles, and propaganda indicates that the Germans were well aware of Soviet conditions: "a dictatorship exists." Brutzer assessed the Soviet Baltic and Black sea fleets as having negligible combat power. He recommended against making any naval ship visits to Russia in the foreseeable future. Nevertheless, he thought the Germans should go "half way" to help the Soviets in the material field, as "we are the only one with anything to offer for the foreseeable future." Because food was difficult to get and very expensive in hotels, Brutzer recommended against sending individual officers to the USSR for language training. In dealing with Soviets, he recommended against praising the Russians and increasing their self-conceit: "The competent persons are grateful for just criticism, even if it is devastating; it increases the impression of the genuineness of the visitor."[40]

The political climate in Germany was in flux. Hitler's view of bolshevism was on its way to becoming German state policy. The Germans apparently requested that the Soviets not return the German navy's August 1930 visit.

Relations Severed—The National Socialist Era Begins

Despite the apparent success of the visit, showing its true colors, the Marineleitung did not follow up on any of the Brutzer delegation recommendations. They stonewalled the Heeresleitung and finally rejected the latter's proposals for increased Russo-German cooperation in a memorandum dated 2 May 1931. Brutzer pointed out that the issue of control of the seas in wartime dictated that at this time the German navy look toward cooperation with the U.S. and British navies, which dominated the world at the time, and that it would do ill to anger either of those forces by an overly pro-Russian naval policy. Finland also needed protection. The Germans had been successful in getting several small and medium sized U-boats built in Finnish yards to German designs.[41] According to Brutzer, no other country at the time could give the assistance the Germans needed. The German navy's final argument against improved relations was that in 1931 there was "nothing we can expect to receive from the Russian Navy in time of peace."[42] Thus, the early Soviet concern about German intentions and interests appears to be correct. In fact, the difference between Ambassador Krestinskiy and Commissar Berzin, to the effect that the ambassador believed the Germans had no intention of changing their pro-Russian policy while the military security chief believed otherwise, presents an interesting conundrum.

Nevertheless, it is interesting to recall that three classes of Russian U-boats received German diesel engines delivered during growing Soviet-Nazi political hostility in the mid-1930s.[43] These engines were built by

Maschinenfabrik Augsburg-Nurnberg (MAN) and constituted a commercial delivery that, somehow, was not halted, despite hostile political relations. Most of the engines went into the Dekabrist-class boats, which served well in World War II against the Germans. This was economic detente driven by the desire to keep Germans employed and Soviet submarines equipped. On many other issues, however, Soviet policy had clearly hostile consequences for the Allies.[44]

The Reichswehr did not intend or support a change, but the German navy believed that the key interests of German sea power lay, in the short term, in defense with the West. Brutzer's statement indicates that in 1930, at least, Berzin was half-right. At the same time the German navy's leadership remained concerned that the Communist bacillus might again infect the crews of German navy ships (as it was thought it had in 1917 and 1918) should they come in contact with crews of Russian ships as documented above. In August 1931 the chief of the Armed Forces Section in the Reichswehrministerium and a representative of the Marineleitung signed a memorandum of agreement—to disagree—on policy toward the USSR. Its last line was: "closer cooperation with the Russian Navy cannot be considered because the Marineleitung has nothing to offer."[45]

The paucity of documentary evidence of further German-Soviet naval cooperation is consistent with official German naval staff attitudes of the early 1930s and also may be directly attributed to the political circumstances that surrounded Adolf Hitler's coming to power in 1933. Nevertheless, this official hiatus did not completely interrupt exchanges in items of naval interest and of German interest or Soviet interest in each other's navy. Specifically, there was the sale by the German firm MAN of U-boat engines, which ended up in the Dekabrist, Pravda, Leninets, and Stalinets Soviet submarine classes built during the 1930s.[46] Ultimately, the German navy, like Germany and the world, was headed into dark waters. The intoxicating first phase of a grand new naval buildup was about to begin.

Chapter Three
Navy to Navy
Competition, 1933–1939

The German and Soviet Navies, 1931–1939

Political developments and perceptions of conflict-ing national interests in both Germany and the Soviet Union continued to have a direct impact on the growth and development of the German and Soviet navies during 1931–39. The Soviet investment in naval forces was greater than the German. The official journal of the Gorbachev-era Soviet navy asserted in 1990 that the Soviet battleship program alone absorbed 33 percent of the entire Soviet *national* budget by 1940.[1] Diffi-culties arose for both powers in obtaining critical materials, and these shortages reduced the number of ships produced in the immediate prewar period. Neither side accomplished their intended fleet construction tar-gets prior to the outbreak of hostilities.

Soviet Naval Reconstruction:
Competition for the Germans and the World

From 1931 to 1939 the Soviet navy established its material base, built and destroyed the core of its officer corps, and grew into its first post-czarist missions. While the 1920s had seen some postwar revolutionary purges, they were only a shadow of what was to come. The Soviet navy, like its German counterpart, was a reflection of the national political milieu and objectives. In the 1930s the Soviet Union carried out a program of forced industrialization and forced collectivization of agriculture and had fully liquidated the "exploiter classes"[2] in constructing the world's first Socialist state. Lenin made the original decision to rebuild the czarist navy.[3] This work had the imprimatur of the Tenth Party Congress of 1921, and Stalin followed through with arrangements already in place. The Soviet military reformer M. V. Frunze, who was reportedly murdered by Stalin, is cred-ited by early Soviet sources "as . . . devoting a great deal of time and energy to renovating and improving the combat power of the navy." The navy also benefited from the early political sponsorship of the Komsomol and the infusion of many of its members into the officer corps of the new service.

By 1930 the navy was beginning to benefit from the high priority it had received in Moscow's early planning. That priority was dictated by Stalin as a mixture of ego and state ambition in the face of many other desperate needs for the Soviet Union. The strength and power of the armed forces of the Soviet Union were dependent upon the industrialization of the Soviet economy. Defense industries got first priority on raw materials. This had serious adverse consequences for the Soviet people, the dimensions of which are becoming increasingly irrefutable under glasnost: "the buildup took place at a time when hundreds of thousands of people were dying of starvation in the Soviet Union, and millions more were dying of cold exhaustion and hunger in concentration camps."[4]

By 1930 the Soviet fleet consisted of three reconditioned czarist dreadnoughts, five cruisers, two dozen destroyers, as well as eighteen submarines and a force of auxiliary ships. This force was divided roughly between the Baltic and the Black seas. There was a naval air force of both fighter and strike aircraft as well as significant numbers of small attack and mine warfare vessels. The Red Fleet was the result of the decision by the USSR Revolutionary Military Council in 1928 to create a fleet whose missions included: "back up of operations of the ground troops in the maritime directions, joint defense with land troops of the shores, bases, of the fleet and politico economic centers on the coast, and operations on the sea communications of any enemy."[5]

In the first half of the decade of the 1930s the Soviet navy began to mature in other directions and lay the foundation for what was to come. The decisions adopted in the prewar years by the Communist party and Stalin's government on the construction in the country of an oceangoing fleet rested on a vision that they would have strong fleets in the Pacific and the Baltic and greatly strengthen the Northern (Squadron at the time) and Black Sea fleets. The need for the fleet to have powerful shore-based aviation for combined operations with ship formations was also recognized.

The priority of the shipbuilding program adopted on the basis of these decisions was to create large surface forces—battleships and heavy cruisers, superior to the corresponding foreign ships. In 1938–40 the first Soviet battleships of the Sovetskiy Soyuz class and the heavy cruiser *Chapayev* were laid down. We now know even Gorshkov was being less than complete in his description of intended fleet strength. In the second issue of *Morskoy sbornik* for 1989 Sergey Zonin notes that the 1940 Soviet program was 4 to 5 battleships (75 tons each), 6 heavy (battle) cruisers and 30 light cruisers, 7 to 8 aircraft carriers, and more than 250 submarines.[6] In fact, subsequent Soviet/Russian authors indicate that Zonin was on the low end of the total numbers planned and probably at the high end regarding the displacement of 75,000 tons. Operationally, these ships were at the upper end of the prewar design spectrum. The Soviets carefully examined the interwar battleships, including the British *Nelson*, the French *Dunquerque*, the German *Scharnhorst* and *Bismarck*. They recognized that these designs were substantially improved technically over their World War I predecessors. According to Zonin, Joseph Stalin "gave especially high priority to major prestige ships." In May of 1936 Soviet designers began *Sovetskiy Soyuz*, the lead ship of Project 23. By the end of 1946 the construction of fifteen battleships and fifteen large (battle) cruisers and dozens of ships of other classes was planned. In working out Project 23, the designers built on the experience of constructing the World War I battleships of the Sevastopol class and the World War I Izmail-class battle cruisers. They also based their studies on an unused design of battleship project design of 1916 from Nikolayev Shipyard in the Black Sea. Stalin's purges, however, interrupted the work begun in 1936. The head of the battleships design bureau, V. Bzhezinskiy, and chief of the project, V. Rimskiy-Korsakov, were victims. The lead ship was laid down on 15 July 1938. The design was only formally presented to the Defense Committee of People's Commissars on 13 July 1939. This date is very close, of course, to the Soviet-German negotiations.

As a result of war games conducted at the Soviet Naval War College in 1939, the Soviets believed Project 23 would have produced vessels superior to foreign battleships, especially as to the antiaircraft (AA) guns.[7] The other facet of the design was that it included fully welded construction, a lesson that the Soviets say they learned from the German armored pocket battleship *Deutschland*. *Deutschland* was built to comply, at least in appearance, with a 10,000-ton Versailles Treaty displacement limit.[8] Of fifteen planned only four Sovetskiy Soyuz class were actually begun.

The Soviets rapidly discovered very significant problems in such an ambitious program. At the Baltic works there were not enough cranes or electric anvils. Construction was begun, but it turned out there was not enough steel either. Not enough blueprints were available to begin work until the first quarter of 1939, although fabrication of key subassemblies was begun in the first quarter of 1939 on *Sovetskiy Soyuz*. The launch was rescheduled from the middle of 1941, with shipyard trials to begin in 1942. The planned construction time was sixty months. These ships were to cost 1,180 million rubles each. The third and fourth ships and following vessels were designated Project 23nu and were improved versions of the original design with an armor belt of increased thickness and all-welded construction.

The Sovetskiy Soyuz class did take from the Germans the concept of single-purpose secondary armament arranged in six twin turrets as in the *Bismarck*. The Soviets had considered weapons as large as 457 mm (18.1 in.) but decided on triple turrets of 40.6 cm (16 in.) because this was considered to be the outside maximum capability of Soviet industry. Consequently, it is probable that Stalin was on a fishing expedition for German technological information, not the actual turrets, when he asked the Germans for so much in the 1939 negotiations.

War interrupted the construction of the class. All were captured or destroyed on the stocks. The 40.6 cm (16-in.) main caliber guns reportedly were used by the Soviets for "creation of powerful permanent long-range fire positions." Material and equipment were diverted from the ships to other vital war uses. A great deal was learned, including how to accomplish electric welding and other technical aspects of ship construction. Nevertheless, the Soviet view *today* (post-Gorshkov) is that the construction of

Figure 1. Originally intended for the "H" class battleship successor to *Bismarck*, the Soviets wanted this 40.6-cm (16-in.) naval gun for their Sovetskiy Soyuz-class battleships. Neither Soviet production nor Western sources proved adequate to supply Stalin's naval production requirements. Hitler refused to cooperate as well. (W. S. Bilddienst.)

such ships was a bad idea because they were the embodiment of Stalinesque global imperium, absorbed far too many national resources, and were less effective for national defense than such resources would have been if given to the army and air force, upon which defense from the Wehrmacht rested. The question also arises about *why* the Soviets did not actually build aircraft carriers. The Soviets, even under Stalin's draconian draft labor could not, according to current Soviet sources, afford them.[9]

Regarding the Kronshtadt class, the Soviets decided that the ships had a number of roles in a modern fleet, including fighting other battle cruisers and battleships, attack and defense of sea lanes of communication, defense of own shipping and support to ground forces. Again, the capabilities and main caliber artillery were designed to be capable of besting all foreign opponents. In the fall of 1936 the basic draft of the project was completed for fifteen "heavy" battle cruisers called Project 69. The draft design was not presented to the Defense Committee of People's Commissars until 12 April 1940, after the lead ship had already been laid down on 30 November 1939. Interestingly enough, the Soviets believed that the ships could adequately handle the German *Scharnhorst*, the Italian *Guilio Cesare*, and the French Dunquerque-class battleship as well as all light and heavy cruisers. The main propulsion unit for these ships was the same as the Sovetskiy Soyuz–class battleships. The design of these ships was based on the experience gained with the heavy cruisers *Kirov* and *Maksim Gorkiy* as well as light cruisers and *Chapayev* (Project 68 classes), the last of which was only completed after the war. The lead battle cruiser was supposed to have been laid down in 1938. According to the Soviets: "The lead heavy cruiser *Kronshtadt* was laid down in Leningrad on 30 November 1939; and a little earlier on the 5th of November, the *Sevastopol* . . . was laid down in Nilolayev. A decision was made (in the middle of 1940) to strengthen their weaponry and accelerate their construction. The Soviets accepted the proposal of the Krupp firm for the installation, on Soviet ships under construction, of six sets of two gun turrets. These were analogous to those installed on the *Bismarck* class battleship.[10] The complete package had not been delivered at the beginning of the war." The metal for the hulls was used for repair and other tasks. The other named ships of the Kronshtadt program (which was to have been fifteen ships in all) included *Sevastopol* and *Stalingrad*.[11]

The building of light surface forces was also continued. At the same time a plan was made to build powerful underwater forces, including over two hundred different submarines.[12] It was not only the European theater, however, that posed threats for the Soviets. The Pacific Ocean Fleet was established in 1932 as part of a series of measures to counter Japanese expansion.[13] Simultaneously, shipbuilding facilities were established and

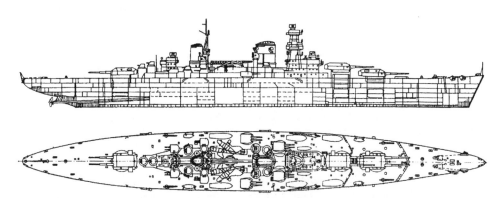

Figure 2. Plan and elevation of Kronshtadt-class battle cruisers known in the Soviet Navy as Project 69. This figure is a re-creation of an illustration from official Soviet sources which appeared in the journal *Sudostroyneniye* (Shipbuilding) in November 1989. Note the telltale angles in the German-designed 380-mm gunhouses. This design shows the maximum physical interaction of German and Soviet naval technology.

construction begun in the Soviet far east and north to support those fleets. Those decisions had their bases in the works of the Sixteenth Party Congress.[14] The decisions also confirmed the top priority accorded to the "complete reequipping of the Red Army with the latest weapons . . . [and] assigned at the same time was the task of securing a significant increase in the fighting strength of the Red Navy."[15] The expansion of the Northern Fleet was advanced by the efforts of hundreds of thousands of political prisoners "undergoing re-education by laboring on the construction of the Baltic-White Sea Canal (*Belomorstroi*), and a reserve [additional ships] for the Baltic Fleet."[16] While the Soviet naval buildup continued, the Soviets diplomatically maneuvered to obtain guarantees that would support greater naval freedom of action in the Baltic (e.g., independence of Baltic states). Further evidence of the buildup included Stalin's attempt to purchase larger-caliber naval guns abroad. He tried first in the United States, where he had deposited the then enormous sum of $200 million dollars for the acquisition of such technology and weapons. Regarding the acquisition of big guns for his ships from U.S. industry, the political judgment of the White House was overcome by bureaucratic opposition from the U.S. navy. Specifically in 1933, the depression was in full force, and all U.S. heavy industries needed orders. A weapons deal with Russia, shortly after the reopening of diplomatic ties, would have suited President Franklin Roosevelt's domestic needs. And the Soviet navy was, per Communist party direction, to get the latest and best equipment possible. Germany was still forbidden by the Versailles Treaty to manufacture 16-inch naval guns, and Britain and Japan were unlikely to sell them to the USSR; the former was regarded as the *Glavniy vrag* (main enemy) and the latter as a de facto enemy; the United States remained the only possible source.

Although President Roosevelt was in favor of a deal in principle, his wishes and those of his secretary of state, Cordell Hull, were frustrated by middle-grade naval officers with tacit approval from both the civil and military naval leadership. United States manufacturers of large ordnance and battleships were reminded that they would have to deal with the U.S. navy in the future and that a Soviet battleship deal was not regarded by the U.S. navy as in its interest.

Stalin either did not trust his own weapons people or, more likely, wanted so much capacity that his own plants could not handle it, or both. Stalin's total program of fifteen battleships and fifteen battle cruisers would have exceeded the total U.S. navy Washington Treaty limited order of battle. Stalin's requirements totalled 135 16-inch guns plus reserves and 135 12-inch (305 mm) guns plus reserves for the battle cruisers. This was in addition to the development and production of a 340-mm mortar by Soviet industry and the regunning of the surviving czarist battleships with new, larger, 340-mm guns. A recent postglasnost Soviet account put it this way: "The future generalissimo was very much in love with big ships, and this little foible cost his country, not yet completely strengthened, millions of rubles, most of which could not be converted into metal because of the outbreak of war. At the time, the industrial resources of the USSR were not adequate to the task of building large surface warships."[17]

The prospect that a Soviet policy existed to acquire a real Weltflotte that actually exceeded Hitler's program surfaces in 1938 when the French naval theorist Admiral Raoul Castex was cited by the Soviet publication *Foreign Military Observer*: "Soviet Russia, naturally, could have [an] incomparably greater . . . sphere of influence . . . if it were to add command of the sea to its land power." A 1938 issue of *Morskoy sbornik* affirmed Castex's authority and said his article "contained much of interest."[18] Admiral N. G. Kuznetzov supported such a fleet at Stalin's direction when he gave the keynote accountability report at the Eighteenth Party Congress (10–21 March 1939) for the navy's activity from 1934 to 1939. According to Herrick, "Kuznetzov focused on the naval threat to the Soviet Union posed by the world naval arms race." He stressed the need for additional protection for the Soviet Union's forty-eight kilometers of maritime borders and asserted that Soviet industry was already in shape to give the country combatant ships of every type, large as well as small. Kuznetzov also asserted: "We already have ships of large tonnage and are mastering the construction of the remaining ships, too." Stalin had, according to Kuznetzov, decided to create a mighty "sea and oceanic Soviet Navy with big ships not inferior in their power to the best military ships."[19]

The Soviets did not intend to be outbuilt. In addition to the final *Sovetskiy Soyuz* design, plans for a carrier battleship were submitted to the Soviet Union by the U.S. naval architectural firm Gibbs and Cox. It displaced about 65,000 tons. It is possible that the Soviets would have accepted such a radical hybrid, especially if they had been given the option and the resources to build it.[20]

There is also another issue in the chronology of these events. Careful review of some published documents connected with additional postglasnost Soviet historical analysis points strongly toward a secret Anglo-Soviet naval agreement: "It is interesting that on 6 July 1938, just nine days before the first battleship was laid down, an additional protocol to the Anglo-Soviet Naval Agreement of 1937 was signed, in accordance with which the maximum standard displacement for this type of combatant ships was increased from 35,000 to 45,000 tons."[21]

Beyond this there is a reasonable prospect that there was a connection between this agreement and British concessions made at the Montreux Convention, which restored Turkish sovereignty over the Dardanelles and Bosporus in 1936. One account that relies on Hungarian diplomatic reports from Moscow says specifically that the agreement included Soviet adherence to "qualitative limits" on warships (the displacement limit of 45,000 tons) and probably 16-inch guns as well. Hungarian diplomatic sources believed that the Soviets decided to sign the pact "in order to avoid the danger of Germany denouncing the 1935 Anglo-German Naval Agreement under the pretext of Soviet naval superiority. It is further alleged the Soviet Union undertook not to bring its Far Eastern Fleet to European waters under any circumstances whatever."[22] Additional British archival sources indicate that the British believed such an agreement provided a valuable pillar to appeasement diplomacy.[23] Stephen Roskill, whose *Naval Policy between the Wars* and *Hankey Man of Secrets* are the standard works on the British and naval political events of the interwar years, provides further insight into the Anglo-Soviet naval relationship, particularly the *Naval Policy* volumes. Roskill confirms that the Germans were sent the draft of a possible Soviet-Anglo naval treaty. The British were attempting to prevent the complete collapse of the 1922 Washington treaty limits. Roskill states that in July and August of 1936 the Soviets and the English negotiated an agreement whereby the Soviets "would accede to the treaty." Roskill refers the reader to the records of the discussions but leaves open the question of whether an agreement was reached brought into force. His judgment about all the negotiations of the 19. being a colossal waste of time is still reasonable. The interlocking relationship among the powers engaged in them, however, including the USSR and Germany, is the important point.[24]

Whatever the outcome of the Soviet battleship design and acquisition issue, the maelstrom of international politics in the mid- to late 1930s made the ultimate size and mission of the Soviet navy of the time largely dependent on Stalin's whims. Two other factors obtained. Stalin reacted to technical and political developments outside of Russia in which he was well informed, and to a lesser extent he also responded to the technical-strategic analysis his own people produced—although he frequently shot them for their efforts. Nevertheless, the strategic rationale for this fleet and the evolution of the Soviet debate surrounding it has been described by Robert Herrick in his masterful work *Soviet Naval Policy: Gorshkov's Inheritance*. Herrick traces the evolution of what was to become "the Soviet School"[25] by the late 1930s. His analysis of Soviet naval theoretical writings points clearly toward that fleet that was needed to protect the Soviet homeland and which could fight an enemy fleet at tactically favorable distances to obtain and maintain command of the sea in a specific area or, as the situation demanded, to deny it to an enemy fleet to allow a strategic objective to be obtained. That Stalin turned to Germany, the enemy par excellence (for a time at least), for help in achieving his fleet is simply an irony of history and a direct result of the fact that such assistance was not forthcoming from anywhere else.

Fleet Admiral, then Captain, Kuznetzov relates an interesting conversation in late July 1935 with the old Bolshevik Sergei Ordzhonikidze.[26] As background to the conversation, Kuznetzov notes the progress Russian shipbuilders had made in building "excellent ships of various classes."[27] Kuznetzov notes that Ordzhonikidze knew all this in general outlines and was looking ahead,[28] pressing Kuznetzov for an assessment of what kind of navy the USSR should build. Ordzhonikidze revealed some of the background to Stalin's policy when he said: "We are now building [in 1935, with very limited German industrial help] pretty good submarines, and even bigger ships will soon make their appearance . . . it's a question of having the metal. The development of large turbines is also hard going, but our industry will master that as well. We have already learned to make guns of any calibre. They will not hold things up. And in general we shall have to depend entirely on ourselves."[29]

From 1937 to 1940 many classes of smaller combatants were under construction in the Soviet Union, and considerable progress had been made with the submarine, destroyer, and cruiser arms of the new Soviet fleet.

That more progress was not made across the board is probably due to the "command methods," or "administrative style," used by Stalin and his minions in support of his objectives. Soviet military glasnost continues to reveal some of the damage wrought by Stalin and his successors. In an interview with *Soviet Naval Digest* the chief of the editorial commission of the authoritative *Sovetskaya voyennaya entsiklopediya* (Soviet Military Encyclopedia), Vice Admiral A. Sarkisov, indicated that a second edition of that magnum opus would soon be issued. According to the admiral captain second rank, M. Golovko, Stalin's decision to build a large battle fleet was strategically disastrous because it violated the principle of balanced armed forces (i.e., adequate and appropriate resources denoted to ground, air, and naval forces) and which subsequent Soviet policy had been to cover up this fact. Further, Stalin's decision-making process was also flawed because it violated the Marxist precept of a scientific approach and used an "administrative style."[30]

Indeed, it was administrative style, which has become a code name for Stalinism, which drove the Soviet navy into the German navy's unenthusiastic embrace. Starting in September 1988, *Soviet Naval Digest* exposed Stalin's injustices and their cost to the rebuilding of the Soviet fleet, from the first great purges forward. Stalin's policy that he should go abroad for designs has already been discussed, but there is more. Kuznetzov also told the Eighteenth Party Congress that Stalin's orders were clear: "We must have a powerful navy . . . and if an enemy undertakes to attack us, the Navy . . . must become an offensive fleet which not only prevents the enemy from reaching our shore but which will destroy him in his own waters."[31] If the Soviets had decided to build a high-seas fleet and had a fairly well-developed naval design and shipbuilding capability, *why* should Stalin be so interested in anything the Germans could provide?

The answer lay in Stalin's politicostrategic maneuvering and was part of the complex of calculations he made in his approach to Hitler. We now know with some certainty that the tilt toward Germany was made because of the rejection of Soviet foreign minister Maksim Litvinov's approach to foreign policy. Specifically, the CPSU Central Committee (i.e., Stalin) was dissatisfied with the results of the policy, oriented primarily, in cooperation with Britain and France, on participation in the League of Nations. The idea of collective security in Europe had little effect, due to the positions adopted by London and Paris.[32] Indeed, the Soviets had concluded that the West was too weak as a consequence of the final negotiations with the British and French military delegations prior to the outbreak of World War II. Not only that—neither the views of Poland with regard to passage of Soviet troops nor the position of Belgium regarding British and French assistance were known. This lack of knowledge was used, together with

Western weakness, as the reason for breaking off the talks with the West and for achieving the brief detente with Germany.[33] The key person was Molotov, who was at the time a true believer in Stalin's ways; Molotov's personality, standards, and mores were defined by Marshal of the Soviet Union Georgiy Zhukov as "one who consciously followed Stalin and supported him in the cruelest actions, . . . proceeding from his own views."[34] Zhukov believed Molotov "had a serious influence on Stalin, particularly on foreign policy questions."[35] Molotov must bear a share of the responsibility for Stalin's deeds. At least one other calculation entered into Stalin's concerns about his course of action in the summer of 1939: the securing of the Soviet eastern front: "the still fresh memories of Khalkin-Gol[36] forced the Japanese military circles to show caution and to link the problem of their entry into a war against Russia."[37]

Stalin's views of world domination with a new navy at the point, aided and abetted by Molotov, make a nasty stew. What is clear is that Stalin was trapped by the consequences of his ideology, ambition, and ruthlessness. When combined with the very similar character of German Foreign Minister von Ribbentrop, a pernicious confluence of interests was truly possible. But were the Soviet navy and the German navy in step with their national leaders and policies? Were both headed toward a Weltflotte and war? Do the lessons of World War I, as appreciated by either service, provide any insights? What did those services do to build their Weltflotte? What did their programs look like?

German versus Soviet Naval Reconstruction

The German navy, like the Soviet navy, was under reconstruction during the 1930s. Like its Soviet opposite number, it had been destroyed by war and revolution. Like the Soviets, the Germans were building a Weltflotte. The Soviets would allege that they were building a defensive navy: should they be attacked, it would respond by destroying the attacker in its own waters. The Germans were less circumspect. Neither Plan Z nor the "program for construction of a large fleet" had benign intent. Finally, both navies intended to profit from analysis of German World War I experience.

There was synergy between German actions and Soviet naval policy in the 1930s. It existed on two planes: Soviet response to German naval ambitions and fleet reconstruction and Soviet response and lessons learned from German naval experience.

The German navy broke out from the Versailles restrictions in stages, and that breakout drove, to a certain extent and at least in the initial stages, Soviet fleet expansion under Stalin. The Germans, in turn, responded to

Soviet construction, and so an arms race was joined in the Baltic. But both were also on a larger playing field, and this is where the Soviets' appreciation for the German lessons learned came into play. Stalin and Hitler both had dreams of world conquest. The war simply came too early for both.

The Panzerschiff design, which resulted in the famous "Deutschland" pocket battleship class, was the deliberate result of a German naval decision to circumvent the intention of the Versailles Treaty to keep the Germans confined to the mud flats of the Elbe. By 1930 the Germans had arrived at a plan that would have seen a rebuilt fleet centered around eight Panzerschiffe by 1946. The French, however, were concerned and replied to the Panzerschiffe with the *Dunquerque* and *Strasbourg*, fast battleships of 26,000 tons with eight thirteen-inch guns. They were thus larger, more heavily gunned and faster than the German ships. Nevertheless, the full German navy plan of 1932, which was the German position at the Geneva naval disarmament conference of that time, was as follows:[38]

> eight Panzerschiffe
> three aircraft carriers
> seven Washington Treaty heavy cruisers
> twelve light cruisers
> eighty-two destroyers
> eighty U-boats

Interestingly enough, the German navy position at the Geneva talks was not coordinated with the Reichswehr.[39] Essentially, the German navy wanted parity with France at 579,000 tons of warships.[40] The plan was only partly realized, even under Hitler. Beyond that, however, was the clear decision the Germans had made to concentrate on overseas cruiser warfare. They recognized that, even in an event of a war with Poland, the navy could play a little role, and the army would dominate.[41]

When Hitler came to power in 1933 this plan, approved by the previous government, was not enough. He brought with him a policy, rooted firmly in his Weltanschauung and documented in *Mein Kampf*, that German naval strength must be rebuilt and that the former German colonies were to be regained.[42] Hitler decided to aim for a naval agreement with England to cover his buildup. In the meantime the German naval leadership planned on a naval strength 33 percent that of the United Kingdom, with eventual hopes for achieving 50 percent. In the end the public figure was 35 percent of British naval strength until early 1939 when the agreement was repudiated.[43] The German naval construction plan of March–April 1934, which was coordinated with the *Heer* (army) and reflected Hitler's temporary priority for the ground forces, was (as seen from 1934) by 1950 to have included:

eight Panzerschiffe (rising from 10,000 to 25,000 tons and armed with
30.5-cm [12-in] guns)
three aircraft carriers
eighteen cruisers
forty-eight destroyers
twenty-four large U-boats (800 tons)
forty-eight small U-boats (250 tons)

This earlier naval construction plan evolved to included three Panzerschiffe, two Scharnhorst-class battle cruisers and the battleships *Bismarck*
and *Tirpitz* (which were armed with 380-mm or 38-cm guns). By 1937 the
U-boat numbers had risen to forty-nine under construction. Most of the
smaller construction was to have been completed by 1943. Hitler had
more in mind, however, and ordered the navy to draw up plans for vast
expansion of its infrastructure. The German navy had a baptism of fire in
the Spanish Civil War, including air attacks resulting in serious damage
to the Panzerschiff *Admiral Scheer*.[43] By 1937, however, the capital ship
construction plan had changed again to include ships beyond the *Bismarck*:
battleships *H, I, J, K,* and *N*. The Germans were beginning to accept sce-
narios of a possible war with France and/or the USSR which began as a
war with England alone or with the other two.[44]

By 21 December 1937 the Z Plan had been expanded to include: six
type "H" (*H, I, J, K, L, M, N*) battleships (406 mm (16-in) guns); ten light
cruisers; and priority to U-boats, M class (battle cruisers).

By 1 November 1938 another modification had been made to add by
spring 1947: twelve new Panzerschiffe (battle cruisers armed with heavy
artillery).[45] Hilter's priority for acquisition had now shifted to the navy. In
fact, Hitler had begun personal intervention into naval construction to the
point of threatening to replace Raeder if he could not increase the pace of
naval construction.[46]

The Soviet and German Plans in Global Context

For Stalin to plan to build fifteen modern battleships and fifteen battle
cruisers appears to be a maximum response to Hitler's program and, indeed, was consistent with the context of the international naval arms race
prior to World War II. What is different from the German program, however, was the size and strength of the battleships and the balanced fleet of
Soviet carriers, cruisers, destroyers, and submarines which would accompany them. At 59,150 tons standard displacement, the Sovetskiy Soyuz
class would have been at the high end of the spectrum among World War
II–era capital ship construction. They would have had balanced offensive

power (16-in. guns) and range as well as innovative heavy armor and protection. In fairness to Soviet policymakers and designers it must be pointed out they would have had to face eight German super-battleships (two Bismarck with 381 mm (15-in.) guns and six "H" class with 406 mm guns). By the mid-1940s had the battleship arms race continued the Soviet ships would have also had to contend with twelve new German Panzerschiffe—to which Stalin would have replied with the Kronshtadt class (at least four of which we now know were to have had German 15-in. guns). That design was finalized in 1940, after Stalin overruled a smaller, less well-armed version. On the world naval scene these ships would have had to deal with U.S. Alaska class (also 12-in. guns) as well as with six Iowa and six Montana, four Indiana and two Washington and eight Japanese Yamato / Super Yamato plus another class of Japanese battle cruisers. Smaller powers were also constructing their own fleets centered around a number of fast battleship designs. These competing programs illustrate the global context of Stalin's naval programs by warship class.

In proportionate terms of national effort the Soviet contribution to the arms race exceeded the 1940 program of the United States and paralleled the Z Plan of the Germans. Indeed, if the "15/15" battleship/battle cruiser numbers are correct, Stalin's effort far exceeded Hitler's final Z Plan. Stalin planned to accomplish it with a much smaller industrial base than the United States or Germany, at much greater cost to his people. The Japanese were a close fourth, as were the British. There is no doubt that the 15/15 plan had carefully taken the Soviet geographic situation into account, absorbed lessons learned from Germany's experience, and reflected an intent to build balanced task forces around their heavy units with the intent to deny local naval supremacy to other powers at key points around the globe to achieve Soviet strategic objectives.

Even had the fleet been built, success against the Germans or other Western or Far Eastern navies was by no means assured. One consequence of the construction of the larger ships in Stalin's naval buildup was a diversion of resources from ground and air forces, which added to the price Stalin forced the Soviet Union to pay to survive Hitler's onslaught on land and in the air.

Ambitions, Delusion, and Reality

From the Soviet view the canvass of naval war included the national issues between Russia and Germany and was complex and interlocking. The decision to deal with Germany militarily was not easy for the Soviets. The ensuing contacts on the naval issues between the mid-1920s and Hitler's accession were not easy, successful, or very significant strategically. The politicomilitary foundations of the navies were actually more potentially difficult than for the armies that did not share a common border. The Soviet navy and the German navy were both military adjuncts to the main fighting strength of their nations. The Soviet navy and the German navy had in common a world that could not accept the designs of their political masters for world maritime dominion. Hitler was defeated in 1945; Stalin's heirs collapsed in 1990, taking their fleet with them. Hitler and Stalin's grandiose political plans for Weltflotte were frustrated by insufficient time and inadequate resources. Both Nazi and Soviet naval establishments were frustrated by insufficient time and resources. The resources dedicated to their respective fleets cost both German and Soviet ground and air forces vital funds and equipment, and depleted order of battle. The chapters that follow describe the events that constitute the full record of intercourse between the two services between 1939 and 1941. The theme that emerges is one of hesitancy and lack of trust delivered on a plate of intuitive national discord.

Part Two

Nazi-Soviet
Naval Relations, 1939–1941

Chapter Four

The Naval Dimensions
of the Hitler-Stalin Pact

Context

Stalin's recent biographer, Alex de Jonge, áttributed the dictator's motivations for a pact with the Nazis as a "keen appreciation of history, awareness of the foolish generosity of Nicholas II, and an understanding that a German alliance would serve the Soviet empire. He had more in common with the Nazi warlords than with the pusillanimous democracies . . . right down to a certain attitude toward the Jews."[1] Stalin's view of Hitler emerged clearly: at a Politburo meeting early in July 1934, shortly after the killing of the leader of the storm troopers, Ernst Röhm, and about 180 others in Hitler's "Night of the Long Knives," Stalin is said to have exclaimed: "Have you heard the news from Germany? About what has happened, how Hitler got rid of Röhm? Good chap, that Hitler! He showed how to deal with political opponents!"

By the time of Munich, four years later, Stalin had come to believe that the democracies had no real standing as great powers. Besides that, Stalin saw the Western allies as dedicated to getting Germany and the USSR to go war.[2] Stalin believed the interests of the USSR and Germany to be coincident and worthy of a detente. Stalin, however, could not be bound, any more than Hitler was at Munich, by a "scrap of paper."[3] Among the Soviet military both admirals A. A. Golovko and N. V. Kuznetzov noted that the Soviet people were uneasy in 1939 about Stalin's deal with Hitler. Admiral Erich Raeder, an anti-Communist and one of the few German Russian linguists and an expert on Russian naval affairs, who was also commander in chief of the German navy, held similar views.[4] Elements of the German and Soviet military, nevertheless, seemed to have had common visions of dividends as well as drawbacks from the decision to conform, albeit temporarily, to the general interests of Germany and the USSR.[5] That Stalin could have thought that Hitler ever meant anything other than a truce is highly unlikely: Hitler had set forth his intentions clearly in *Mein*

Kampf. It reveals the true intentions that underlay Hitler's behavior toward Russia's leadership. Hitler labeled Russia's leadership unprincipled evil fanatics whose intentions were driven by racial stereotypes of the most vile nature.[6]

It reveals Hitler's perceptions of Russia's leadership, among whom Stalin was, of course, the principal antagonist. It is insightful and a testimony to Stalin's ego that he thought he could waltz around Hitler's depth of feeling. Like others, Stalin overestimated his abilities to influence Hitler and underplayed Hitler's commitment to ideology. Stalin probably did believe he could outsmart his German adversary. Soviet-German detente was really a series of agreements—first, of the exchange of telegrams on terms that constituted the nonaggression pact.[7] This was followed quickly by a German-Soviet commercial agreement.[8] There were a number of subsequent protocols.[9] The Germans had to reassure their Italian allies, who were most concerned. Hitler had abandoned their collective anti-Bolshevik stance as expressed by the Berlin-Rome and Berlin-Tokyo pacts of 1936 and acted against Mussolini's interests.[10] Actually, it was the trade agreements that constituted the opening for most of the technical agreements between navies which are described in the following pages. There was an additional German-Soviet commercial agreement signed on 11 February 1940.[11] The Soviet army was still staggering from the results of Stalin's purges and was, with limited naval support, involved in a very costly war with Finland. By 11 April 1940, however, the German Scandinavian operation had succeeded and the war with Finland was over, obviating some German needs for strategic position.

What did the Germans and Soviets attempt to get from each other? The Germans wanted U-boats, Soviet supply ships, bases, logistic support, and even naval and air cover for coastal convoys. The Soviets wanted technology, plans, and inspection tours of the Kriegsmarine. Beyond that they wanted armor plate, guns, fire control equipment, and insights into German technical planning. All of that unfolded against a background of Anglo-French conflict with Germany and a behavior on the part of the United States which was increasingly hostile. Japan and Italy were German and Soviet concerns as well. Japan had just been militarily deterred at Khalkin Ghol. Italy was furiously restive over perceived German concessions to Stalin against Finland.

Valentin Berezhkov, an eyewitness to the entire negotiations and much of Stalin's career in the capacity of translator, has recently provided the world with another view of this complex issue. Berezhkov asserts that, in spite of the then only one-month-old treaty with Nazi Germany, the Soviets had concluded that serious agreements with Britain and France were only ruled out in September 1939.[12] Berezhkov's arguments are based on

Soviet assessment of Western capabilities and intentions and the record of appeasement up to 1939. These views, when combined with de Jonge's analysis of Stalin's tactical flexibility, made the Soviet decision to deal with the Germans seem perfectly rational. Nevertheless, in retrospect, the Soviets now label what Stalin did as a grievous "error in judgement."[13] The rationale of Soviet actions gets stronger when predated to the context of the 1930s, and specifically the conflict between the USSR and the West over Spain. Current Soviet historical opinion obliquely blames the West for the demise of pro-Western Soviet foreign minister Maksim V. Litvinov and his subsequent replacement by Vyacheslav M. Molotov:[14] "It becomes known later why Maksim Litvinov had been removed. In the CPSU Central Committee, they were dissatisfied with the results of a policy oriented primarily on cooperation with Britain and France on participation in the League of Nations. The idea of collective security in Europe had little effect due to the position adopted by London and Paris."

There were other reasons for replacing Litvinov: Molotov accused Litvinov of creating a commissariat for foreign affairs which was insufficiently Bolshevik and that "nonparty attitudes" had begun to prevail. Subsequently, "a new wave of arrests and reprisals swept through the commissariat." Whatever Stalin's motives for the 1939 pact, he had made certain he would receive no advice contrary to what he wished to hear from the Ministry of Foreign Affairs.

Berezhkov believes that the Soviet military viewed that a military containment of the Germans by a Soviet-French-British entente was, because of inadequate Allied forces, "potentially doomed to failure."[15] Once the decision to side with the Germans had been taken by Stalin, a positive response to a German feeler about a "willingness to come to terms with Russia about the fate of Poland" was inevitable.[16] Stalin considered Poland's eastern boundary "unfair" in any case: it was too close to Minsk and Kiev, and many Ukrainians and Belorussians lived under Polish dominion. Hitler offered a deal, but at the same time said that, if the opportunity was missed, that would be it.[17] By 16 August Germany had told the USSR that it would pressure Japan to improve relations with the USSR and, in addition, the Germans would sign a nonaggression pact with the Soviets. The other thing that impressed the Soviets was German high-level decisiveness vis-à-vis Allied low-level dilatoriness: the Allied delegation was judged too low ranking and tardy by 18 August 1939.[18] Interestingly enough, Stalin believed that the trade treaty was more important to Moscow than a nonaggression pact, probably because Stalin wanted benefits up front before the inevitable conflict; this in fact happened.

Berezhkov notes that Stalin's fundamental error in judgment seems to have occurred subsequent to a personal communication received from

Hitler dated 20 August 1939. Stalin apparently believed Hitler was "willing to accept far-reaching Soviet demands," and "[Stalin] interpreted Hitler's message as evidence of his desire to cooperate with Moscow over a long period." In essence Stalin had been duped by Hitler at this point. Stalin thought he had bought breathing space, especially in light of the planned attack on Poland and the dilatory attitude of the West. Hitler's "concrete and definite" stance appealed to Stalin. This, of course, also conforms with Alex de Jonge's personality assessment. Subsequent to the nonaggression pact, with its secret protocol, which delineated spheres of influence being announced 23 August, and the 1 September invasion of Poland, Hitler's stance provided sufficient demarcation lines. A Treaty of Frontier and Friendship was signed with Germany on 28 September 1939. Hitler continued playing to Stalin's ego. Discussing a possible meeting with his Soviet fellow traveler, in November 1940, Hitler said, "I consider Stalin an outstanding historic personality. Well, I also expect to go down in history. So, it is natural that two political leaders, of the kind we are, should meet." Stalin's assessment of the timing of Hitler's attack on the USSR was probably twisted by this offer. To some extent, the mutual admiration was genuine: Albert Speer even spoke of Hitler's purported desire to have Stalin rule the USSR after its conquest by Germany.[19]

Stalin and the Economic Agreement of February 1940

The Germans were called to the Kremlin after midnight on 31 December 1939 for serious negotiations regarding an economic agreement, with Stalin once more taking a personal interest in the negotiations. The principal issues discussed included metal production, naval armament, machine tools, and aircraft. Presiding over a meeting of the economic delegations, Stalin insisted on the reduced Soviet demands but, for the first time, used the expression "mutual assistance," indicating that Germany could expect raw materials in exchange for its manufactured goods. Once Stalin had made the Soviet position clear the tone and pace of the negotiations intensified. A German eyewitness provides valuable record and insight into the Soviet leader's behavior as he conducted the December 1939 negotiation, which contained significant naval detail: "I remember the officers and obedient manner in which people's commissars like [Naval Commissar] Tevosian would rise from their seats like school boys when Stalin would deign to ask them a question. In all the conferences at which I saw Stalin, Molotov was the only subordinate who would talk to his chief as one comrade to another."

Indeed, whatever technical details or procedural efforts his naval minions had made, naval policy was Stalin's and Stalin's alone to make.[20] In fact, Schulenburg had an additional discussion with Molotov on 7 January, in which it was indicated that the Soviets were willing to make deliveries of raw materials on an accelerated basis, in return for extended deliveries of war materials.

By mid-January Hitler had reacted favorably to the Soviet proposal. The German embassy then urged the Foreign Office to pressure German arms firms to accept Soviet orders. As general issues were reviewed, Stalin was interested in the detail and substance, often making small changes and improving the documents in a general sense. Stalin was particularly interested in and competent on the details of military issues.

Naval Issues

Hilger again observed: "[I] . . . was similarly impressed by Stalin's technical knowledge when . . . he chaired a meeting of German and Russian experts discussing the ordnance specifications of the turrets for a cruiser which Germany was to deliver to the Soviet Union. . . ."[21] This discussion took place on 8 February in the Kremlin and covered the conclusion of the trade treaty between Germany and the USSR. The memorandum of conversation indicates that economic and naval issues were discussed, and the Germans raised the matter of the delivery of six gun turrets for battle cruisers, which Molotov had said was to be over a "rather extended period." Stalin asked two questions. First, would it be possible to use (German) 28-cm turrets in place of (Soviet) 30-cm turrets in battle cruisers already under construction? Stalin said he knew 28-cm turrets were in production in Germany and therefore available. Ritter replied that 28-cm turrets were available and could be delivered five months sooner if the Soviet Union would be content with the "current" version, although manufacture had actually ceased on 28-cm turrets, with the last being made for the *Gneisenau*. Stalin had his battle cruisers in mind and recent Soviet publications indicate that fifteen "heavy cruisers" originally designed to carry 12-inch (30.5-cm guns), were the intended recipients of the guns. Perhaps Stalin's requirements from Soviet industry for their own very good improved 12-inch weapon exceeded capacity, or perhaps he wanted the German technology. Regunning the three old czarist dreadnoughts requires a minimum of thirty-six barrels plus reserves. The Soviets also had underway an extensive coastal defense artillery effort, which required several dozen more barrels. Finally, the fifteen heavy cruisers (battle cruisers by any other name), called the Kronshtadt class, would have required nine large-caliber guns each. Whatever his motives, Stalin wanted the German guns.

Stalin then asked if displacement, weight, and offensive power would be compatible with the earlier design if twin 38.1-cm guns were substituted for the triple 30.5-cm guns originally planned in the battle cruisers. Ritter deferred but promised he would get the answers for Stalin's questions from technical offices of the German navy. One wonders what Stalin knew of the German plans to execute a 38.1-cm up-gunning for *Gneisenau*; Krupp had agreed as early as 1935 that a twin 38.1-cm turret could be set on the 28-cm triple barbette, but the turret support decks would have to be reinforced. Ultimately, the answer to Stalin's question was no, even though the Germans agreed to deliver the turrets and other naval material Stalin requested.

Ritter told Stalin that his questions on the compatibility of gun turrets could be resolved if the Soviet navy would agree to provide the plans of their battleships to the German navy. Stalin pressed the matter, inquiring whether the Germans had any plans to manufacture 40-cm turrets. As in the matter of the 28-cm guns, Stalin's concern was for the main armament of his battleships as well as to draw out the Germans on their own programs.[22] The Germans had 16-inch gunned battleships on the drawing board; these were put on hold on 30 September 1939; Stalin may have been trying to divine German plans there as well.[23]

Stalin also followed up on the matter of armament for *Lützow*. This was the one large combatant, which the Germans had agreed to deliver in an unfinished state. Although he was assured the ship would be delivered with 20.3-cm turrets, Stalin complained that the 150 million Reichsmark price tag for the cruiser was excessive. Finally, Ritter observed that Stalin "proved particularly well-informed on these matters and devoted special interest to the question of the construction of 40-cm turrets, . . . for which the Germans had promised to provide plans." Ritter said *Bismarck*'s plans could be included in the list of war material to be delivered to the Soviet Union.

A memorandum of the conversation was sent to Berlin. The führer reacted favorably, and the agreement was signed 10 February 1940. Soviet demands fell into several categories. The naval items on which contract negotiations were to begin without delay included naval construction, shipbuilding material, and underseas weapons. The Soviets wanted "the cruiser ex-*Lützow* [see discussion in chap. 6]; information on the trial results of *Seydlitz* and *Prinz Eugen* or *Admiral Hipper*; plans for the *Bismarck* and a large destroyer with 15-cm guns; and complete machinery for a large destroyer." There were also requirements for "electrodes for welding armor plate; boiler tubing; propeller shafts; electrical equipment; various boiler tanks; and motors; naval artillery including one fully equipped 38.1-cm double turret, to be delivered by 1 March 1941; preliminary sketches for a 40.6-cm triple turret; and working drawings for a 28-cm turret."

Finally, Stalin required samples of "mine gear; torpedo gear; a periscope; and marine acoustical devices" and "precision technology items including marine clocks and watches and hydrographical instruments."

These items were to be traded by the Germans for several hundred million Reichsmarks' worth of goods from the Soviet Union. These were to be delivered during the course of the year, from 11 February 1940 through 11 February 1941. The Soviet raw materials included smaller quantities of manganese ore, metals, lumber, and numerous other raw materials and, in general terms, the following:

> 1,000,000 tons of feed grains and legumes
> 900,000 tons of petroleum
> 500,000 tons of phosphates
> 500,000 tons of iron ore
> 300,000 tons of scrap iron and pig iron
> 100,000 tons of chromium ores
> 100,000 tons of cotton
> 2,400 kilograms of platinum

The Soviet goods were due during the same period, from February of 1940 to February of 1941. A second delivery period, from 11 February 1941 to 11 August 1941, promised another set of exchanges for both sides. These exchanges were to include more of the same commodities—this time to a value of 220 to 230 million Reichsmarks, or about half the value of the deliveries during the first period.[24]

The other significant German exports to the Soviet Union were primarily in the areas of naval construction and artillery. Complete details of the German *deliveries*—especially major ones—are difficult to glean from the war diaries, intelligence documents, and works published to date. This issue suggests itself for future research in the German military and naval archives in Freiburg and possibly in Russia.[25] There seems little doubt, however, that a great deal of Soviet oil was delivered to Germany. It would appear that five floating cranes, five aircraft, an electrode shop, and additional ship construction tools were actually delivered. Several turrets, some of which were fully equipped with fire control apparatus and spare parts, and two submarine periscopes also appear to have been shipped. The Soviet Union, for its part, commenced deliveries of raw materials and maintained them for several months after the agreement was reached.

Nevertheless, as early as 15 March 1940, Ritter was reporting difficulties in getting German deliveries to the Soviet Union. His sources indicated German business bureaucracy had managed to erect mountainous paper barriers, and only five Messerschmitt aircraft had been delivered. Germany had exported a number of other finished products to the Soviet

Union.[26] To facilitate deliveries Ritter requested a list of German firms behind in deliveries, but his Soviet counterparts responded by naming only the major companies with which they were experiencing problems, apparently frustrating Ritter's effort for whatever motives. With regard to Soviet purchases of German ships already built, the Soviet Union changed its plans several times. Each time the requests changed the negotiations had to be started again.[27]

Although the British contributed to his discomfiture in the *Altmark* affair on 16 February 1940, by 18 March 1940 Hitler was securing his southern flank at a meeting at Bremmer Pass with Mussolini, who told him Italy would be ready to join the Nazis in three or four months. Hitler was about to conquer Norway and France. As spring turned into summer in 1940, Nazi Germany rolled up victory after victory. The Panzers that drove to the channel, the aircraft that flew, the raiders that scoured the seas against Allied shipping—all benefited from the additional fuel flowing into Hitler's supply lines.[28]

Such was the profit the German military reaped by sending a sample of its harvest of technology, some of which must have directly aided the Soviet war machine, eastward. A message from the naval high command's attaché section to its offices in Sofia and Rome shows that much, if not all, of the Soviet crude oil went by rail from Varna in Bulgaria directly to Wilhelmshaven, the principal locus for operations of the German navy in the first half of 1941: "The supply of Russian crude oil to Germany is proceeding according to plan, due to the efficient and valuable cooperation of all officers concerned . . . for the past five months, 150,000 tons have been delivered as a monthly average. About 900 German tank cars are reserved exclusively for this traffic. . . ."[29]

Although the German need of Russian oil was "most pressing," as Hitler put it, "This will not become critical as long as Romania and Russia continue their supplies and hydrogenation plants can be adequately protected against air attacks." Hitler was looking down the road, although this statement was made during a discussion of what possible help England could expect in the summer of 1940.[30]

But by August of 1940 Germany was 73 million Reichsmarks behind in deliveries under the economic agreement. The Soviet Union had, in fact, supplied over 300 million Reichsmarks worth of raw materials, whereas the Germans had delivered only about half that amount in finished products in compensation. As a result, the Soviet Union suspended deliveries. Worse, from the German point of view the "Russians had canceled all long-range projects in the commercial treaty of 1940. . . . They had further restricted themselves to goods which will benefit their rearmament within the next eight to 10 months."[31]

Short on delivery, the Germans resorted to promises of future cooperation and to negotiating away other people's lands. A particularly revealing letter from Ribbentrop to Stalin illustrates the Nazi approach to the solution of problems between these two powers when they wished to act in consort: "From time to time personal contact is indispensable in authoritarian regimes such as ours." Later on Ribbentrop offered Stalin nothing less than division of the world: "I should like to state that in the opinion of the Führer . . . it appears to be the historical mission of the Four Powers—the Soviet Union, Italy, Japan, and Germany—to adopt a long-range policy and to direct the future development of their peoples into the right channels by delimitation of their interests on a worldwide scale." Although Stalin later purportedly told his daughter that Russia allied to Germany would have been invincible, he decided that he could push the limits of his relationship with Germany in the middle of 1940, when he decided to annex the Baltic states of Lithuania, Latvia, and Estonia, "extending the frontiers of the Soviet empire beyond those of Peter the Great's Russia."[32] Nevertheless, negotiations on a second treaty progressed at a desultory pace in the second half of 1940. But, as early as November 1940, Hitler was again stating that he was "inclined toward a demonstration toward Russia."[33]

Other than the cruiser *Lützow*, the most important items agreed for delivery (and possibly delivered) were three 38.1-cm twin turrets. The German military were all initially concerned about the impact of deliveries of such war material to the USSR, and, in fact, by 18 January 1940 the Oberkommando der Wehrmacht (OKW [German Military High Command]) had instructed a lower echelon unit to find out how many guns twenty centimeters and larger were available in German navy stocks. This was so all could be converted to long-range artillery, once the German navy's ships were disarmed. Raeder and his staff were not pleased. Hitler, however, instructed that the navy delay delivery of the cruiser *Lützow* and the plans for the *Bismarck* as long as possible, hoping to avoid delivery altogether if the war developed favorably. Nevertheless, the largest items apparently delivered to the Soviets, other than *Lützow*, appear to have been at least three and possibly six 38.1-cm turrets.[34]

The USSR placed an order for sixteen guns of 38.1-cm (15-in.) caliber. At least eight of these were completed in 1941. Seven ended up in Norway: three on Engeby Island in the Vest Fjord near Navrik, called Batterie Dieft; four to Vara near Kristiansand; and an additional gun was placed in Oslo Fjord by May 1945. The famous Batterie Todt absorbed another four guns to guard the Dover Straits, with one additional gun of four installed in Octeville near Le Havre. All the French-based guns were destroyed during the Normandy invasion campaign. Three of the sixteen

Figure 3. Forward 381-mm guns firing aboard battleship *Tirpitz*. Some of these weapons were delivered to Stalin's Kronshtadt-class battle cruisers but never installed. (W. S. Bilddienst.)

guns became railroad guns in 1943–45, and one was sunk in transit to Norway. None ever ended up in Soviet service.[35]

On 21 April 1941 Krupp wrote the naval high command asking to which Soviet ports in the Black Sea deliveries should be made. The German navy's answer was to deliver three to the Black Sea and three to Leningrad, indicating some of the turrets were going to Kronshtadt-class heavy cruisers under construction in Leningrad and others to battle cruiser construction in the Black Sea. Soviet sources clearly show that the guns were intended for the Kronshtadts, although it is not known if any of these 38.1-cm turrets were actually delivered to the Soviet Union before the German invasion. It is very likely that some of the orders were delivered. An assessment that appeared in *Warship International* in 1982 provides a good overview of the entire German larger gun production effort.

It is also known that the Germans produced six of the 40-cm guns for which the Soviet Union had requested drawings. The guns were installed in coastal defense positions in France and Norway.[36] The fire control equipment that the Soviets desired was enough to affect completion of the aircraft carrier *Graf Zeppelin* and, indeed, the rest of German naval construction. Erich Raeder's view of the provision of this material to the Soviet navy was one of concern driven by the limits of German production, regardless of what the treaty required. For naval strategic reasons he is also constantly on record in the führer conferences as having been thoroughly opposed to the invasion of the USSR. Raeder, who was retired as navy chief in 1943, surrendered to the Russians when they captured Berlin in 1945, instead of fleeing to the West, and was taken to Moscow. He was extensively debriefed. Although later evidence shows that Raeder was an imperial naval officer at heart, and he continued his dreams of Weltflotte and had no fundamental disagreement with his führer on foreign policy, the Soviets consented to release him from prison after only ten years of a life sentence.[37] Raeder's pro-Russian stance is seen as a deferral until the Western powers were defeated, not an abandoning of Hitler's war aims. Raeder could not have been unaware of the importance of Soviet resources, especially oil, for the conduct of the war to this point, but he had no choice but to accept Hitler's assurances that the eastward and southeast conference expansion would generate revenues the navy would need to pursue the Atlantic and U-boat war against the West. Perhaps, glasnost will yield what he told his interrogators.

Turning to the commercial agreement and boundary treaty Germany reached with the Soviet Union early in January of 1941, it is clear the agreement was no more than part of the diplomatic mask that complemented Wehrmacht cover and deception operations related to Hitler's plan to invade the Soviet Union. Hitler knew that Germany would have to occupy both Polyarny and Murmansk if his invasion was to succeed, saying as much to Raeder (in one of the führer conferences as cited) at the beginning of April: "Such action was militarily necessary to close off the access to seaborne supplies which the Germans knew must come from the west to aid the USSR."

Thus, the first negotiation in 1941 culminated various ongoing trade and military talks. In addition to some actual exchanges of goods and technology, agreements of 19 August 1939 and 11 February 1940 provided for the Soviet Union to act as an intermediary to circumvent the Allied blockade by purchasing items on consignment for Germany and then transshipping these items to the Reich.

Soviet-German negotiations in the summer and fall of 1940, subsequent to the three-power pact, were clearly an attempt by Hitler to divert Stalin in the grand strategic realm, dividing up the world on paper while preparing to remove the Soviet Union from the map. Hitler's strategy was to use the negotiations to buy time for a military buildup and to obtain the element of surprise. The Soviet leaders, on the other hand, appear to have viewed the negotiations following the initial nonaggression pact as a follow-up to a fundamental political settlement. Instead, these follow-up negotiations failed to yield substantive results and eventually trailed off into war.

The Military-Technical Relationship

Indeed, Hitler dedicated a large section of *Mein Kampf* to the naval issue and had grasped the technical truism that ships had to be built which were individually more powerful than *any* English counterpart. Nevertheless, political expediency had caused the führer to depart from his doctrine on occasion. Hitler's naval policy had generally remained a repudiation of the "cost-effective" building policies of Grand Admiral von Tirpitz, whose legacy was a lost naval war. Hitler did not intend to lose and, up until the Polish campaign, had given the navy primacy of place in capital expenditures.

"Sedulous" Behavior and Erich Raeder

"As for the two navies themselves, they had sedulously carried out their agreements and there had arisen no matters of major friction." Or so said Erich Raeder. This assertion is not entirely correct.[38] Some elements of Erich Raeder's relationship with the Soviet Union remain shrouded in mystery to this day. As discussed in chapter 1, Raeder led a navy that had ceased totally its dealings (even as a junior partner to the *Heer* [army]) with the Soviets in 1933. Raeder was considerably more in tune with Hitler's foreign and military policies than his self-serving memoirs would indicate. At the same time he also spoke and wrote Russian and had, because of reading translations of Russian works about their 1905 disaster, a profound appreciation of the Russian strategic situation. Raeder's assertion that he opposed the attack on the Soviet Union is well documented in the *Führer Conferences on Naval Affairs*. Perhaps, like many of the German elite, he thought he could manipulate the dictator to his own ends—in this case the reconstruction of a battle fleet.

Considering the institutional naval dimension of Soviet-German military relations, the evidence concerning Cruiser "*L*," Basis Nord, and the Soviet "wish lists" for German naval technology, there was at least some degree of disingenuity on the part of the high command of the German navy. The Soviet navy, on the other hand, also true to form, created considerable friction with its extensive demands for military technology as well as through several incidents of Soviet forces firing on or even sinking German merchant ships and uncertain treatment of German ships in Soviet ports. There were, in fact, few issues of substance between the Soviet and German navies which were handled in such a fashion as to support Raeder's statement about "sedulous" behavior.

Nevertheless, there was some truth in Raeders' assertion: beginning with assistance for the large passenger liner *Bremen*, which used Soviet harbor as sanctuary from capture by the British blockade in late 1939, these additional issues reflect quite a different relationship than that proposed by the grand admiral. This is not to say the relationship as documented below was totally "sedulous." There were incidents of Soviet attacks on German ships and German mistreatment of Soviet ships in German ports. Taken together, these elements of Soviet-German naval relations reveal a military relationship and history that reflect the mixed behavior of totalitarian powers in consort and conflict as well as significant military aspects of the Soviet-German naval relationship. This relationship also did not take place in a vacuum.

In early October 1939 Soviet troops had just occupied eastern Poland and had helped the Wehrmacht divide that hapless border state. On 6 October 1939 Hitler made a peace offer to the Western allies which amounted to nothing more than a proposal that he keep what he had and that hostilities should cease. It turned out that the English chose to interpret the secret protocols of the *Anglo-Polish Treaty of Alliance* as applicable for clear *causus belli* only in the case of the Germans and not over the Soviet attack on Poland. The British rejected Soviet excuses and German blandishments of armistice and continued to fight at sea while engaging in a war of position on land. The 28 September treaty signed between Hitler and Stalin was seen by France and Britain as de facto allegiance to protect territorial gains of Russia and Germany against third parties.[39] The Soviets did well by this: Ribbentrop instructed the German ministers in Estonia, Latvia, Lithuania, and Finland on 7 October 1939 that the small Baltic countries filled in the Soviet sphere of influence.[40]

At sea other affairs obtained. In early October the British battleship *Royal Oak* was sunk at its moorings by *U-47* early on 14 October, a military accomplishment that particularly impressed the Soviets. In fact, the Germans were facing an enemy whose war plans had taken into account a German-Italian alliance, as well as Japan, but not the Soviet Union.[41] The Germans had to face blockade at sea of imports but on land had access to the vast natural resources of the Soviet Union and opportunities thereby for blockade circumvention.[42] Because of the pocket battleship *Admiral Graf Spee*'s operations in the South Atlantic, the British had been forced to draw down severely their cruiser forces in the Norwegian Sea, and they were not able to respond to the seizure of the U.S. steamer *City of Flint* on 15 November by the pocket battleship *Deutschland*. The German ship put a prize crew aboard the American neutral and sent it to Murmansk, much to the embarrassment of the Soviets.

Soviet Naval Attaché Activity

The Germans and the Soviets, who the Western powers treated as cobelligerents, in December 1939 were still faced by an undefeated France as well as Britain. The Soviets had attacked Finland on five fronts and were doing badly in all but one sector, but the numbers were such that Finnish capitulation, without outside help, was only a matter of time. The British and French wished to prolong Finnish resistance and to stave off an Axis-occupied Scandinavia, but they had divergent views. The United Kingdom believed that the Soviet attack on Finland might cause Germany to enter the conflict to protect Swedish iron ore supplies; the French agreed but believed that the way to prevent German seizure was to stop Soviet aggression and help Finland. Essentially, Sweden and Norway were to be invited to go to war with the USSR.[43] Nothing was decided. Although the respective governments were very concerned about it, the respective German and the Soviet military establishments did not have to counter Franco/British action against the Soviets as well as the German base.[44]

During the brief years of Soviet-German detente the invitation of the Soviet naval attaché in Berlin to visit German naval operating bases represented a high point in normal diplomatic activity and in Soviet-German naval relations. In a gesture of goodwill, apparently originating from Raeder, Captain Second Rank Yuri Vorontsov was given permission to visit Kiel and Flensburg between 11 and 13 December 1939.

In Kiel Vorontsov viewed a battleship, destroyers, and U-boats, toured the naval shipyard, and visited a coastal defense battery. In Flensburg he was to visit the naval school at Mürwik and, possibly, a torpedo or intelligence school. Vorontsov's escort was to be a senior naval doctor Kaull. The reason the German escort officer was neither line nor intelligence but, instead, a medical doctor was quite pragmatic: Kaull was one of the few officers available in the German navy who spoke Russian. Fortunately for Vorontsov and for German naval intelligence, Kaull appears to have had a good technical naval background as well.

Vorontsov and Kaull arrived in Kiel early on the afternoon of 11 December. Vorontsov toured the coastal defense installation Batterie Tirpitz and called on Vice Admiral Rolf Carls, chief of the Baltic Naval Station, at 1700. The next day the Russian and his escort drove to Mürwik and visited the naval school, commanded at the time by Captain Walter Lohmann. While at the school, Vorontsov was very curious about underwater communications devices, as well as the 800-watt, long-range wireless transmitters used on board German ships. The Soviet attaché's specific technical interest followed the thrust of what is known about Stalin's objectives: collect information and buy time. The Soviet attaché was impressed by the "size and thrust" of the talent at the naval training complex in Mürwik, describing the barracks rooms and quarters at the school as "kulturny" (cultural, or sophisticated/civilized).[45]

Before returning to Kiel about 1630 the inspection party proceeded to the torpedo school in Flensburg. During the tour of the torpedo facility, in accordance with the German assessment that Vorontsov was on a fishing expedition, Vorontsov was not answered when he asked about the speed and propulsion of torpedoes. Further, Kaull and the German escort officers attempted to deflect questions that might prove embarrassing to the Germans at all of the facilities visited, especially those questions that were sensitive.

On the final day of the tour they inspected the submarine *U-46*. While visiting the U-boat, the Soviet officer noted that the *U-46* was a sister ship of the famous *U-47* commanded by Günther Prien, who had sank the British battleship *Royal Oak*. Vorontsov and Kaull then toured Kiel Navy Yard and met with its director, Rear Admiral Otto Hormel. The technical officers at the navy yard in Kiel gave Vorontsov a good explanation of a submarine escape apparatus, including the escape suit. Vorontsov asked detailed questions about the 105-mm antiaircraft guns, which were the standard long-range weapon in the German fleet, as well as the rate of fire of the 280-mm coastal and shipboard heavy guns, the main armament of the Scharnhorst battle cruiser and Deutschland pocket battleship classes. He was interested in the loading arrangements for the guns and was even curious about the average age of officers in admirals' billets.

The tour was capped by a visit to the battle cruiser *Gneisenau* and lunch with its commanding officer, Captain Harold Netzbandt, whose ship had just returned from a successful North Atlantic sortie. The specific details of the armor of the turrets on the *Gneisenau*—which the Soviets knew were heavier than the earlier pocket battleship models and probably were a motive for Stalin asking about the triple turrets during the negotiations—were one line of dogged questioning pursued by Vorontsov. He did not get much from his hosts, according to their records.

While the Soviet attaché was persistent in questioning his German hosts, he also volunteered some potentially significant information on a reorganization within the political-military control structure of his own navy. In 1939 the status of the shipboard political commissars was altered to that of being deputy commander for political affairs, and, thus, they became militarily second-in-command to the commanding officers. Vorontsov, in an uncharacteristic exercise in candor, said that the political commissar now outranked the commanding officer unless the commanding officer was a Communist party member. The political commissar, the shipboard representative of the party, had the authority to countermand the orders of the captain or to oppose their implementation if, in his opinion, the orders were improper. The commissar was attached to the officers' mess so that he might monitor the political views exchanged by the ship's officers. Although there were a large number of Nazi party members in the Kriegsmarine, nothing quite like the commissar system existed.[46]

Vorontsov remarked to Kaull that the trip "had been very valuable" and had "cleared up many questions." "The situation of a navy attaché," he said, "is very difficult. It falls to me to get information about everything my regime desires, without appearing to damage the defenses of the country where I am working." Vorontsov realized that his counterpart faced the same problem in Moscow, perhaps to an even greater extent, "because foreign attachés were not to be given any information"—again, some uncharacteristic, if possibly useful, candor.[47]

Some months later, on 17 April 1940, Vorontsov called on the attaché department of the German naval high command to request information and opinions on the various enemy losses during the Norwegian campaign (see chap. 1). At first Vorontsov was referred to the Armed Forces High Command's public releases on the campaign and was told that military results could not be provided to friendly powers while the action was still underway. Naturally, Vorontsov was also curious about German losses, having heard in the foreign press that *Gneisenau* and *Emden* had been lost and the *Königsberg* seriously damaged. The attaché department of the naval high command then reiterated standing German policy, which was not to address individual enemy press releases, especially if this might result in the enemy getting a clearer picture of the German position. The facts were that *Königsberg* had been immobilized and later sunk at Bergen on 9 April 1940 during the successful Norwegian invasion.[48] *Emden* took part in the invasion also as part of the *Lützow*'s group on Oslo but survived the operation.[49] At the time of the conversation with the Soviet attaché *Gneisenau* and *Scharnhorst* were in port, and damage suffered in the Norwegian operation was being repaired.[50]

The Germans were not about to lift the fog of war, erstwhile "friendly" or not. Vorontsov went on to assert that von Baumbach had visited the Soviet high command in Moscow a great deal more often than he had visited its counterpart in Germany. The German attaché replied that he had seen the Soviet attaché twice a week since November and that it was well known that the Soviet navy was a "foreign but friendly service" in German eyes. Vorontsov was also reminded that his navy had asked a great deal more of the German navy than the German navy had asked of the

Soviets and that much effort had been put into addressing Soviet wishes. With regard to the British forces in Norway, Vorontsov drew some response. The Soviet attaché was told that the British had landed in places where German troops were already ashore but that Norway was firmly in German hands and the British landings were not expected to yield any important results. In fact, that was the case. The British tried valiantly to use sea power to cut off German naval forces, extracting a terrible price, especially among the German destroyer force, of which some ten were sunk. Yet, in the end, because Germans used air power and interior lines of communications, and because of real disasters for the Allies on the western front, the Allied Norwegian campaign was doomed. Indeed, as the British official history admits "the Germans successfully gained local command in the southern North Sea to carry out their plan to invade Norway."[51]

The Soviets were in the process of deciding their policy on the German invasion of Norway at the time of Vorontsov's visit. The report that Vorontsov sent back from Berlin had an impact on Soviet policy, with the Soviets subscribing to Germany's "defensive measures" in Norway. In the end, however, it would appear that the Soviets did not get much more information about German losses from Vorontsov than could be gleaned from press reports. Although he informed the Soviet attaché about the general state of affairs in Norway, the German naval high command practiced tight-lipped diplomacy in its relations with the Soviet service.

In July 1940, in the professional journal *Morskoy sbornik* (Naval Digest), Rear Admiral Professor Vladimir Belli of the Soviet Naval Academy published a major study entitled "Scandinavian Naval Operations and Their Lessons." Belli, who was one of the leading Soviet naval theoreticians of his day, concluded that the Germans had recognized that the German strategic objective in Scandinavia was a campaign to "gain a favorable strategic position. The Germans had made the British naval task of blockade much more difficult. German Baltic sea communications and vital imports of Swedish ore were secure. All of the United Kingdom's naval bases were within German bomber range." From a military-technical point of view the Soviet writer concluded that the operation had succeeded because the Germans "operated under a single strategic plan that required strict coordination of operations of the three branches of the armed forces: Army, Navy and Air Force." The Soviets naval brain trust[52] had deduced the key lessons of the Norwegian campaign using their own analysis rather than whatever other sources Vorontsov might have collected.[53]

In an attempt to gather more useful intelligence Moscow sent an assistant to its naval attaché in Berlin in April 1941. Very probably, Major Viktor Smirnov was a member of Soviet intelligence and security services.

The Germans accepted the additional posting of an assistant naval attaché—Norbert von Baumbach, after all, had at least one assistant in Moscow—but they did not permit any other trips by the Soviets to the naval "front." In fact, after the one trip to Kiel and Flensburg the Germans appear to have made an effort to keep the Soviet naval attaché in the dark.[54]

When the time came to exchange diplomatic and other personnel caught in Germany and Russia during the 1941 invasion, one Soviet intelligence officer observed that the Germans "had a three-to-one superiority over us [the Soviet Union] in numbers of people stationed in the respective countries at the outbreak of hostilities—quite an intelligence advantage."[55]

The Germans appear to have enjoyed a slight edge in the effectiveness of their man in Moscow over the Soviets' naval attaché in Berlin. Although each attaché received an invitation to tour naval bases in their host countries, Soviet naval attaché Vorontsov managed only to tour Kiel and Flensburg-Murwik before the turn of events between Russia and German prevented further access. Von Baumbach, on the other hand, appears to have had somewhat better access to the Soviet high command.

Trust, the Soviet Military, and the German Military

Soviet assistance in the escape of the *Bremen* and their help to German steamers using Murmansk as a port of refuge, the establishment of Basis Nord, the sale of Cruiser "*L*," and other elements of the Soviet-German naval relationship all represent elements of the Soviet-German military interface, which involved the invocation of trust. But there was also a negative side to the dealings. In December of 1939, while the first Soviet-German economic treaty was still being negotiated, von Baumbach wrote a telling letter to his head of section in Berlin. It reveals that these negotiations were being kept in "back channels" and that there was real concern on the part of the German military that the Soviets were being deceptive. The attaché's letter seems almost a cri de coeur and says in part: "The political negotiations going on between our government and the Soviet government have been kept a close secret by the head of the German mission to Russia. Despite our requests, no precise information has been given to us attachés of the armed forces and we have been forced to pool our scanty knowledge and can claim only a limited degree of accuracy for our conclusions."

The naval attaché asked Hilger: "the Russians have deceived us or not?" Hilger's reply was, "This is not the case . . . they remained within their own sphere of influence, the boundaries of which were determined by our interests."[56] Diplomatic niceties aside some members of the German military could not believe it was "in accordance with German policy to deliver a decent, hardworking people like the Finns to Soviet barbarity . . . it throws the question of our dependence on the Soviet Union into sharp relief. It appears the Soviet government is showing a surprisingly great willingness to cooperate with us in many things, in order to ensure our silent toleration of her own plans." The letter went on to express concerns about possible German economic dependence on the Soviet Union which might result in significant political leverage for the Soviets.[57]

In December of 1939 the Germans were not about to make life more difficult for the Soviets. The latter's raw materials provided significant clout. In August of 1940, when the Soviets wished to support politically their own policy in the Balkans in the face of an unexpectedly rapid victory by the Germans over France and Britain during that summer, it suspended deliveries of Soviet raw materials, and the Germans were in a bad way— just as von Baumbach had predicted.[58] The resource issue in itself was the major Soviet leverage over the Germans. German control over Balkan resources checkmated traditional Russian hegemony over the Balkans and provided a major portion of the resources needed to support the Germans and the German navy's war effort.

Returning to the smaller maritime issues, the German government took the position that Soviet merchant ships were friendly neutrals, which were to be treated as vessels in official service, with the ensuing extraterritoriality accruing to the Soviets. Even so, problems between the two navies continued. On 8 August 1940 two merchant raiders intercepted by Soviet ships in Arctic waters while making the passage to the North Atlantic were forced to stop and identify themselves as German warships. The naval high command fulminated that, if operations were to be carried out in the Barents Sea, "it cannot be ruled out that Russian, not English, destroyers will have to be dealt with here!" It should be pointed out that the Germans were willing to risk an attack on the Petsamo nickel trade out of northern Finland to England and Russia using the cruiser *Hipper*. The Germans had intended to disrupt the trade and would have sunk any of the nickel carriers, Soviet or British. But no Russian ships were encountered, and it turned out to be a markedly unsuccessful operation.[59]

Dinner in Moscow

It was a short leap from naval operations to diplomacy and back again during mid-1940. In the strategic arena Soviet-German relations were at virtual impasse. The complete German victory in France had forced the evacuation of the last British troops by the end of the first week in June. On 16 June 1940 the Soviets were reassured that the Germans desired a "settlement" in the Balkans on terms that would not disrupt the 1939 nonaggression pact. France, attacked by Italy on 10 June, sued for an armistice on 17 June. Nevertheless, Stalin was also pressing the Germans on Bessarabia, an eastern province of Romania, and on Bucovina as well. On 24 June Hitler authorized the German ambassador in Berlin to cede to the Soviets a sphere of influence as far as the Turkish Straits including Romania and Bessarabia. The same day Hitler dictated the armistice to the French at Compiegne.[60] As always, Stalin pressed his advantage wherever he could. At sea the British were recovering from the Dunkirk evacuation and were planning to defend the British Isles from invasion. Because of deployments and attrition, only two heavy cruisers were available to support a German invasion of England in June 1940. The summer of 1940, however, allowed the German U-boat forces much free reign among poorly escorted British shipping.[61] Back on land in the summer of 1940 the Nazis decided to pressure Romania into ceding territory to the Soviets. Stalin, for his part, rebuffed an Allied mission whose purpose was to bring Russia into an alliance against Germany in mid-July. By the end of August German diplomats had redrawn the Hungarian and Romanian borders and settled Bulgarian claims. The Balkans were quiet.[62]

More important, the Royal Air Force (RAF) had checked the Luftwaffe over Britain in the summer of 1940. On 2 September the U.S.-British destroyer deal was signed, prompting Stalin to conclude that the war was to be a long one. In Germany, despite intensive bombing efforts, the new battleships *Bismarck* and *Tirpitz* were nearing completion, and battle cruisers *Scharnhorst* and *Gneisenau* were almost ready for service again. The Soviet destroyer, cruiser, and battleship program continued apace, but the Sovetskiy Soyuz–class battleships were far from complete.

Despite the rocky course that Soviet-German relations were following, von Baumbach decided to press his acquaintance with the Soviet high command. In September of 1940 von Baumbach issued a personal invitation to the commander in chief of the Soviet navy to dine with his family in his Moscow quarters. Tendered in the context of an official thank-you for the use of Basis Nord, which was closed in the fall of 1940, the invitation was cleared with naval high command in Berlin as something of a litmus test of the state of Soviet-German relations. The Soviet navy did not reply until 9 October, when a functionary of the Soviet naval attaché affairs office, Captain Second Rank Zaitsev, told von Baumbach that the chief of staff of the Soviet commissariat of naval affairs could not accept an invitation to dinner at any foreign military attaché's house. By October 1940 the Germans had signed the Tripartite Pact with Italy and Japan (27 September), and the Soviets were concerned. But there was more trouble: German deliveries to the USSR were behind schedule, and Soviet deliveries to Germany were beginning to dry up.[63] In point of fact, the last time such a senior officer, then a chief of the Soviet general staff, had accepted such a German social invitation was in 1932, when the late Marshal M. N. Tukhachevskiy did so.[64] He was a key player in earlier Soviet-German military exchanges, while head of Soviet army ordnance in the early 1930s, and worked with the German general Ludwig on technical cooperation.[65]

Perhaps because the talks between Molotov and von Ribbentrop in Berlin had begun moving in a positive direction, the Soviets modified their policy and accepted the German invitation. On 14 December 1940 a dinner was given in the name of the German ambassador, with several embassy staff members and the following Soviet guests—including the chief of staff of the admiralty—in attendance: Admiral L. M. Galler (deputy commissar of Soviet Naval Forces, 1940), commander in chief of Soviet Naval Forces for Ship Construction and Naval Armament, murdered by Stalin after World War II; Rear Admiral V. O. Alafuzov, deputy chief of the admiralty staff; Captain First Rank Ivanov, aide to the chief of the admiralty staff (this officer could have been academician Lev Ivanov, who in the 1960s wrote a book on *Anglo-American Naval Rivalry* and translated Corbett's *Principles of Maritime Strategy* into Russian; he also defended balanced fleets and command of the sea in the 1930s, when it was dangerous to do so); Captain Second Rank Zaitsev, chief of the naval attaché group (could have been an OGPU officer, later KGB technical éminence grisé).

Not a great deal of intelligence was gleaned from what was apparently a pleasant occasion. Von Baumbach confirmed that Galler was a former czarist officer with thirty-eight years of naval service, having entered the Russian navy in 1902. Galler was professionally interested in the progress of the war and believed it could not but result in a "favorable outcome." Although he knew German from his earlier czarist service, Galler spoke only Russian at the dinner party. He apparently did not want to reveal his German ancestry, although he was listed in the 1914 rank list of the Imperial Russian Navy as von Galler![66] According to the Germans, Galler appeared more intelligent and clear-thinking than the average Russian officer; the admiral described himself as a Russian patriot whose nonpolitical status would have to remain as long as he was in such a high position. V. A. Alafuzov, on the other hand, was a young officer who wore a lot of medals and was assessed as a rapid riser. The Germans believed Alafuzov was a fortress commandant in Soviet Lappland (Lappland refers to that part of Finland annexed by the Soviets after the Winter War) and Estonia during the 1940 Soviet takeovers of those countries. In fact, we now know Vladimir Antonovich Alafuzov (1901–66) joined the navy in 1918 and completed the Naval Academy in 1932 after participating in the civil war.

He served as a battleship navigator, as executive officer of a cruiser, and as the deputy chief of the main naval staff.[67]

Soon after the dinner the Russians were asking questions about actions in the Norwegian campaign, centering the questions on the reportedly successful attack on *Hipper* and later *Gneisenau* by British naval torpedo bombers. *Gneisenau* was actually damaged twice in Norwegian waters. The first instance was the running sea fight with the battle cruiser *Renown* on 8–9 April 1940.[68] The second time was *Gneisenau*'s torpedoing by British submarine *Clyde* on 20 June on its return from Trondheim.[69] In fact, as the dinner party was going on, *Gneisenau* was preparing for sorties, albeit abortive, with *Scharnhorst*. The former was seriously damaged by heavy seas off the Norwegian coast and had to return to base.[70] With regard to the heavy cruiser *Admiral Hipper*, the British destroyer *Glowworm* rammed *Hipper* in a daring and extraordinarily gallant attack.[71] On 8 April 1940 the Soviets were fishing for information, using knowledge acquired from other sources.[72]

The Germans did not respond directly, reminding the Soviets that they had already been informed in April that the *Hipper* had not been hit by torpedoes. The Germans related part of the story to a Soviet officer: several destroyers had been hit (in fact, more had), and some of the torpedoes had actually landed ashore and gone off there. *Scharnhorst* was also the target of such an airborne torpedo attack, but it too had failed, with a destroyer allegedly taking the hits again.[73]

Unfulfilled Expectations

Whatever their uneasiness about Nazi-Soviet political detente, the militaries of Stalin's Russia and Hitler's Germany hoped that significant military-technical benefits could possibly be obtained with the Molotov-Ribbentrop Pact. The Germans envisioned raw materials to support their naval war effort and bases to help them break out of the "wet triangle" of the North Sea. For the Soviet Union, German technology and additional industrial support for construction of a modern oceangoing navy and air force surface as two possible objectives.

The first indication that Raeder's navy thought it could derive real benefits under the new pact appears in the *War Diary* of the German naval high command. An entry for 14 September 1939 observes that "the purchase of additional U-boats from . . . Russia is considered necessary and is proposed . . . Commander-in-Chief Navy agrees in principle and . . . he will ask for the Führer's decision." Unfortunately, the Soviets have not released the full record, including an equivalent war diary of their commissariat of naval affairs for the period, although they may yet do so under glasnost; indeed, we do have the earlier records (as seen in chap 1). It is regrettable that neither Golovko nor the official history of the Soviet navy in World War II say anything about these dealings.[74]

Acquiring U-boats from Soviet sources was one of three major cooperative proposals raised by Grand Admiral Raeder with Hitler in a meeting on 23 September. Raeder also suggested that German warships might use Soviet harbors and that German merchant raiders could be supplied at Murmansk. Hitler said he would instruct the foreign minister, Joachim von Ribbentrop, to raise the issues in Moscow on his next visit to Moscow.

By 27 September Captain von Baumbach reported that he considered the idea of purchasing submarines from the Soviet Union "very promising" because the USSR had already agreed to equip several German auxiliary cruisers. This objective eventually was partially realized by the planned later Northern Sea Route transit of auxiliary cruiser *Thor* to the Pacific. Other operations, however, never came to fruition. The assistance had geopolitical, strategic, and military-technical implications at a time when pocket battleships *Graf Spee*, *Admiral Scheer*, and *Deutschland* were preying on British shipping lanes. Von Baumbach had no hard information on the state of readiness of Soviet submarines, but he was aware that the Soviet navy had an almost legendary record of submarine breakdowns and technical losses in the Baltic Sea.[75] Von Baumbach was instructed to pursue the matter with the Soviet government in order to ascertain the Soviet position.

The next day, 28 September, was marked by the signing of diplomatic instruments by the Soviet Union and Germany, including a joint political declaration, a border and alliance treaty, and an economic plan. Given these larger agreements of 28 September, it was hardly a surprise when Grand Admiral Raeder informed his flag officer submarines that his impression from talks with the German Foreign Office indicated that "with regard to Russian assistance, the Reich Foreign Minister believes that he can count on far-reaching support." The actual matter of purchase, however, was to be pursued "after a decision had been made on continuation of the war."[76] At this point the German leadership continued to entertain the thought that it would be a short war and that a negotiated peace with England was possible. France was still regarded as a formidable power by both Germany and Russia. Neither regime contemplated the Anglo-French debacle of the spring of 1940.

By 3 October Raeder asked his staff to produce a more extensive list of requests which the foreign minister could take to Moscow, including the refueling of German warships in both Atlantic and Pacific Soviet ports. Although Raeder thought bringing combined Soviet and German political pressure to bear on Norway might make it possible to establish German bases in that country, the acquisition of U-boats from the Soviet navy remained the top priority of the preliminary list. Germany entered the war with fifty-six operational U-boats. There had been no time to achieve the planned submarine order of battle, even for the smaller mid-1930s plans. A possible 20 percent increase in available hulls was militarily significant.

The German naval high command concluded that the U-boat war against England could be intensified if ten Soviet submarines built from German plans and equipped with German engines could be acquired quickly. Beyond the ten boats the German navy wanted to explore the possibility of building U-boats in Soviet Baltic and Arctic Sea shipyards, where German engineers, technicians, plans, and assistance could work without danger of British air attack. Knowledge of the prospect of such an agreement, or others like it, would have added to British hostility toward the Soviet Union in the fall of 1939. The level of knowledge by French or British governments of German dealings with the Soviets was minimal to nonexistent, however, especially regarding secret protocols. The effects of the pact on the German navy's situation were quite clear and positive. First, the German fleet was able to concentrate its efforts against England, and, second, it was able to secure the Baltic. Ultimately, the German naval high command proposed that a unit of ten newly commissioned former Soviet submarines operating out of Soviet harbors could be supplied by support ships flying the Soviet flag.[77]

But the German naval staff's plans regarding U-boat purchases were never realized. A week after Raeder requested his staff to prepare a more extensive list, Hitler decided for political reasons that he did not want Stalin to know that a key weakness in German military-industrial planning existed. The U-boat purchase issue was brought forward once more by General Wilhelm Keitel, Wehrmacht chief of staff, but Hitler again rejected the plan, citing the poor quality of the Soviet boats. Von Baumbach's earlier reports on Soviet submarine disasters in the Baltic were probably relevant.[78] Ultimately, the Germans did not buy U-boats from any other nation; they depended on a large-scale program of their own.

After further consultation with Hitler, Raeder asked the German Foreign Office to pursue several major items with the Soviets, other than U-boat purchases. The German naval "wish list" was forwarded to the Soviets via diplomatic channels.

First, it included a request from the German navy for the Soviet Union to provide supply ships to extend the radius of action of German surface raiders and submarines. The supply ships were to be escorted by Soviet warships to their rendezvous. The Germans admitted this would strain Soviet neutrality somewhat, so an alternative arrangement was proposed whereby the Soviet supply ships would leave harbor as "neutrals" and be taken "prize" by German ships, until after the support function was completed. Such a plan of operation was on the edges of the international law of the times. It is likely the British and French would have treated such ships and their escorts as combatants—or, at the least, as naval auxiliaries.[79]

Second, the German navy proposed Soviet transport of surface raider and submarine supplies to a Soviet transshipment point where they would be taken aboard German supply ships.[80] Third, the Germans suggested the Soviet Union could supply U-boats and commerce raiders with fuel and provisions in Soviet harbors. In addition, they suggested that a transfer of munitions and spare parts sent from Germany could be accomplished in Soviet ports. Fourth, specialized technical support from Germany for the repair and refitting of German cruisers, submarines, and auxiliary vessels in Soviet shipyards was proposed, as was the conversion of German merchant ships to armed raiders. Such actions, taken together, seriously compromised Soviet neutrality. Because of other British concerns, however, the Soviets avoided the adverse consequences rightfully consequent to such behavior because it did not vitally affect the interests of Britain, or so they thought. By December, however, the Soviets were emboldened to attack Finland. The prospect of a Soviet advance across Scandinavia put a different twist on the issues. By December 1939 the Allies were searching for a way to gain the initiative. True, Germany had been isolated and most of its commerce swept from the seas, but there was no balance to the entire weight of the German army hitting France and the Low Countries.

For France and Britain a Scandinavian project was important because, as the by-product of helping Finland against Russia, the Allied forces would have to pass through and, by implication, occupy a section of northern Sweden which contained one of the main sources of German iron ore supply. The ore was shipped out via Narvik or Luilea (in Sweden): "An expedition . . . which landed at Narvik, and followed the railway to the Gulf of Bothnia, would, literally take the ore-fields in its stride and thus deprive the Germans of a commodity essential to their war production." To some degree the Germans had to take such possibilities into account. According to British estimates, Germany imported twenty-two million tons of iron ore in 1939. Nine and a half million tons came from sources that the Allies were able to cut off; nine million tons came from Sweden. If the supply from Narvik were stopped, the loss would be between two and a half and three and a half million tons.[81] Soviet-German agreements had politically blocked at least one plan to use naval power against Norwegian ore traffic in 1939.[82]

Raeder did not believe the loss of the Finnish ore would have been critical for German war industry, but the British did. Accordingly, the ore trade became a very tempting target. Meanwhile, the British had faced the prospect in late October 1939 of having to declare Russian cargoes on their way to Germany as contraband. On 22 November the British war cabinet instructed "the contraband authorities to avoid, as far as possible, action likely to lead to serious disputes with the Soviet Government." Moreover, the British chiefs of staff concluded that a declaration of war on the USSR would result in increased submarine activity (from the Soviet fleet) *and* increased economic cooperation between Germany and the USSR. Iran, Iraq, and Afghanistan would have to be secured without additional resources. By mid-December 1939 the Finno-Russian War had broken out, and the Allies, for the reasons previously outlined, did nothing.[83] The German navy was about to play a large successful role in securing Norway for the Reich.

The German diplomatic agenda with the Soviets in the fall of 1939 also included important details of naval arrangements. These included protection of Soviet harbors or sea areas used by the Germans, intelligence support of German naval operations against both enemy merchant shipping and naval forces, and use of the Soviet flag to cover German coastal convoys along the shores of Norway. Cancellation of all direct or indirect Soviet exports to enemy countries was to be requested. The German military, at least, had a complete plan that would have made the Soviets true cobelligerents against the Western democracies.

The German Foreign Office received a series of requests from the naval high command on 12 October. Raeder was most interested in obtaining the supply and repair of German naval ships and U-boats from Soviet harbors. The other points were subordinate to the principal strategic objective of escaping the wet triangle of the North and Baltic seas, which was the limited strategic basis for German naval operations. Again, in the fall of 1939, Raeder could not know of the forthcoming successes or losses his navy would have. The conquest of Scandinavia, albeit at the cost of half the German navy, would solve the strategic problems of the "wet triangle" for the rest of the war. Yet we do know that he planned for the conquest of Norway at the same time, exploiting the geostrategic advantage derived from good Russo-German relations.[84]

Of course, the German Foreign Office presented the German naval requests to the Soviet Union, emphasizing: "the supply of cruisers, submarines and auxiliary ships with fuel and provisions in Russian harbors. . . . Other munitions and material could be transshipped from Germany; overhaul of German warships could be accomplished in Russian ports; equipment and provision of Russian supply vessels to supply German cruisers and submarines was also desired."

Meanwhile, German naval attaché von Baumbach had followed his orders to explore informally the support the Soviet Union would actually be willing to provide.[85] Following his visit to the naval commissariat on 13 October 1939, von Baumbach reported the Soviet attitude. He observed that he had been called to the Soviet commissariat for naval affairs—an unusual situation even in those days. At the commissariat he met with a Lieutenant Commander V. Skriagin, who informed him that orders had been given to facilitate the desired floating base in the Murmansk area. The Germans were to be given a bay and could place as many ships there as they wished. Von Baumbach raised questions concerning the Soviet attitude toward the arming of auxiliary cruisers in the bay and of basing support ships there. He reminded Skriagin that, because Murmansk was a civilian port with a great deal of traffic, the military nature of the undertaking was likely to "complicate matters." German concerns about cover were transparent. A busy commercial port was not a good place from which to run a secret submarine base. The Soviet officer agreed to explore the "problem" of neutrality further. The Soviet naval leadership offered to provide semiskilled and unskilled workers supervised by German technicians and engineers to support for German ship repair and conversion efforts. Von Baumbach replied that the German floating base would be fully equipped with qualified German technicians. The Soviet high command also discussed the difficulties caused by the German transatlantic super liner *Bremen*, which had recently run the British blockade into "neutral" Soviet waters. They said that the ship should proceed to an outlying bay in the Kola Peninsula so as to be less obtrusive than it was in Murmansk. The *Bremen* was not intercepted on the way out but was detected by the British submarine *Salmon* on the way back. It was not attacked because the British admiralty orders of the day forbade submarine attacks on unarmed passenger liners. The final point discussed was the safe transit of two Soviet floating cranes on order in Holland, which was staffed properly through the German system by von Baumbach. While German-Soviet naval relations seemed to be on a firm footing in Moscow, the German request to have overt repair and resupply facilities at Soviet ports was not to be fulfilled. The war diary of the German naval high command says:[86]

> The desire of naval staff, at [regarding] Murmansk and Vladivostok, [included] the possibility of completely overhauling in Russian dockyards German warships (pocket battleships and submarines), making repairs, equipping auxiliary cruisers and

replenishing supply ships, cannot be fulfilled. Reasons are of a political and technical nature as follows:

> The secrecy required would be in doubt as the harbors are open to foreign merchantmen at all times.
>
> Although the Russians are willing to accommodate us to a great extent, they wish to maintain outward neutrality.
>
> Work at Russian dockyards does not compare with that of Germany. The naval attaché does not consider overhauls by Russian labor very promising.

While mulling over the German requests, the Soviet naval leadership was preparing its own requirements. Soviet commissions on naval construction and artillery manufacture arrived in Berlin on 29 October 1939. Political officers led their delegations. They requested a visit to the battleship *Scharnhorst* immediately and promptly asked to view all equipment and weapons for sale. Their attitude was that the Soviet Union had made it possible for Germany to continue the war because of the economic and material support that it had been provided. Therefore, they should be able to buy anything they wanted. Soviet requests grew each time they were submitted. The Soviet delegation asked the Germans for their most important secrets, including torpedo fuses, naval mines, and detonators. The Soviets broached the purchase of the half-finished cruisers *Lützow* and *Seydlitz*, aircraft carrier "B," and plans for the *Scharnhorst*. They also wanted to visit the heavy cruiser *Hipper*, a modern destroyer, a U-boat of the type that sank HMS *Royal Oak* (a battleship torpedoed in Scapa Flow by *U-47* in early 1939), and a minelayer.

These Soviet delegations showed great mistrust of the data with which the Germans provided them. For example, the Soviets purchasing commissions thought that the Germans actually had mounted heavier-caliber guns aboard ships and in coastal batteries than they were willing to reveal.[87] The chief of the German naval construction office, who wrote the memorandum from which this account is drawn, indicated that the price asked for each individual request on the Soviet request list should be decided only after discussion with Hitler. The document indicates that the middle levels of the German naval command were in no hurry to provide anything to the Soviets. Indeed, beyond the highest political levels it was not certain whether significant benefits really accrued to the relationship and that at most only a patina of trust existed.[88]

The members of the Soviet commissions, for their part, expressed the desire for everything from 38.1-cm (15-in.) guns to binoculars. These guns were a possible substitute for the U.S. guns, which were not available.

There had been enough opposition from the U.S. navy that no weapons were ever purchased, much less delivered.[89] This American naval attitude and bureaucratic obfuscation were ultimately supported by the formal arms embargo that resulted from the Soviet-German treaty.[90] As pointed out earlier in this work, the 38-cm guns were desired for the Kronshtadt-class battle cruisers to arm the first pair of a class of fifteen.[91]

This was only the preliminary Soviet request and represented a catalog of naval high technology items of the day, some of which the Germans did not have themselves. The Soviets wanted virtually every sensitive item in the German navy's inventory—eighty-nine categories in all—and they wanted the weapons and equipment in amounts that would have had an adverse impact on German capabilities. It is very likely that the list was the result of Stalin's objectives to learn as much as possible about his future enemy and, if possible, to hobble its expansion. Insight into how the Soviet navy hoped to use German technical and material assistance is indicated by its request during the negotiations for 15,000 tons of German armor plate to equip a class of four light cruisers and several smaller ships. The request included armament, electrical supplies, parts of the ships' structure, and all machinery, except for the main turbines and boilers.

The Germans were also asked to provide everything but the scantlings and basic steel framing for two Hipper-class heavy cruisers to be produced in the Soviet Union as well as complete plans for the Scharnhorst-class battleships and the Graf Zeppelin–class aircraft carriers. The Soviets went so far as to request 40.6-cm (16-in.), 38.1-cm (15-in.), and 15.5-cm (6.1-in.) coastal artillery armored turrets, "with directions for firing and supply of ammunition, etc."[92] These requests were followed up with even more detailed lists accompanying the two Soviet delegations' visits to German shipyards in November 1939.[93]

The composition of the Soviet naval construction commission is, itself, interesting. Led by commissar of shipbuilding Ivan T. Tevossian, who was directing Soviet Stalin's fleet buildup, it included eight experts on ship construction, four gunnery specialists (including a head-of-section named Ustinov, who might well have been the late defense minister), three experts on turbine construction and electric motors, various experts on machinery construction, torpedoes, mines, and radio, and one "trade representative" named (possibly L. S.) Zaitsev, who may have been the very successful KGB official later responsible for science and technology efforts.

In the German view the Soviets were technical experts who had done all the paper homework they could but had no practical experience in the modern methods of ship construction. The delegation was most interested in ship's armor, especially that directed against plunging fire or air attack.

The delegation visited three shipyards: Blohm and Voss in Hamburg, Germania Werft in Kiel, and Deschimag in Bremen. They were taken to sea on the heavy cruiser *Hipper* and allowed to compare it with the still incomplete ships *Lützow* and *Seydlitz*. During a discussion of the Soviet delegations' goals at naval headquarters, the Nazi high command concluded that the Soviets would " above all . . . like the cruisers *Seydlitz* and *Lützow* in exchange for delivery of goods."

While another source indicates that the Soviet delegations also visited *Scharnhorst*, *Blücher*, *Graf Zeppelin*, *Bismarck*, and the destroyer *Anton Schmidt*,[94] Germany's naval attaché to Moscow was not accorded reciprocal visiting privileges and, in fact, only saw the more sensitive aspects of the Soviet fleet program after the shipyards were captured by German forces.[95]

The Russians wanted the Germans to help in the construction of their navy, but Germany was already beset by a labor shortage. The Germans decided to continue with the negotiations in November 1939 with the following objectives:

1. Every effort should be made to meet the Russian demands, but the limitations of the German shipbuilding industry working to full capacity for the war effort must be made clear.
2. The delivery of the *Seydlitz* is quite out of the question, but the cruiser *Lützow* and aircraft carrier "B" can be offered to the Russians.
3. We cannot allow our own vitally necessary strategic building program to be held back . . . by making deliveries of new construction or other kinds of material and machinery to Russia. Weapons and equipment can only be delivered within the limits of the capacity available.[96]

High-Level Progress and Impasse

By November of 1939 the key issues had reached Hitler, and the German military establishment was beginning to balk at the volume of Soviet technology transfer requests. In a conference with Hitler and General Keitel held 10 November 1939 Raeder pointed out that negotiations with the Soviets were "proceeding satisfactorily" but warned that deliveries of ships' equipment should not be made at the expense of armed forces quotas: "The Führer and the Chief of Staff, O.K.W., state [concur] that such deliveries are to be made only from export quotas."[97] The Germans wanted to lead Stalin on to convince him of honest intentions without compromising their German interests or German war aims.

In fact, in late 1939 the German military viewed its relationship with the Soviet military as one of absolute German superiority. The Germans were confident, as of 25 November 1939, that "as long as Stalin is in power, it is certain that she [Russia] will adhere strictly to the Pact made." Stalin was "in the bag." By the middle of January 1940 the German Foreign Office representative in Finland had concluded that Soviet military weakness was such that the Germans could take a free hand with the Soviets after the war. Nevertheless, Hitler did realize that problems could arise: he opposed the sale of *Seydlitz* and *Prinz Eugen* and delivery of 406-mm turrets from battleships "H" and "J" and suggested that Raeder delay as long as he could on providing plans for the *Bismarck*.[98] In November 1939 the battleship *Bismarck* was not yet complete, the battleships "H" and "J" were suspended, *Prinz Eugen* and *Seydlitz* were also not complete, but, taken together, this was the future of the German navy, which Hitler would not, at that point, mortgage. The German Z Plan might yet come to fruition.

Yet the pact with the devil (Stalin) had exacted a price in the form of domestic opposition to Soviet Union's invasion of Finland. Hitler had to deflect opposition to the Soviet policy against a fellow Nordic people, even by Nazi party stalwarts. Von Baumbach, in fact, wrote an interesting letter to the chief attaché of the naval high command in which he noted the adverse impact of the treaty on Germany's foreign relations, even lamenting Soviet aggression against a "decent people" like the Finns.[99] Such low-level concerns about the treaty did not prevent Raeder from recommending "that Russia be accommodated, for example, in the matter of oil supply for submarines, as Russia also offers us practical advantages, e.g., holding foreign ships in Murmansk for three days after the departure of the *Bremen*." The führer agreed.[100]

The führer may have agreed, but the problems of a war economy were not solved by Russian deliveries of grain and oil. The navy believed that German submarine construction would be delayed because of a shortage of metals in the first quarter of 1940. About 170,000 tons of steel were needed, with only 140,000 tons actually available. The position of the German navy was that the most valuable deliveries, that is, oil, should be traded for the incomplete *Lützow*, plans for the battleship *Bismarck*, destroyers, and submarines. On 7 December 1939, when the German naval high command reviewed the latest Soviet requests, they found that the Soviets had requested physical transfer of the incomplete heavy cruisers *Seydlitz*, *Lützow*, and *Prinz Eugen*.[101] This was particularly ironic because the cruisers had been built as replies to Soviet cruiser shipbuilding programs.

Hitler decided to minimize ship sales to the Russians. *Lützow* alone would go, in its incomplete state. The 203-mm guns belonging to *Lützow*, then in the army's possession, would have to be returned to naval stocks. These guns were only to be sold as a last resort, and no heavy turrets at all were to go to the Soviets. Hitler did not want to give up any heavy guns because he was concerned lest a war of position ensue after the planned German offensive in the West. No decision on the sale of the plans for *Bismarck* was made at the meeting: Hitler wanted to know what the price would be. Since the German navy still intended to build more advanced types of battleships after *Bismarck* and *Tirpitz* were complete, the technology in ships represented in Hitler's view, excellent "bargaining counters." Raeder estimated that it would take the Russians six years to reverse-engineer the *Bismarck*.[102]

The German naval high command soon took advantage of the difficulties the Soviet Union was having in Finland and advocated playing German military strength to its maximum diplomatic effect. Hardening their position on all Soviet requests, as of 17 December 1939, the naval staff was "of the opinion that the military and political weakness of Soviet Russia brought to light in Finland should be taken into consideration in our attitude toward Russia. In making plans and decisions we should . . . let our military and political power add weight in all negotiations with Russia more than . . . it has done so far."[103] The naval staff was much more prescient of the intuitively obvious in this issue than the Foreign Office.

Progress and Obstacles—Winter Negotiations

When negotiations reopened in January of 1940 the Soviet Union too had hardened its position. The cost had been high, but it had succeeded in defeating Finland, and Japan had been checked at Khalkin Ghol in July and August 1939 in the east. In fact, additional commercial agreements were being considered. Stalin decided to focus on obtaining *Lützow*, heavy turrets, and naval equipment, but the Soviets now focused on obtaining the plans of the improved sister ship of *Bismarck*, the *Tirpitz*. Stalin himself conducted the negotiations with special German ambassador Karl Ritter on 10 January 1940. During the course of negotiations the Russians moderated their demands, requesting only one cruiser, the *Lützow*, but still three twin 15-inch turrets, three triple 280-mm turrets, and four triple 5.9-inch heavy turrets. In return the Germans were to get iron, ore, scrap, nickel, copper, tin, and oil.[104]

Although we now know the 380-mm turrets were to go to some of the Kronshtadt class (as described in chap. 1), the 11-inch turrets destination would have also been for those ships, probably the third and fourth units. It is highly probable that all the heavy turrets were to be reverse-engineered so Stalin could take advantage of any German technological developments. The number of guns Stalin requested was inadequate to arm all the ships he was having built. At the same time the German naval attaché was pursuing arrangements for use of the Soviet-developed Northern Sea Route through the Arctic Ocean to the Orient by German warships and merchant ships. He was instructed to proceed through political channels via the Foreign Office and Molotov if no progress was made on a navy-to-navy basis. For its part the Soviet Foreign Office was busy requesting that Teriberka Bay, instead of Murmansk, be the locus of the repair facility for German warships and U-boats. The Germans, having gone to the trouble to get the base in the Kola Peninsula and having planned to use the Northern Sea Route, now had to consider taking Norway to protect their extended sea lines of communication. This subject, a significant subtopic in German naval strategy, will be examined in a later chapter of this work.[105]

Meanwhile, the Germans were working to get the most out of the Soviets, mostly in exchange for territorial or to influence changes in Eastern Europe. Grain transports had been sailing for Germany since 18 December 1939, and "the actual effect on the very considerable Russian exports remains to be seen; the German Naval High Command's impression was that the war in Finland was bound to have a prejudicial effect on the Soviet Union's industrial production and ability to meet treaty commitments. It was clear to the high command by mid-January of 1940 that Soviet losses to the Finns were of 'catastrophic proportions.' " By late January there were more indications that Hitler was disingenuous. On 26 January he said Germany should drag its feet with regard to delivery of *Lützow* and the plans for *Bismarck*, apparently "hoping for favorable developments in the course of the war." On 28 January the German ambassador telegraphed the foreign ministry that the Soviets were getting suspicious about German willingness and/or ability to make the deliveries required under the treaty. Shortly after Hitler made his statements, however, the German naval attaché in Moscow reported that the way had been cleared for German use of the Northern Sea Route. This the Germans took as an indication that the negotiations would develop favorably. Berlin authorized the raider *Komet* to use the route on 2 February 1940. Yet this positive indication was followed a few days later by a contraindication in the form of the Soviet demand that German naval operations in the Baltic be limited to west of 20 latitude east longitude, the remainder of that sea being a Soviet sphere of influence. The Germans acquiesced.[106] The Germans did not have much choice. The winter of 1939–40 was one of the worst on record. Much of the Baltic was frozen, Hitler's fleet was preparing for the invasion of Norway, and the "first wave" of auxiliary cruisers was preparing to savage Allied sea lanes. A review of the German "wish list" in Moscow by von Baumbach highlighted the agreement, in principle, concerning the use of the Soviet Northern Sea Route. The attaché, however, reminded Berlin that every single issue had to be decided within the labyrinthine naval and political bureaucracies of the Soviet Union. Von Baumbach also told the high command that everything Germany needed had to be accomplished in absolute secrecy and away from foreign eyes. Therefore, use of Murmansk or Vladivostok was out of the question. Two other issues of interest to Germany—the conversion and outfitting of auxiliary cruisers for commerce warfare and technical support of operations and ships in northern Russia and the Far East with help of Soviet shipyards—had not reflected much progress. This was largely because of practical difficulties: a Soviet claim of a lack of technical capability at either Murmansk or Vladivostok and Soviet concern of discovery by foreigners.

Although the Molotov-Ribbentrop Pact included a change in policy, whereby Germany no longer shared information on the Soviet Union with any other country, von Baumbach apparently did not believe there was a way to make workable arrangements for intelligence exchanges with the Soviet Union. Exchanges of intelligence on hostile powers would only be possible with the approval of Stalin and Admiral L. M. Galler, chief of the Soviet admiralty staff. Both sides seemed to appreciate that the compromise of such exchanges would lead to far worse consequences than any possible benefits they might bring.[107]

Von Baumbach was also concerned about the dangers of German ships using unfortified Soviet naval bases. He concluded that this might seriously compromise the thin cloak of Soviet neutrality and pointed out to Berlin that German ships would be at anchor under foreign guns (either Soviet or enemy) and subject to foreign controls. Von Baumbach considered Soviet naval escort for German convoys off the Norwegian coast or transport of naval supplies for German warships by Soviet support ships out of the question. He discouraged establishing bases in the calm, but relatively empty, Sea of Okhotsk or near Vladivostok, which would be close to areas of potential operations but too near waters under Japanese control. Again, in the spring of 1940, barely nine months had passed since the guns of Soviet and Japanese armies had fallen silent at Khalkin-Gol. While the eastern coast of Kamchatka had the advantage of unrestricted access to the Pacific, it was a long way from an advantageous naval operating area and was filled with Japanese fishing fleets.

The German navy viewed the acquisition of a base as fraught with difficulties. The acquisition would bring with it a Soviet partner, no fortifications, and a lightly armed ally. The Soviets had not had time to build up their forces in the Far East. Von Baumbach noted that German naval activities in the Far East were risky due to limited secondary support possibilities in Japanese waters. Worse, German ships operating from such a base at the time would be at the mercy of the Soviet bureaucrats running the base. Soviet neutrality would be constantly at issue.

Von Baumbach evaluated potential Soviet docking facilities in the Far East at Vladivostok and Petropavlovsk as well as at Morshchovoya Bay on the east coast of Kamchatka, which he thought could serve as a possible anchorage for ships up to 15,000 tons. Even so, he consulted the German naval attaché in Tokyo, Admiral Paul Wenneker. Wenneker believed that passage through Japanese waters was possible under cover of darkness and did not represent an obstacle to effective use of Soviet Far Eastern bases.

Turning to another possible use of Soviet territory, von Baumbach said that U-boat passage through the Soviet White Sea canal might prove attractive during the ice-free months so long as the northern Norwegian Sea was not mined. In any event, the Germans had already asked the Soviet Union for use of the Kamchatka Peninsula or the Belkin (Vladivostok) coasts in December of 1939. Although the initial reception was positive, the Germans still had no solid answer as of 15 February 1940. Nevertheless, von Baumbach still considered the establishment of a floating support base and machinery overhauls in Siberian Russian waters aboard a German repair ship to be real possibilities. His assessment, accomplished in early February 1940, appears to have been the last thorough review of Germany's requests under its pact with the Soviet Union.[108]

Although Soviet access to German production information was described as "unprecedented" by both Ribbentrop and Molotov as they hammered out the final details of the initial pact (i.e., 23 August 1939), it is probable even in October 1939 that the Soviet leaders were not at all satisfied with the attitude of the Germans about the transfer of military technology and the armaments assistance that followed. Later the Germans were pressed by Stalin to help with supplies during the Finnish War. The Germans, however, pleaded that they were feeling the full weight of the Allied blockade and the demands of their own war production. They were in dire need of additional raw materials.[109]

The extensive nature of the Soviet requests had alarmed many Germans, including Reichsmarshal Hermann Göring, Raeder, and Keitel, all of whom apparently came to the independent conclusion that "the Russian delegation in Berlin expected too much in the way of inspection and procurement of German materials of war" and that "things in the testing stage or otherwise secret should not be shown to the Russians." It was, however, also obvious to the Soviets that the latest German achievements were being held back, as Commissar Tevosian pointedly remarked in conversation with Göring during a reception at the Soviet embassy in Berlin on 7 November 1939. Stalin's objective was clearly to obtain as much information about the German war machine as he could and perhaps some real military dividends as well. Neither side was really interested in true peace—the process had become a grindstone for both sides. In fact, the German negotiator (Schnurre) noted that the Soviet requests consisted only of lists of manufactured goods and war material and that Soviet bottlenecks coincided with German industrial bottlenecks. December was also a bad month for the Kriegsmarine: *Graf Spee* was scuttled off Montevideo, and the British submarine *Salmon* sank *U-36* and torpedoed light cruisers *Leipzig* and *Nürnberg* in the North Sea. Negotiations on the Soviet requests reached a low ebb during December 1939. Serious problems had arisen: Soviet demands for 70,000 tons of iron per month would have necessitated serious cuts in German programs. Germany was accused of complicity in an Italian shipment of aircraft to Finland and publicly accused of shipping munitions to Finland. Finally, Stalin's request for extensive military deliveries was rejected.[110]

Ambassador Friedrich von der Schulenburg pressed for progress in the negotiations, telling the Soviets that their demands for military supplies were excessive. On 11 December 1939 the Soviet economic delegation in Berlin presented further demands, which, in the German view, far exceeded those previously agreed upon. The Germans proceeded to reject a Soviet demand that the German military deliveries should begin immediately, as being contrary to an understanding reached between Ribbentrop and Molotov in September. On 23 December von der Schulenberg and Molotov discussed the unsatisfactory progress of the negotiations. Molotov conceded that the Germans did have a war on and that this would explain some problems with military deliveries but complained that deliveries were few and the price exorbitant.[111]

Many other specifics of the Russo-German detente relating to naval issues were never fully resolved. Diplomacy, however, proceeded apace, and two major additional agreements were signed after the nonaggression pact was concluded in August 1939. The first was an economic agreement signed in Moscow on 11 February 1940; the second, a commercial agreement and boundary treaty was signed 10 January 1941.

While both these agreements indicate some very practical results of the Soviet-German detente, the record of negotiations for the economic agreement of 11 February 1940, between the German Reich and the Union of Soviet Socialist Republics, is of particular interest, because it formalized most aspects of the Soviet-German naval agreements, which traded technology for raw materials. In fact, these negotiations continued the diplomatic underpinning for the Soviet-German naval relationship. It was under this umbrella that the major transfer of Cruiser "*L*" (heavy cruiser *Lützow*) and the 38.1-cm guns were arranged.

The political-strategic issues in which naval issues were embedded were reflective of a much larger canvas, which allows them to be placed in historiographical context wherein the German navy's strategic desires and its Continental role came into conflict. Hitler did not hesitate to bargain technology for raw materials to feed his juggernaut. He probably believed the Soviets were incapable of assimilating much of value in time, anyway. Raeder's imperial naval geist thus had to cope uneasily with the Communist greatcoat so that he could fuel and feed *most* of his ships for the campaign against England.

Part III

Operations

Chapter Five

Basis Nord

Strategic Position beyond the North Sea

As the Soviets painstakingly examined the lessons of World War I at sea and followed the German debate on the strategy to be derived from that conflict in the interwar years, they concluded one of Germany's principal failures had been lack of free access to the oceans. The Imperial German Navy had failed to break out of the "wet triangle" of the North Sea. That the Soviets should be willing to provide any sort of extraterritoriality on Soviet soil to Nazi military is a conundrum of history. Yet from October of 1939 through August of 1940—well after the conclusion of the Norwegian campaign—the question of German naval bases in the Kola Peninsula of the Soviet Union remained a live issue.[1]

Was this base one of the great deceptions in history? Did it represent Russia's desire to break out of political isolation or Germany's solution to geographical isolation, or was its function simply a political or military expedient for Stalin and Hitler? If the strategic implications of a German naval base in the Soviet Union, German use of the Northern Sea Route for support of commerce warfare, or Soviet protection and aid to German maritime trade are understood, it is clear that this base was more politically than militarily significant in terms of the course of World War II.

Basis Nord was by no means the first effort the German navy or German intelligence had attempted to provide afloat logistics support for overseas operations. As early as 1902, in support of German naval operations off Venezuela, a Hamburg-America line ship, the *Siberia* was hired to provide supplies for the German East African cruiser squadron. In World War I the German plan was quite extensive and provided for the establishment of several floating bases.[2] Essentially, each *Etappe* (military base) consisted of all German merchant ships prepared for naval support in peacetime and commanded by a naval officer stationed overseas to support

German naval operations abroad. There were also a number of prizes taken which added to this naval equivalent of "living off the land."

In World War II the German effort was extensive and the mission the same. Basis Nord was part of a much larger establishment. Many of the *Etappe* ships served as auxiliary armed merchant raiders, and, in addition to German or chartered vessels, several prizes ended up on *Etappe* rosters.[3] That the Germans should wish to include a Soviet base in their clandestine naval support effort is operationally consistent with both historical precedent and operational requirements.

The political origin for the German base on Soviet territory was, of course, the signing of the Soviet-German nonaggression pact in 1939, which provided unparalleled openings for both sides to mutually exploit their respective resources and technology. The Soviet Union could offer precious little technology, but it could provide valuable raw materials and geographic position important to the success of German sea warfare. The Germans, on the other hand, had the technology the Soviet Union needed to build a blue-water fleet. The German naval archives have left us a record of behavior, first to chronicle and then to explain.

At the beginning of the relationship the Soviet Union was willing to show that it would exchange strategic maritime position for technology. The USSR was ready to provide a northern base to the Germans, as von Baumbach had reported, but not a busy seaport. Militarily speaking, the base would be tenable only as long as the Soviet Union was willing to tolerate its German tenants. It was deep enough inside Soviet territory and sufficiently isolated that no German operations were possible without Soviet observation. On the other hand, such an operation *had* to be politically isolated as well. It was, after all, a very belligerent act. Therefore Murmansk, according to Soviet Foreign Minister Molotov, was "not sufficiently isolated for this purpose." The Soviet Union's initial position was that Teriberka Bay, situated northwest of Murmansk, and not a port of call for foreign ships, would be a suitable location. On 16 October 1939, Raeder reported to Hitler that the Soviets "have placed at our disposal a well-situated base west of Murmansk. A repair ship is to be stationed there."[4] At the same time, Raeder had urged the seizure of Norway, which was, in fact, accomplished in the spring of 1940. By 14 December Hitler had authorized appropriate planning, driven mostly by fears of British intervention. The base also featured in the planning for the operation against Norway, but it was not used.[5] Details of the arrangements for the establishment of the base were to be worked out through the people's commissar for foreign and international trade, Anastas Mikoyan. The German naval high command had objections to the initial Soviet offer outside Murmansk, as the bay in question lacked good shelter as an anchorage and possessed no facilities whatever.[6] From the Soviet perspective Molotov was reportedly opposed to any use of Murmansk or Vladivostok, in the Soviet Far East because the Soviet side believed that the use of these facilities by the German navy could not be kept secret because of the use of these ports by vessels of other states; repair of German naval vessels would not be possible for the same reason; and Russian (Soviet) officials would like to satisfy the German request but were afraid of charges of violations of neutrality.

The Soviet proposal was discussed at length within the German naval high command and with the German naval attaché in Moscow. On 11 October 1939 the high command sent a memo to Captain von Baumbach asking for his recommendations on setting up a base with repair and support capabilities for surface vessels and U-boats in Teriberka Bay. The high command suggested that mobilization of German merchant ships lying in Murmansk might be a way to establish the base quickly but noted that there were physical disadvantages. This included exposure to wind, poor anchorage, and poor logistics, attendant to the location proposed by the Soviets. The Germans wanted these points checked before accepting the Russian proposal, but the Seekriegsleitung still forwarded as "good news" the Russian offer of a naval operating base in northern waters to Hitler on 16 October 1939.[7]

The next day Attaché von Baumbach informed the Seekriegsleitung that the Soviets had modified their offer of Teriberka Bay. Agreeing with the German assessment that the bay's "situation, harbor conditions and repair facilities are, however, most unsuitable . . . a new offer [October 1939] was submitted by the Russians placing Zapadnaya Litsa at our full disposal." The Soviet offer was unequivocal: "In this bay, Germany may do whatever she wishes; she may carry out whatever projects she should consider necessary. Any type of vessel may be permitted to call there (heavy cruisers, submarines, supply ships)." This broad offer would later prove to be considerably less useful in detail or true in practice than its language appeared to promise: "As a result of negotiations, the place for the creation of Basis Nord was chosen in Zapadnaya Litsa in Motovskiy Gulf where German ships could secretly enter during any season of the year."[8] Further, the Soviets asserted: "The Germans intended to build the frontline naval base with repair shops and warehouses in very little time. The invasion of Norway was already approved and the Hitlerite admirals understood the need for supply points for ships in the Arctic."[9]

Nevertheless, the German naval high command assessed Zapadnaya Litsa as being much better than the initial Soviet offer. It was wholly surrounded by Russian territory and closed to all foreign and Soviet domestic shipping. Its entrance prevented observation from the open sea. Even so, there were some disadvantages. Zapadnaya Litza was totally undeveloped, there were no naval facilities available, and there were no communications by rail or road with Germany; even ground connections to the rest of the Soviet Union were nonexistent. Only long-range seaplanes suggested themselves, along with wireless telegraphy, as means of rapid communications to the fatherland. Nonetheless, the Germans decided to accept it on 17 October.[10]

Von Baumbach initially thought that the high command's concerns over adequate communications between Berlin and the base were not an insuperable obstacle to operations from the base. Once German supply, barracks, and repair ships arrived at the bay the German navy could function from it. Apparently, he believed the Soviets would eventually have some solution to the problem of operational isolation and recommended communication by wireless telegraphy to Berlin via Moscow as an interim measure. The attaché said unexpected visits from warships would have to be signaled to Moscow from the naval high command, with Moscow then informing the base. As for ships entering the bay itself, the procedure would be to identify first in wireless, then by flag hoist, and finally by flashing light. German ships entering the bay were to inform the base if they had any damage so that the support ships could be ready.[11]

Murmansk as a Safe Harbor

Before the Germans could get Basis Nord operational they were taught a salutory lesson in the need for secrecy in relying on support from the USSR. The U.S. cargo liner *City of Flint* had been taken as a prize by the pocket battleship *Deutschland*. The Germans asserted that *City of Flint* was carrying contraband to Britain, and after its capture on 9 October *City of Flint* was sailed into Murmansk by its prize crew. When it arrived in late October 1939 the Soviets promptly interned both the ship and the German prize crew.[12] *City of Flint*'s American flag and neutral status underlined the political dangers and difficulties that were attendant to smooth Soviet-German naval relations, especially when the actions of a combatant state involved and endangered the interests of two neutrals, whose respective alignments were considerably different. The United States supported Britain as far as it could on 19 December, when the large German liner *Columbus* was forced to scuttle itself while under the watchful, if appropriately "neutral," escort of the U.S. cruiser *Tuscaloosa*. The latter did not interfere when British destroyer *Hyperion* intercepted the German ship off the U.S. coast.[13]

The German naval high command instructed the dogged attaché, von Baumbach, to get the German prize crew out and obtain release of the prize. He was also to see that the *City of Flint* was replenished and that orders were provided for its return journey. This von Baumbach did with dispatch. Three days after the ship was interned, the internment was canceled. Five days later *City of Flint* was replenished and on its way to Germany. In the meantime twelve German ships had set sail from Murmansk on 25 October. Soviet authorities forbade other ships from leaving port for twenty-four hours, giving the Germans a significant head start.[14]

The report of the master of the *City of Flint*, Captain Joseph A. Gainard, delivered to the U.S. minister in Bergen some time later, indicated that the Soviet approach to the American ship had been initially friendly—until word was received from Moscow to permit the Germans to continue their voyage. As Gainard viewed the situation in Murmansk, "it was evident that my position with the Russians became worse daily, while that of the Germans improved."[15]

The Soviets rather unneutral pro-German actions regarding *City of Flint* were not without political consequence: the Germans made strenuous representations to the Soviet government pressing their advantage, while the United States also protested Soviet handling of the incident. The United States' first knowledge of the incident came from the Soviet news agency Tass report of the arrival and subsequent internment of *City of Flint*. The U.S. ambassador was instructed to request release of the ship and crew and to request the Soviets to intern the prize crew as "failure to so act would compromise the neutrality of the Soviet Government."[16]

Despite subsequent U.S. protests, Soviet obfuscation continued. The Soviets were essentially claiming that one part of their government did not know what the other was doing, which may not have been too far from the truth. Since they released *City of Flint* with a German prize crew, however, it seems fair to say that they succumbed to German pressure instead of American. In the end, the State Department recognized the obvious: "the Soviet Government has throughout this incident been acting to protect German interests while holding itself out as faithfully complying with the principles of international law."[17]

While U.S. diplomatic protestations accomplished little with the Soviets in the matter of *City of Flint*, the German naval high command did send new instructions to its pocket battleships: "Owing to American objections, political complications have arisen for Russia through *City of Flint* (taken in prize by the *Deutschland*) putting into Murmansk. Russia requests that repetitions be avoided. In the future dispatch prizes to Kiel via neutral territorial waters, calling at intermediate ports only in accordance with Article 21 of the Hague Agreement."[18]

The *City of Flint*, however, was not yet a prize in a German harbor, and, for fear of interception by British warships on the high seas it was taken down the Norwegian coast, almost entirely in Norwegian territorial waters, and headed for Germany. At Tromso, however, it was promptly interned by the Norwegians. The British, meanwhile, had attempted to release the American steamer prior to Norwegian internment, but the attempted intercept by cruiser *Glasgow* and its accompanying destroyers was not accomplished.[19] At Tromso, the Germans were detained, and the U.S. ship and crew were set free and allowed to proceed to their next port of call.

The *City of Flint* made the agenda for the führer's conferences on naval affairs on 10 November. The assessment was that German actions in the case were "mismanaged." Indeed, von Baumbach could not determine why the prize officer took the ship into Murmansk in the first place. The attaché admonished Berlin in trenchant terms, observing that the Hague agreements, which the Soviets had signed, applied and pointing out that the Soviet Union had been placed in a very difficult position by what was apparently an inexperienced prize officer.[20]

While the German mishandling of the *City of Flint* incident put the Soviets in an awkward diplomatic situation, the Soviets certainly did all they could to help the German prize crew after appropriate pressure had been applied by von Baumbach. Soviet actions with regard to the *City of Flint* were probably influenced by the timing of two Soviet delegations bearing lists of requests for technological and military assistance. The delegations were scheduled to arrive in Germany within the week. In any case, the Germans had the last word. The *City of Flint* was sunk by a U-boat in 1943 while straggling from a convoy.

Escape of the *Bremen*

The SS *Bremen* was a 52,000-ton liner that had succeeded in evading the British blockade and capture by proceeding to Murmansk from New York. A large ship used on the North Atlantic run, the *Bremen* was making a return voyage to Europe from America shortly after the war broke out. The main body of the British home fleet main body actually carried out a sweep for the liner but were too far to the south.[21] The ship avoided the British blockade, heading for Murmansk. Ignoring Soviet interests and pushing the spirit of Molotov-Ribbentrop to the limit, the *Bremen* sailed right into Murmansk harbor, which was full of Russian, German, British, and other Western shipping. There the Soviet naval authorities gave the liner all requisite help to return to Germany. Indeed, the Soviet actions compare with the unneutral behavior of the U.S. authorities, who desired that the British cruisers *Perth* and *Berwick* find the *Bremen* and sink it. *Bremen* sought refuge in a Newfoundland fog and escaped to Germany.[22]

Figure 4. German transatlantic superliner *Bremen*, whose escape from the British blockade was facilitated by Soviet authorities and regarded as co-belligerence by the British. The whole incident strained German-Soviet relations almost as much as Soviet-British relations. (W. S. Bilddienst.)

The Soviets notwithstanding, *Bremen* almost did not reach Germany safely. The British submarine HMS *Salmon* intercepted the liner, but did not try to sink it. *Salmon* had already put a crimp in German dealings with Russia by upsetting plans for Basis Nord through sinking *U-36* on 12 December 1939. *Salmon* did not attack *Bremen* because the British rules of engagement forbade the sinking of passenger liners, although it may have been that. *Salmon* actually dove because it spotted a Dornier DO-10 flying boat sent out to escort the liner.[23]

Although the Germans never used Polyarny as a naval support base, Raeder's account of *Bremen*'s escape has the ship putting into Polyarny instead of Murmansk. Raeder also credits Polyarny with being the port of refuge for German shipping and a "base for German naval forces." The German admiral Friedrich Ruge, in his account of the German navy in World War II, *Der Seekrieg*, has *Bremen* proceeding to Germany via Murmansk, which is the truth. In any case, the arrival of *Bremen* in Germany on 14 December 1939 was greeted with great enthusiasm by the Germans. As Propaganda Minister Joseph Goebbels put it: "A great triumph for us,

ıch by the entire world, and for Churchill, a terrible loss
e same time, Raeder also passed on thanks for the help in
ord set up. *Bremen* was not the only German maritime
939. Battle cruisers *Scharnhorst* and *Gneisenau* conducted a
November which took them into the northern Norwegian
Sea and thence to the Greenland, Iceland, and United Kingdom gap,
where they sank the armed merchant cruiser *Rawalpindi*. This event was
coincidental, but, even though Basis Nord was hardly operational, it must
have given encouragement and comfort to German battleship commanders to know there was some potential solace in the Russian Murman
fjords.[25]

Establishing the Base

By late October the naval high command had decided to establish Basis
Nord. The coordinates for the base were 69° 25' north longitude; 32° 26'
east latitude. This was to be kept secret, and the term "Basis Nord" was to
be used as the cover location in all official communications. The document
establishing the base as a German "naval entity" is dated 31 October 1939.
Perhaps reflecting a degree of German anxiety to get Basis Nord established, three messages were sent to pocket battleships overseas, a day before the high command had formally organized Basis Nord. The messages
said that, since Murmansk was not suited as a supply base, the Soviet
Union had provided "Zapadnaya Litza in the closed boundary area west
of Murmansk." Executed in Berlin, the concept of operations for Basis
Nord was sent to the relevant German naval entities: Naval Group Command East, based in Kiel, the Naval Group Command West at Wilhelmshaven, the flag officer U-boats, and the Armed Forces High Command
Overseas in Russia. Basis Nord was to have three missions: as a logistics
base, as a safe harbor, and as a repair base (as support ships became available). Supplies for ships at the base were to be drawn, initially, from the
German merchant ships trapped by the British blockade in Murmansk.
Very little of military significance, however, was available from these ships
other than fuel and provisions. The high command also ordered lubricants
and supplies for U-boats from Germany. Emergency calls by German warships were possible at the base, Soviet neutrality notwithstanding. There
is no question the Soviets were very concerned. In fact, they assumed that
"British intelligence would find out about project Basis Nord sooner or
later."[26]

SS *Phoenicia*, a merchant vessel lying in Murmansk, was to be requisitioned as the supply vessel for the base. According to the plan, another
German merchant vessel, also located in Murmansk, was to be assigned to

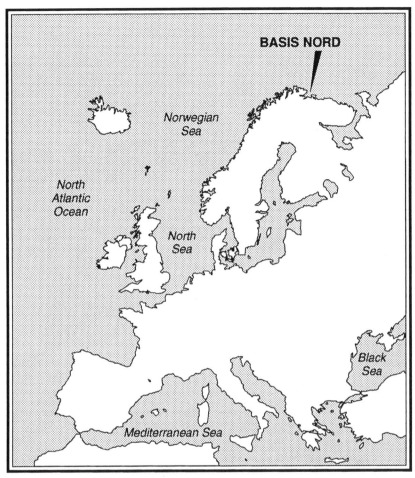

Map 1. Basis Nord was located in Zapadnaya Litza in what was then the Soviet Arctic, in a fjord with access to the Norwegian Sea and the North Atlantic.

the base as a barracks ship. This was a combination passenger and freighter ship, the SS *Cordillera*. No vessel that could serve as repair ship was in Murmansk at the time the naval high command established Basis Nord. The German Navy set to searching among the dozens of merchant ships idled but safely in German ports in the fall of 1939.[27] While searching out appropriate barracks and repair vessels, the Germans procured the supplies needed to service U-boats and pocket battleships in port and at sea and sent them from Germany to Murmansk.[28]

The Soviet Union's Arctic Fleet Command had been informed by its headquarters in Moscow of this arrangement. The rationale for such a base was to allow the Germans to support their blockade of the British Isles.[29]

German records provide details on discussions about procedures for German ships passing through Soviet defensive barriers, and how they would be serviced once they arrived remained the subject of continuing discussions. Indeed, if a German warship needed to make emergency use of Basis Nord, the visit was to have been cleared beforehand through a cumbersome maze of bureaucratic channels.

This assumed too much of Soviet intentions and capabilities, and even German capabilities, not to mention the course of the war. From the beginning of Basis Nord's operations the Germans did not wish to be hostage to Soviet intentions with regard to all provisions, and especially fresh water. Sanitary conditions in the Murman wilds were more primitive than in metropolitan Russia, where dysentery was rife under Stalin, and the German navy did not want to risk operational effectiveness. In the high command's plan for the base the permanent support ship was to carry a supply of fresh water for Basis Nord in addition to ninety days' supply for a battleship.

Soviet Admiral Golovko's description of the physical conditions in the Soviet Northern Fleet operating areas apply equally to those at Basis Nord, which were, of course, similar to those in the Northern Fleet: "We inherited from Tsarism a vast sea theatre which, however, was practically unexplored and little was known about conditions for naval operations there. The coastline was unprotected. There was not a single naval station for thousands of miles. Everything had to be planned, built and linked up with roads. The Soviet government had accomplished that by 1940. . . ."[30]

Connecting the Murmansk complex to Leningrad, there was a rail line built by Stalin's prisoners, and there was also the infamous White Sea–Baltic Canal. The construction of the canal was the end result of one of Stalin's more ambitious forced labor projects. It was designed to allow the inland transfer of warships from the Baltic to the White Sea without exposure to vulnerable external lines of communications. Murmansk was turned into a real port. The Soviets knew the importance of a fleet base in the north: it was astride the line of communications to the west and constituted the terminus of the Arctic route from the east. Golovko was sent north, however, to remedy the defects in the situation, to help make the transition from political enthusiasm to genuine operational readiness. When the Germans got there the transition had not been made, and gulag labor was still in force on Soviet facilities. In fact, when the first ships from the West arrived in Murmansk they could not understand the unenthusiastic welcome from the workers on the dock. Most were the unwilling prisoners of the gulag. Yet little more than two years before the first hard fought North Russian convoy, the Germans planned their first U-boat replenishment from Russian waters.

On 5 November 1939 Attaché von Baumbach received a signal in Moscow from the naval high command indicating that the first U-boat resupply from Basis Nord was to take place between 18 and 23 November. *Phoenicia* was to be the ship providing the U-boat support. Berlin said the ship was to proceed from Murmansk to Basis Nord and there receive supplies from other vessels being sent out from Germany, principally *Jan Wellem*. Thus, well before the conquest of Norway and France by German forces in the spring and summer of 1940 Admiral Karl Dönitz had a base for his U-boats in the Soviet Union. Dönitz, in fact, was named as the action officer responsible for the base. As such, he was responsible for operations carried out at sea supported by the base and any associated sea lanes. Dönitz understood the strategic significance of a Kola Peninsula base for his U-boats. In principle, this was the long-awaited opportunity to break out of Germany's geographical cul-de-sac, which was delimited to the Jutland peninsula and the shores of the North and Baltic Sea.[31]

Dönitz and the Base

On 5 November Admiral Dönitz outlined both a strategic plan and specific tactical requirements in his reply to the navy high command. Dönitz viewed Basis Nord as a highly desirable instrument for underseas warfare, in that it offered an opportunity to attack the sea lane between northern Russia and England as well as a base for U-boats operating in the Atlantic. Dönitz cared little about the adverse effects of such attacks on Russian shipping; he wished to keep the English merchant fleet in his periscopes. The access was valuable because it offered a relatively secure entry to the open ocean, entry not subject to British interdiction. Even though it cost an additional three hundred nautical miles, Dönitz believed the longer transit and shorter on-station time were acceptable trade-offs, in view of the dangerous passage that had to be made to break out of the North Sea to almost any attack position. Dönitz, of course, was pursuing here a logic laid down in his paper written in 1937, which stated that the naval lesson of World War I was that the U-boat was "suitable for threatening enemy sea communications, the enemy trade," and concluded that "the U-boat would always be an excellent, perhaps only means . . . effectively to threaten the vitally important enemy sea communications, and under certain conditions to be able to damage them war-decisively."[32] Politically, Basis Nord could be considered an advance Nazi toehold on the East and a clandestine overseas naval base—a minuscule manifestation of the plan of overseas colonies and world power which risked English opposition.

Dönitz posited: "German policy has to reckon with two hate-enemies, England and France, to whom a stronger German colossus in the middle of Europe would be a thorn in the eye, whereby both States would reject a further German strengthening as much in Europe as overseas. . . . In the erection of German bases overseas both countries would see a threat to their sea communications and a security for German trade resulting in a strengthening of the German position in Europe."[33] So much for the ideological-strategic justification for Basis Nord. More time and distance from the transatlantic sea lanes meant, however, that U-boats deployed to the base would have to be longer-ranged and larger. In Dönitz's view, as of late 1939, no matter where German U-boats were to operate, longer transits could be expected "for the foreseeable future," and U-boats required greater endurance "in any case," if they were to be effective upon arrival in combat zones. Dönitz believed the issue would become more important as the war became a battle of the Atlantic sea lanes. The Germans did not occupy the Atlantic coast of France and commence effective U-boat operations from it until late 1940. In November 1939 such an occupation was still regarded by Dönitz and his staff as a dream.

Dönitz was reticent to commit himself to a major effort in the development of the Russian base without first getting a clearer picture of its potential capabilities. Overall, he believed it was correct to develop the base as a large U-boat support facility within the context of a war situation, which he realized could change in a moment. Dönitz surmised that efforts to establish Basis Nord were warranted only if a more westerly base was not available and logistical support to make the base operational could be provided. He envisioned one U-boat at a time using the base, with three to four weeks between boats. Such a base was small indeed by later standards, when whole flotillas of U-boats operated out of French or Norwegian bases. At the same time, Dönitz realized that Basis Nord's operational effectiveness depended greatly on the ability of the German navy to get supplies to the base and that this could only be demonstrated by a practical test. In late November two submarines were sent to visit the base to test its operational effectiveness.

Turning to the organization of the base, Dönitz proposed that the officer in charge should be a submariner—of course. The merchant vessel *Cordillera*, pressed into service as a combination supply and barracks ship, was to provide physical comfort for submarine crews conducting extended service in the arduous northern waters. Dönitz planned to have the crew on the accommodation ship supplemented by additional personnel to manage the supplies at the base.

Although he did not specify a location, Dönitz ordered that a communications station be established to support U-boats deployed to Basis Nord and to communicate with naval headquarters in Berlin as well as with his own command. He suggested the communications equipment be sent with the first U-boat. Dönitz felt that secure land communications and support, including a rail link to Murmansk, were especially desirable. A survey of the bay was needed, as the navigational charts available were primitive. Also required were active measures for military security against surprise attack, as Dönitz did not believe the base's existence could be kept secret from the British for more than eight to twelve weeks.

A small, highly maneuverable support ship that could get into and out of small bays and inlets would be provided to support clandestine U-boat operations at Basis Nord. Dönitz believed this ship could operate in several places, including Motovskiy Gulf (33° east longitude), Dolgaya Bay (35° 10′ east longitude) and Yarnishanaya Bay (35° 5′ east longitude). The crew for the ship would be minimal: a U-boat officer, a communications petty officer, a cargo officer, a doctor, and probably a complement of enlisted men for support. It was believed that such a ship could be on station by the end of November.[34]

Dönitz's staff examined further details concerning provisions, fuel, lubricants, water, and other supplies to be arranged for the base. The Seventh U-boat flotilla, based in Kiel, was to provide both the submarines and support ships. Communications facilities for Basis Nord were to consist of an 800-watt long-range surface transmitter; a U-boat transmitter as reserve; two large ships' receivers; and two universal (broad-band) receivers. These were to be powered by a diesel generator with transformers.

The German naval high command responded to Dönitz's recommendations on 9 November 1939. They asserted that base security in the areas in question were the responsibility of Russian naval vessels. They noted that Kola Bay was also guarded by antisubmarine barriers, including nets. The German high command believed from tactical wireless intercept that this was the case; they also knew that overt German fortification of Basis Nord was a political impossibility. The Germans had to trust the Soviet Union, depending on its well-known concern for "reliable defense of the fatherland."[35]

The next day following Attaché von Baumbach's suggestion that the quickest way to proceed on the details of the arrangements to support U-boats out of Basis Nord was to raise the subject at the highest level, a personal note from Raeder was passed to fleet admiral and naval commissar N. G. Kuznetzov in Moscow. Von Baumbach reasoned that, if Kuznetzov got the German requests, he would rule on them and the details could be more easily worked out at lower levels. Within the week Kuznetzov told the attaché to pass on his greetings to the grand admiral and to say that his response to the German requests would be in "deeds, not words."

Von Baumbach recorded both the Soviet words and deeds in a memorandum, "Final Arrangements by the Soviet Navy Concerning the Impending Use of Basis Nord for U-boat Support." The major points included sailing directions, Soviet recognition signals, a detailed description of the entrance to Teriberka Bay, identification of guard ships, special procedures to be followed to enter Basis Nord from Teriberka Bay, and a request for German recognition signals.

These arrangements were provided to *Phoenicia* and *Cordillera*, which were to proceed under cover of darkness to the Motovskiy Gulf from Murmansk and to enter Zapadnaya Litza by first light. As a temporary arrangement, orders were to be sent through Berlin to Moscow then forwarded over Soviet communications to the Kola Peninsula. Ships off the coast were to communicate with Moscow on designated frequencies.

Meanwhile, *Phoenicia* had been ordered to take on supplies for the base from the German steamer *St. Louis*, which was in Murmansk at the time. *Phoenicia*, however, had to dispose of 700 tons of cargo to make space for the needed naval stores. The Germans had suggested that Soviet dockworkers move the cargo, but apparently this was not feasible until the end of December.

Although *Phoenicia* was to assume twenty-four-hour readiness to move from Murmansk to Basis Nord, its movement actually required seventy-two hours advance notice via Moscow—the Soviet bureaucracy extracted its due. The movement of *Phoenicia* was further complicated by the fact that its decks were only capable of taking limited weights and its crew was not outfitted with winter clothing. From Moscow von Baumbach approached the Soviet authorities with a request for winter clothing for all the German merchant crews in Murmansk. This was speedily provided by the Soviet navy. Von Baumbach again credited this swift reaction to a personal letter Raeder sent to Kuznetzov—and the concession to the Russian mind-set that such German action at the highest levels represented.

By now a third ship to support Basis Nord had been found and requisitioned in Germany, the steamer *Jan Wellem*. *Jan Wellem* was to bring a doctor, medical staff, and supplies to the base as quickly as possible. While the ship was en route, several practical problems prevented the rapid establishment of Basis Nord. First, both the *Cordillera* and *Phoenicia* still had to move from Murmansk to the base. Second, the issue of how communications were to be maintained with the base had to be resolved.[36]

The Mission of *U-36*

Not trusting the Soviet Union's intentions or its sailing directions, the Germans decided to conduct a clandestine reconnaissance of the Kola Bay to make a U-boat's periscope assessment of Basis Nord. They dispatched

Figure 5. Motorship *Phoenicia*. This ship was mobilized from German merchant marine assets interned in the Soviet Union. It was then assigned to Basis Nord as an accommodation ship for tired U-boat crews. (W. S. Bilddienst.)

two submarines to evaluate the proposed location of the base and the state of Soviet readiness. The mission of *U-36* is contained in a top secret German naval intelligence document in the records of the operations division of the Naval High Command (SKL). Dated 17 November 1939, it was a detailed order accompanied by charts carried by night courier from Berlin at Dönitz's request.

The commander of *U-36* was to signal the high command two days before he anticipated entry into the Kola coast waters so the German embassy in Moscow could be informed with some lead time. The *U-36* was to steer surfaced through Teriberka Bay until it reached a position fifty nautical miles from Teriberka lighthouse. There it was to signal the local Soviet naval authorities on 330 kilohertz with the call sign "572" and give the recognition signal "FPQRG." The Soviets were to answer with the signal "275." The U-boat was then to steer due south with all navigational lights lit.

The German submarine was to be met by a Soviet watch vessel displaying a white-and-red light on its mast. The U-boat was to again signal "FPQRG" with flashing light or wireless as well as by displaying a flashing

Figure 6. The covert submarine and pocket battleship support ship *Jan Wellem*. Sunk by the Germans at Narvik to avoid capture, it was salvaged and served as a depot ship in German waters until the end of the war. (W. S. Bilddienst.)

red light. The Soviet vessel was to answer with the recognition signal "36." The U-boat was then to follow the Soviet vessel to the base at a distance of two-to-three cables astern. In case the Soviet ship was not in position due to fog or storm, *U-36* was to proceed unescorted to Motovskiy Gulf, where a guard boat would pick up the escort and take it into the base. This procedure was not followed, however, as *U-36* was torpedoed and sunk on its mission by HMS *Salmon*, a British submarine in the Norwegian Sea, on 4 December 1939.[37]

Again, it is necessary to provide some perspective on the first German attempts to use Basis Nord. As Sir Maurice Hankey's biographer and author of the British official history of the war at sea, Captain Stephen Roskill so noted: "The phoney war period between September 1939 and April 1940 was a very active one for the Royal Navy . . . the battle against surface raiders, U-boats, and mines began on the day war was declared."[38] Indeed, it was against this background and the fact that "the Baltic was frozen for an unusually long period, and the carriage of Swedish iron ore to German ports suffered . . . this greatly enhanced the alternate routes for such traffic from Narvik in North Norway to the ports on the North

German coast . . . [that] the Admiralty became increasingly anxious to extend its blockade to ships using that route."[39] The British, in fact, made the decision to mine Norwegian territorial waters to stop such traffic. The obvious question with regard to *U-36*'s mission is whether the British knew or cared about its objectives? We do know that British intelligence watched the Russo-Finnish war and, by implication, any German activities dealing with the Soviets very carefully.[40] The British were able to piece together a pattern of operations based on aircraft sightings, but not from signals intelligence on German U-boats in the early port of the war. *Salmon*, however, not only was to sink *U-36*, but it also torpedoed and crippled for some months the German light cruisers *Leipzig* and *Nürnberg*.[41]

Although not equipped with all the special instructions given the ill-fated *U-36*, another German submarine, *U-38*, managed to carry out a successful Arctic Ocean reconnaissance to the approaches of Basis Nord. It left Wilhelmshaven in early November 1939. After an uneventful transit through Norwegian territorial waters, it rounded North Cape and was off Teriberka Bay by mid-afternoon on 26 November. Running silently into the bay on a bright, moonlit night, it found no shipping and made no signals to anyone. Lurking about the bay, the U-boat reported the sortie of a naval vessel out of the adjacent Kildin Bay after dark. The skipper of the *U-38* noted that the Soviets were operating with navigational lights lit, spotting two guard boats east of Kildin Island.

The fishing traffic was heavy, and so was the guard kept by the Soviets. *U-38* was apparently on the surface most of the night, diving at dawn on November 28. At 1600 it headed for the Kola Bay, entering it at 2000 hours. As it passed into the bay, *U-38* had to avoid a large steamer with a destroyer escort. While not detected, the U-boat was prevented by Soviet torpedo boats and coast guard vessels from examining some of the inlets.

The commanding officer of the German submarine reported that the Soviet watch was so good as to constitute a great danger to his visit. Parenthetically, for a German U-boat commander to say he believed it inadvisable to follow a large steamer, to achieve entrance to the bay, indicates that some of the German navy at sea held a higher opinion of the professionalism of their Soviet counterparts than the high command in Berlin. The tactic that prompted the U-boat commander's comment was standard procedure for U-boat operations and would only fail if the watch kept was particularly good. The war diary of the U-boat commander reflects that he had picked up evidence of the Russo-Finnish crisis on his radio and submitted that this might be the reason for the high degree of Russian alert. Later that night a target of opportunity seemed to offer itself but

Figure 7. *U-38*. This U-boat performed a clandestine reconnaissance of Basis Nord which proved it satisfactory for German U-boat operations. (W. S. Bilddienst.)

turned out to be a Soviet ship. *U-38* inadvertently revealed its own position with its periscope, and no attack was made.

At 0800 on 29 November, in accordance with a message from flag officer U-boats, *U-38* proceeded back to Teriberka Bay with orders to extend its patrol in that area for six days. While there, its crew heard heavy explosions and later observed aircraft headed westward. The commander attributed this action to the Soviet-Finnish conflict. Shortly thereafter the U-boat headed west and again began searching for targets of opportunity. The captain's final comment was that, in the area of North Cape and the Kola Peninsula, he had observed thirty to forty targets and regrettably had been "harmless to [all] of them."

This successful clandestine submarine mission confirmed that Basis Nord, inside the Soviet Kola watch lines, was not an easy target for attack from the sea. It also indicated that the Soviet navy was highly proficient at maritime border defense and inshore antisubmarine warfare, especially during an alert. An examination of the war logs of the flag officer U-boats indicates that *U-38*'s reconnaissance satisfied Dönitz's earlier requirement to evaluate the utility of this area for German submarine operations.[42]

Bureaucracies and Black Oil: Ships in Place at Basis Nord

Meanwhile, the bureaucracies in Berlin, Moscow, and Murmansk began working to establish Basis Nord. The problems that arose between the Soviet and German authorities during the opening and operation of the base illustrate the rigid character of Soviet-Nazi institutional behavior. Although the points of contention were small—replacing a lost anchor, establishing communications, and obtaining potable water—practical solutions proved difficult. A penchant for clandestine dealings, a Soviet unwillingness to yield control in any but the most elementary circumstances, and a striking lack of initiative characterize the responses of Soviet shore-based officialdom. Other important points include a German tendency to run things on a shoestring, lack of realistic limits, and elements of Nazi extraterritoriality.

While *U-36* was on its ill-fated voyage to the base, the German assistant naval attaché from Moscow, Fregatten-Kapitän John [*sic*] Ross, arrived in Murmansk on 28 November 1939. He was to ascertain exactly what was going on in the base itself. He arrived at 0530 and met with Erich Auerbach, a shipping control officer and intelligence agent, aboard the German merchant ships *Cordillera* and *Phoenicia*. Ross delivered sailing orders to the masters of both ships, who indicated that the vessels were seaworthy and ready for service.

Both ships, however, were in need of water, and *Phoenicia* needed provisions, especially for a long deployment in a support role to Basis Nord. The Soviets were approached and were requested to provide the water as quickly as possible. The German liner *St. Louis*, which was not carrying any passengers at the time, was requested to provision *Phoenicia* with foodstuffs. It should be pointed out that these provisions were not fleet supplies but, rather, those that the German merchant vessel had on board to carry out its normal mercantile role.

Later that afternoon Ross called on the Soviet Northern Fleet command and began his liaison with Captain Third Rank Korolev, who was apparently a professional naval officer. With an acute sense of demands of survival under Stalin's rule, in which any contact with a foreigner was dangerous (especially a foreign officer and naval attaché), Korolev quickly and badly brought Ross's request to the attention of one Captain First Rank Lagovskiy. Lagovskiy was the senior NKVD officer in the Arctic Fleet and the appropriate and safe authority to deal with the German attaché. Lagovskiy told Ross to turn his requests over to a Senior Lieutenant Sysin.

The next morning, after being certain he was not followed, Sysin arrived at the hotel where Ross and Auerbach were staying. (Officers of the

NKVD disliked dealing with foreigners, as it could always be used against them in Stalin's Russia.) There Sysin was briefed on the whole operation. According to records in the German naval archives Basis Nord file, Ross requested that the NKVD assigned officer raise the following issues with the Soviet fleet command:

> Permission for departure of both ships from Murmansk.
> Arrival of the fishing steamers loaded with U-boat stores.
> Auerbach's request to travel to the base (refers to German in his capacity as port representative/liaison).
> Licensing *Cordillera*'s and *Phoenicia*'s radios.
> Provisioning of both ships with water as promised.
> Permission for arrival of U-boats.
> Permission for departure of the steamers and recently arrived U-boats.

As Sysin took the requests and promised quick responses, Ross repeated the request for water for the two support ships. The NKVD officer said that all the requests would be laid before the fleet command that evening. The Soviet representatives seemed to move with uncharacteristic speed. Ross was informed the next morning that water barges would be alongside *Cordillera* in three hours. Five hours later a barge that could provide thirteen tons of water an hour arrived. Twenty-two hours later *Cordillera* was full. Both it and *Phoenicia*, which needed only about one hundred tons of water, were fully provisioned with water by 0600 the following morning. At the same time, cargo transfer from the *St. Louis* to *Phoenicia* was approved, and the loading of required provisions was begun. The Soviets, however, delayed answers to the other German requests, especially giving the permission for the ships to leave.

Although the ships had been cleared much earlier, there was some thought among the German officers in Murmansk that a change in policy had been made in Moscow. The reason was that the Russo-Finnish War had severely tightened up things in Murmansk. Armed troops were stationed in every egress point of the city, with contingents loaded in most of the transport ships in the harbor. Extensive air raid measures, including temporary blackouts and antiaircraft weapons practice firings, had been mounted by the Soviets. Some citizens reported that gunfire could be heard from the nearby Finnish frontier—a report that the assistant naval attaché could not confirm. From the standpoint of the German crews on the ships destined for Basis Nord, however, the Soviet naval authorities were doing everything possible to facilitate their departure, in spite of the fact that the Soviet navy was engaged in several operations in support of the Finnish War.[43]

On the morning of 1 December 1939 both *Cordillera* and *Phoenicia* were cleared to leave port. Sysin noted that Auerbach's intention of accompanying the ships was a difficult matter, because he did not have an exit visa. Worse, Sysin informed Ross that the two wireless installations on the ships had to remain sealed. German protestations to the contrary did not avail. By 2300 hours the two ships still had not left. This was because the Germans wanted to take *Sachsenwald* with them, and it had not been given permission to leave. The Soviets, having given clearance for *Cordillera* and *Phoenicia*, were exasperated at yet another German requirement and insisted that the first two ships leave. After all, Russian customs, *Inflot* (the state shipping line), and frontier points had been notified of two German ships, not three.

An attempt was made to resolve the problem created by the third ship leaving, a conference was called aboard *Cordillera* at 1500. Although the Soviets would not specify their reason, the real problem was not the movement of the ship but, instead, the German port agent.[44] It can be surmised that the Soviets suspected that Auerbach was the German espionage agent in charge in Murmansk, and they did not want him going to a base where he would no longer be under their surveillance. In fact, Auerbach *was* working for German intelligence and headed the German net in Murmansk. During the conference the Soviet port authorities at first refused Auerbach permission to go to the base and would not clear *Sachsenwald* to depart. After referral to the highest NKVD officer, however, the Soviet bureaucrats decided that Auerbach could go as long as Ross went too—better to keep track of two spies at once. But in the end, for reasons not revealed in German reports, neither Auerbach nor Ross sailed with *Cordillera* and *Phoenicia*, which proceeded out of Murmansk, turning north toward Zapadnaya Litza in a snow squall and fog at 1600.[45]

Three days later the two Germans in Murmansk were notified by the NKVD that the ships had reached Basis Nord. The following day, 4 December 1939, Ross was told that the *Cordillera* had moved its position improperly and that the Soviets did not know exactly where it was. Apparently, *Cordillera* had worked its way out of a snow squall and found its anchorage at Basis Nord but, in doing so, had lost its reserve anchor. Anywhere but in the Soviet Union such an occurrence would have been a relatively minor problem. *Cordillera*'s anchor loss is related here precisely because the difficulties that resulted reflect the problems inherent in the Soviet system and its wooden reaction to a German exigency.

Ross requested that *Cordillera* be allowed to return to Murmansk to get a new anchor but was told that a visit to Murmansk was out of the question. The Soviets pointed out that the German supply ship already had a second anchor on board and that the Russian navy could provide another if it were absolutely necessary. When a replacement anchor for *Cordillera* was finally brought out by *Sachsenwald*, the Soviet guard boat would not let the German tender through until it had been cleared by the fleet high command, which took several days. Meanwhile, *Cordillera* was in some danger without a reserve anchor.

It seems that the anchorage assigned to the Germans was a very bad one, indeed. Both Lagovskiy, who was also the port control authority officer, and Sysin, who had previously asserted that he knew nothing about the base, described Zapadnaya Litza as a poor anchorage. The Soviets said the bay could be freed of shipping and that good anchorage could be had in late January or early February. The collective Soviet-German opinion was that the anchorage was not sheltered from storms—terrible in bad weather, only marginally acceptable in good weather. Weather at Zapadnaya Litza had proven so severe that Auerbach recommended extra precautions for *Jan Wellem*. Auerbach also suggested assigning a harbor tug to the anchorage, if Moscow would approve. *Cordillera*'s master insisted that his ship, due to its "high sides" and great sail area, was not suited for work at the base. He suggested that a small "less high-sided" passenger steamer be assigned to the unpopular anchorage. This recommendation evidently did not evoke much sympathy from von Baumbach, as the *Jan Wellem* had the same vulnerabilities as the *Cordillera*.

Besides weather, problems with the Soviets continued. On 6 December, when Ross again asked to visit the base, the NKVD asserted that no transport boat "was available." Yet the following afternoon, permission was given for both Auerbach and Ross to go to the base and to Teriberka Bay. Apparently, the Soviet authorities were extremely concerned about the security of the operation. Ross believed it was the Soviet intention to watch every event at the base closely and not to remove the guard boat without the express order of the Soviet fleet command and, of course, appropriate political authorities.

Indeed, the same was the case with the *Sachsenwald*, one of two ships readied for the support of *Phoenicia*, when it arrived off the Kola Peninsula. *Sachsenwald* was scheduled to arrive in late November, the U-boats about the beginning of December. Von Baumbach had sent a message to the naval high command with a password cleared by the Soviet naval high command for *Sachsenwald* on 18 November. Von Baumbach had even obtained copies of the relevant sections of the Russian naval handbook of the Murman coast relating to Zapadnaya Litza. Despite that, Ross had to refer to Moscow, to get the authority to have *Sachsenwald* proceed to the base. All three ships were in Basis Nord on or about 9 December 1939, but it was fortunate for the Germans that no U-boat needed support in November or early December.[46]

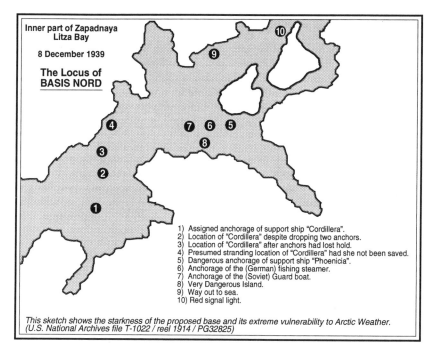

Map 2. Basis Nord in December 1939. This illustration is based on the report of the German assistant naval attaché to Moscow. The only change until the base's closure was the provision of safer anchorages.

Cordillera, Phoenicia, and now *Sachsenwald* were moored under the watchful eye of a Soviet guard boat. Since the ships had been interned in Murmansk since the outbreak of war, they were not armed—even to wartime merchant standards—carrying nothing other than a few hand weapons. Thus, one of the greatest fears of the German naval high command had been realized: the German base was hostage to foreign, in this case Soviet, guns.[47]

Command and Control of Basis Nord

With three ships in place at Basis Nord the German naval high command specified the authority and responsibilities of its new commanding officer, who was to command the floating base from the support ship *Jan Wellem*. All ships and boats were subordinate to him, and all were under military discipline. Anything afloat in Basis Nord was to be considered a warship. The base commander was also responsible for the resupply and armament of ships serviced in the base. In this activity all ships' personnel were answerable to him, including embarked naval officers and ratings. If land-line communications were established, the German naval attaché in Moscow would be responsible; otherwise, radio communications were to be the appointed responsibility of the commanding officer of the *Jan Wellem*. The masters of the various ships assigned to the base were responsible for navigational safety and day-to-day operations of their ships.[48]

Effective communications with Basis Nord could not be established without the arrival of *Jan Wellem*, which carried the necessary communications equipment. Further efforts by Attaché Baumbach to establish a link with the base in Moscow were frustrated. The German had suggested that a field telephone line to the ships be set up from Murmansk; the Soviets vetoed the idea. A request for local radio communications with coastal traffic was also denied. The Soviets wanted to do this either ashore or afloat on a coastal guard vessel so that they could keep tabs on ships and continue reading German agents' traffic in Murmansk and preclude, no doubt, other unfriendly powers from listening to the traffic generated.

Von Baumbach's port captain/representative in Murmansk fared no better. It seemed that Molotov's offer to let Russia's new ally operate freely in the base was heavily circumscribed, as the Soviets were preventing any direct communication with Basis Nord. The Germans all agreed that what was needed was a service support vessel that the Murmansk agent could use to maintain regular contact with the base, preferably one with an armored bridge and a military crew of about twenty individuals.

In the meantime, despite Soviet obfuscation and delays, Auerbach had managed to charter the Soviet steamer *Belomorsk*. Dedicated to the town (and concentration camp) of the same name, *Belomorsk* was a comical example of socialist efficiency. Half of its crew was not on board at the time it was given permission to leave Murmansk; four hours later they had been mostly scraped together, and the vessel proceeded north to the base. About an hour after getting under way, *Belomorsk* had to heave-to because of a severe snow squall. Finally, after a five-hour passage in heavy seas, *Belomorsk* and its escorting guard boat arrived at Zapadnaya Litza. It took the steamer another hour to find *Phoenicia*, *Sachsenwald*, *Cordillera*, and the second Soviet guard boat stationed in the bay.

Nevertheless, Basis Nord was operational. In addition to the stores provided by *Sachsenwald*, *Phoenicia* had all requisite provisions on board for the support of U-boats. Codes and ciphers of the latest available type were provided to the ships so that they could read the blind transmissions coming out of the main German naval communications station at Norddeich. The *St. Louis* had provided additional boats to both ships. Manpower shortages at the base were to be filled with personnel brought by the *Jan Wellem*. To attract as little attention as possible from passing Soviet fishing fleets, the Germans flew no flags at all in the anchorage. Finally, *Sachsenwald*, a trawler "taken up from trade," had made the transfer of its U-boat-associated supplies. Its mission complete, it was to head back to Germany, fishing on the way. That this ship had just been on a secret mission, was going to have to pass through enemy-infested waters, and intended to fish along the way reflects the improvised nature of German fleet logistics at the time.

But the Soviets wanted to keep the *Sachsenwald* for their own operations and created obstacles for its return to Germany. Thus, in their usual fashion, the Soviets made "the easiest things bureaucratically complicated." When the Soviets renewed their request for *Sachsenwald*, the Germans at the base and in Moscow reminded the naval high command that a vessel was needed to communicate between Murmansk and the base. As it was, a formal turnover of *Sachsenwald* was not contemplated. Instead, *Sachsenwald* would be informally run by the Soviets and would fly the Soviet flag. Von Baumbach warned the high command that the proposed transfer of the trawler would create endless difficulties between Moscow and the base as well as between the base and Berlin. The attaché also recommended a Russian-speaking agent be assigned to the ships at Basis Nord as well as in Murmansk.[49]

By the middle of December the situation concerning Basis Nord had evolved somewhat, with von Baumbach reporting to the naval high command that initial arrangements for communications were finally being worked out. There was, however, still no way for the high command in Berlin or its attaché in Moscow to receive classified messages from the base; the only transmissions possible were Russian texts in the clear. There were several reasons for this. First, the interpreter the Germans had assigned to the base would not arrive in Murmansk until 17 December (von Baumbach requested that an interpreter cleared for classified material be carried on the *Jan Wellem* if it had not yet left harbor). Second, use of German code books for transmission over Russian circuits was anticipated to be very difficult. Third, there was a serious technical problem in that

German ciphers were set up to use Roman letters, whereas Russian ciphers were in Cyrillic. Finally, there was the Soviet Union's strong desire to control all communications with the base and its operations. In spite of a full understanding by the Soviet navy of the German need to transmit orders in secret, this remained a problem. Even with good intentions, the Soviets often misread their own script.[50]

Von Baumbach reassured the high command that the problems encountered at the front were mostly a case of the lower echelons not knowing Moscow's policy. As he put it: "All [the attendant difficulties] are children's sniffles which can be cured over and over with calm and patience." Moreover, Auerbach's report of foul weather in the anchorage was apparently colored by severe seasickness (as was the Soviet escort officer's assessment). The reality was that the weather in the outer bay had been bad, but the base itself was sheltered. As for the *Jan Wellem*'s ability to weather wind, no problems were expected. The difficulties with *Cordillera* had also been investigated by German naval authorities and had been seen to be exaggerated—probably by a merchant crew that did not relish wintering over in Russia.

The ability of large warships to anchor in the bay without special buoys or other mooring devices was, however, by no means certain. Ships sent to Basis Nord were, henceforth, to be equipped with additional gear to deal with bad weather. It was also questionable if support ships for U-boat replenishments could supply the base during the two months during which the bay was iced over. The communications vessel had to be strengthened to break ice between the support ships as well as to have the ability to get in and out of the bay.

The foreign section of the German Armed Forces High Command had suggested (against naval wishes) that the commander of Basis Nord be vested with civil authority. Von Baumbach realized that this would be utterly unacceptable to the Soviets: "they would feel much more at home dealing with a military authority who was overt in nature." The attaché understated the case here. The Soviets, having fought hard against the "foreign interventionists" in the same area during their civil war, were likely to be hostile to any hint of foreign civil authority establishing itself on Russian soil.

The German high command appeared to show incredible ignorance of Soviet sensitivities in this regard—or a deep desire to extend Nazi power in a consistent, if shaky, manner at every opportunity. They embarked a political plenipotentiary aboard the *Jan Wellem* when they sent the ship to Basis Nord. It is unclear who the individual was; what is clear is that full civil authority at Basis Nord was to be vested in him. There is no evidence that the Soviet authorities knew that such an authority was embarked on

Jan Wellem, but they surely would have objected had they had a scintilla of proof. From the Soviet point of view there were enough problems already with the German port agents.

The winter of 1939–40 was upon Murmansk and Basis Nord with a vengeance. The German port agent could not visit the German ships lying in the Murmansk roadstead because of ice, storm, and bad weather (and quite possibly his own seasickness). True to von Baumbach's predictions, every telegram sent from Murmansk in code was unreadable, possibly because of the inability to transliterate from the Roman to the Cyrillic alphabet in ciphers, but more likely due to "helpful" NKVD personnel. Given the previous pattern of Russian delay, there was probably some benign neglect on the part of higher authority as well.[51]

Perhaps someone else was listening, however, because on 28 December the first security problem arose concerning Basis Nord when the Danish newspaper *Nationaltidende* published an account of a German submarine base reportedly located in "Hitovaiia" Gulf. A similar radio report had also surfaced from France. The French account apparently located the German submarine base in Sayda Bay. The following day the magazine *Paris Soir* published an article asserting that the Germans had a secret naval base in Murmansk. Von Baumbach and Ambassador Schulenburg worked on a German denial for the Soviet regime, to the effect that no such thing existed. There was additional correspondence about the magazine article, but no indications about where it may have originated. German authorities dismissed the reports as rumors, not breaches of security, possibly resulting from the known return of German merchant ships from Murmansk. Meanwhile, the steamer *Sachsenwald* returned to Germany and was being loaded with replenishment supplies for the ill-fated *U-36*.

The ice and fog settled in over Basis Nord and nothing was accomplished in January or February 1940, although the base was now semi-operational. The first major use of the facility was for the planned raid by the heavy cruiser *Admiral Hipper*, which was to be sent to prey on Allied shipping in the Arctic sea lanes. The Germans, anxious to provide support for the *Hipper* in its operation, asked the Soviets if they would provide fuel for the heavy cruiser. The Soviets agreed to fuel the *Hipper*, requesting only "to be informed of specific time in advance as appropriate," The intention was to refuel in Basis Nord. The Soviet navy indicated that the base was passable by heavy ships without icebreakers, as ice was twenty-five centimeters thick in the bay, but the gulf was ice free. The appropriate elements of the German naval high command were informed that *Phoenicia* could sortie and conduct an open-ocean replenishment. The *Hipper's* fueling was intended to take advantage of the displacement of the British fleet from Scapa Flow, which had been caused by the sinking there of the

battleship *Royal Oak* by a German submarine. The *Hipper's* sortie to 61°
north in early February was, however, without result. The Germans believed that the British had prior warning and had cleared the area of merchant traffic. In fact, this was the case. The *Hipper's* sortie in February
1940 was cut short by a chance sighting by an aircraft of Royal Air Force
(RAF) bomber command.[52] The fueling at Basis Nord never occurred, and
the heavy cruiser returned to Wilhelmshaven on 20 February 1940. As is
now known, *Hipper's* second sortie was the subject of communications that
were not yet broken by the cryptanalysts at Bletchley Park. Meanwhile, a
tolerable working relationship was developing with the Soviet authorities
concerning Basis Nord. The German port agent arranged for the movement of *Phoenicia* as needed, and progress had been made on other issues.[53]

About the same time, the *Jan Wellem* had received its sailing orders and
a realistic cover story from the Germans. Declared to support German
ships in the Barents Sea, the ship was to load supplies and personnel for
Basis Nord at Kiel and proceed under the German merchant flag. "Special
passengers" were to be embarked as civilians, and the trip was to be considered a "private contract" undertaking. The voyage was to be made primarily in Swedish and Norwegian territorial waters, where the German
navy believed there was less danger of attack. In the event of attack or
discovery *Jan Wellem* was to be scuttled. Communications outbound were
to be on coastal waters frequencies supported from the main German
transmission station at Norddeich. Fortunately for the Germans, the British were not reading that traffic at the time. Soviet authorities had been
briefed to receive the ship on 30 January, and special coded communications had been arranged for it. The *Jan Wellem* was to enter Basis Nord—
much in the same way the ill-fated *U-36* would have—but it was also to
remain fifty nautical miles off the Kola Peninsula because of the Russo-
Finnish War. The supply ship was to rendezvous with a Soviet guard ship
off the Russian coast while following a course due south toward the entrance to Teriberka Bay which was frequently fog bound; worse, the inner
bay was sometimes covered with ice. Following the Soviet ship in, after an
exchange of recognition signals, *Jan Wellem* was to proceed on the southern side of the Motovskiy Gulf and to enter Zapadnaya Litza, where *Phoenicia's* master would tell it where to anchor. Upon arrival at the base *Jan
Wellem* was to remain on three-hour alert, ready to go to sea at a moment's
notice to support operations of any kind. It was also to keep the communications watch for the base, standing in readiness to receive messages from
either the naval attaché in Moscow or the high command in Berlin.[54]

The Germans assigned the 500-ton trawler *Kehdingen* as a dispatch and
support vessel to supply the base from Germany. The mail home was to
be carried by the *Kehdingen*. The chief censor was to be the commanding

officer of the base. Even so, the Germans were still looking for a traffic vessel for trips between Murmansk and the base. Arrangements were also made with Soviet authorities for a radio link. Transmissions to the naval attaché in Moscow were to be routed via the German port agent in Murmansk in special code. Only under very unusual circumstances was direct communication by wireless with Germany to be permitted.

These orders were, naturally, most secret and were to be destroyed if it appeared that they might fall into enemy hands. Meanwhile, the designated base commander and "civil authority" took ill and had to be replaced. The commanding officer of Basis Nord during its short existence was an engineering lieutenant commander, Karl Nieschlag, with no civil authority here. The duty may have been accurately perceived as too rough.

The German high command signaled to the naval attaché in Moscow and Nieschlag that *Jan Wellem* had departed for Basis Nord on 22 January 1940. The base was to inform the ship of weather conditions through von Baumbach in Moscow. Two days later von Baumbach informed Berlin that ice in the bay was only twenty-two centimeters thick and that the *Phoenicia* could move at any time. While the number of transmissions to and from the base slowed after mid-January, all the messages were clear, properly encoded and enciphered. This may have been due to progress on other larger Soviet-German issues, such as the Soviet-German economic agreement being negotiated in Moscow which was then reflected by greater cooperation at lower levels.

Von Baumbach persisted in trying to obtain Soviet permission for direct radio transmissions from the base, but he was unsuccessful. He had the impression that the Russians were willing to do almost anything rather than permit this freedom. Still, they would not directly reject his request. The Soviet reaction was to improve the present communications in such a way that the system became functional, but all traffic still passed through their hands. Meanwhile, the delay in transmission time from the base had risen to eight hours.[55]

By 30 January 1940 von Baumbach informed the German high command that orders to Basis Nord would get through, but only after being approved by the Soviet military authorities in Moscow. For example, if *Jan Wellem* were to leave Basis Nord, a special request for a Soviet escort through the frontier zone would be necessary. Since passing through Soviet frontier zones without prior clearance could be deleterious to the health and safety of the traveler, the request would have to come to the attention of the Soviet North Sea Fleet Command. Thus, any signal for a sortie had to be simultaneously sent by blind transmission from Norddeich to *Jan Wellem* and read at the German embassy in Moscow. The embassy would inform military authorities in Moscow, who would then inform

Murmansk to arrange for an escort. The Armed Forces High Command issued orders approving this cumbersome network, which must have been less than satisfactory to everybody but the Soviets.

The *Jan Wellem* left Kiel and headed for Basis Nord on 20 January 1940. Laden with supplies for the German war effort, it was to provide support—with Soviet collusion—for ships the Soviets would later label as "pirates." Its outfit included ninety days worth of provisions and consumables for a pocket battleship and enough supplies to care for eight U-boats as well as the needs of the base itself.

Jan Wellem arrived at Basis Nord with medical, communications, and administrative staff for the base, as well as technical experts for repair and maintenance, on 4 February 1940. It arrived four days late, and it was probably only bad weather and luck that saved the *Jan Wellem* from attack by Soviet ships. Its arrival was a textbook case of how not to follow Soviet border entry procedures. First, the headquarters staff in Berlin was either unaware or oblivious to Soviet custom and planned *Jan Wellem*'s arrival on a holiday, 30 January. Second, after waiting two days, the Soviet guard ship assigned to meet it had returned to port. As the Soviet liaison officer in Murmansk pointed out, *Jan Wellem* entered the bay without making the requisite signal, and the communications system detailed above could not support communications. A lack of understanding of Russian customs by the Germans and a lack of willingness to deal with unplanned contingencies by the Soviets led to a wooden performance by both sides. Disaster was narrowly avoided.

The Germans could not get Soviet permission to have uncontrolled naval access, much less make free sorties from their base. Under the circumstances a request for access to the base through Soviet air space seems unrealistic. Even so, in early February of 1940 the German high command "requested that arrangements be made at Basis Nord for intermediate landings by transoceanic planes." The command directed von Baumbach to make an official inquiry and to determine Soviet reaction to this request, which concerned two long-range aircraft with water-landing capability: a *Blohm and Voss Ha-139* and the *Dornier Do-26*. The estimated range of the *Ha-139* was 3,075 miles and the *Do-26* 4,412 miles. Both planes, however, were in limited service because of spare parts shortages. In any case, few of these aircraft existed, and the Germans did not know if it would be possible for either type to reach Germany without refueling after a water take-off from Basis Nord. Given the Soviet obsession for control of their air space, however, air traffic at the base was likely to be tightly controlled and directed by the Soviets, not Germans. At best, this was another indication of the high command's excessively positive interpretation of Molotov's somewhat disingenuous statement that Germany "could do anything" at the base. The issue of transoceanic landings at Basis Nord was ultimately postponed and later abandoned by the high command.[56] It became moot with the acquisition of Norwegian and later French airfields.

Basis Nord in Winter

It became increasingly clear that Molotov's promise was fraught with delivery problems and that the base might not turn out to be all that the Germans wanted. Conditions on the ships themselves were not ideal. The crews had to remain at constant readiness day or night in all weather; they were almost totally isolated because of the need for secrecy; and, except for an occasional change in anchorage, the lack of activity made for crushing boredom. On 19 February *Phoenicia's* captain reported that the strain was beginning to tell on his crew. These difficulties loomed larger in light of the reduction of the crew from thirty-seven to twenty-one members before deployment to the base from Murmansk. Von Baumbach did what he could to moderate the conditions, replacing the older and married men with men from the crew of the German commercial steamship company Hapag Lloyd, whenever possible. Several days later the authorities in Berlin requisitioned a traffic boat for Basis Nord, which also promised some relief. Oil powered, about 250 tons displacement, and capable of seven to 10 knots, it was an old whale hunting boat named *Viking V.* Indeed, the balance of the work at Basis Nord fell to the German merchant navy—an indication of the shoestring basis on which the regular navy operated.[57]

A Possible British Attack

In mid-February of 1940 the German naval high command thought reconnaissance was being performed to prepare for military operations against Basis Nord. The Germans knew the British were patrolling the North Sea, hunting German merchant ships and raiders. On 22 February German intelligence reported that the British cruiser *Southampton* had left Scapa Flow and was proceeding to the north coast of Norway.[58] Other reports from Sweden intimated that British forces off North Cape were operating against German submarines based in Russian Arctic ports and in Norwegian territorial waters. There may have been some truth to this. The British government regarded the Soviet Union up until the fall of France "as an expansionist state which regarded the British Empire as its main target."[59] The German naval high command also apparently believed that a British aircraft carrier was at sea with the objective of delivering planes to Finland, which would not bode well for Basis Nord. The high command was aware that the French had already given substantial help to the Finns, including about 145 aircraft, 496 heavy guns, 5,000 machine guns, and millions of rounds of ammunition.[60]

Moreover, a report from Reuters asserted that "British warships in the North Cape area have orders to attack and cut off the Russian-German trade via Murmansk. The Soviet Government takes a very serious view of the situation. . . . Russia, however, will take no action, so long as they remain outside Russian territorial waters. Otherwise, Russian forces will attack."[61] Further political complications were also beginning to tell on the Soviets' already delicate position. On 28 February the British minister for economic warfare declared Soviet exports to Germany were breaking the British blockade.[62] But the attack never materialized, probably because the Russo-Finnish War ended sooner than the British had expected.[63]

March saw the recurrence of rumors of a German U-boat base in northern Soviet waters. The *Stockholm Daily Press* reported from London that such a base existed in Murmansk. At the same time, German intelligence observed English naval movements in the vicinity of Basis Nord. While there were naval movements around Norway and the Shetlands-Faeroes blockade, the official British history gives no indication of British knowledge of the base or planned operations against it. Nevertheless, the Soviet government remained afraid: "British intelligence would find out about project Basis Nord sooner or later. The Soviet government was afraid that the building of the base could be seen as direct assistance to one of the warring sides."[64]

The Soviets, Basis Nord, and the Invasion of Norway

Also in early March 1940, the German naval high command and Hitler in Berlin were formalizing plans for the German invasion of Norway. From Raeder's standpoint the base in the Soviet Union could be of considerable use in the undertaking. Raeder sent a proposal to the Armed Forces High Command which "pointed out the difficulty of synchronizing occupation in the south [of Norway] by air force transports and in the north [of Norway] by naval transports. Troops would be moved by merchant ships. Transports carrying material, perhaps also troop transports, should proceed first of all to Basis Nord, since the approach route is shorter."[65]

Additional Soviet analysis indicates that the Russians recognized "the political and military situation in Northern Europe was getting more and more complicated with each passing day."[66] Indeed, the Soviets noted that the German naval attaché was particularly concerned about finalizing the base's terms as late as 5 April 1940: "The occupation of Norway worried the Soviet government, but as a result of it, the problem of Basis Nord on the Kola Peninsula was avoided. It is thought that this prevented a possible conflict between the USSR and England. Besides the latter was thinking of occupying Norwegian and Finnish ports in the north. This possibility was confirmed by an official statement by Churchill in the House of Commons on 16 January 1940. In this speech Churchill confirmed that Great Britain was assisting Finland and providing her with military materiel."

Recent insight has been provided on Soviet behavior vis-à-vis the German invasion of Norway. The Soviets at the time were impressed with the boldness of the German occupation of Norway.[67] So impressed, in fact, they had decided that the Germans were a little *too* successful and had rewritten the book on certain types of naval operations. Further, they recognized that the German victory in Norway had had the effect of improving Germany's strategic position. According to the Soviets, "Britain's task of blockading German naval and merchant shipping as well as neutral shipping had been made more difficult." Germany had access corridors to the Atlantic and had secured the Baltic; aircraft from Norway could easily strike all British naval bases.[68]

There can be little doubt about the early realpolitik motives for Soviet political support for German objectives in Norway. The German presence would prevent the introduction of Allied forces into Scandinavia or perhaps even result in an Allied defeat. First indications of this came when the Soviets refused to support a Scandinavian alliance to deal with the German threat on 19 March. The Soviet Union certainly did not want a Scandinavian bloc emerging on the heels of its war with Finland. A further indication of the Soviet stance came on 28 April, when the Germans were assured that the Soviet Union would not attack Bessarabia "in order to avoid any possible disturbance to the German conduct of the war."[69]

As it turned out, all German ships involved in the invasion went directly to Norway from Germany. No U-boats or surface warships appear to have been supplied out of Basis Nord. But the base did support the German invasion of Norway in other ways. The German naval attaché in Moscow was ordered by the high command to send the *Jan Wellem* to the northern port of Narvik on 2 April 1940. The German naval high command insisted that the ship was "particularly important to Narvik's supplies," but the Soviet authority felt otherwise. Although the Soviets tried to delay *Jan Wellem*'s departure, the ship left for Narvik four days later. The Soviet attitude was "apparently motivated by political considerations and a high degree of nervousness about the future Franco-British attitude toward the USSR. They were, therefore, at pains to avoid any action in the slightest degree non-neutral which the enemy could use as a pretext for action." In effect, the Soviets made Basis Nord very difficult to use—at least until they decided that the Germans were going to win the Norwegian campaign.[70]

Meanwhile, the Germans had again requested permission to lay a telephone cable to the base from Murmansk and had been rebuffed. The communications problems never were solved, and the *Jan Wellem* was only released on the condition that it would not return to Basis Nord. Its departure meant more than a loss of good communications facilities by radio. From both the Soviet and German points of view *Jan Wellem* was the most capable of the ships assigned to the base. It was the only vessel expressly outfitted for the mission of the base, and its departure carried the base commander with it.[71]

Meanwhile, despite some difficulties over Soviet demands for German products, the German consensus was that the combination of Soviet deliveries and transit facilities provided by the USSR had decisively weakened the British blockade.[72] When the Soviet government was notified of the German invasion of Norway, Molotov declared that he understood the German action and wished "Germany complete success in her defensive measures."[73] Shortly thereafter, on 11 April, the Germans noticed marked relief on the part of the Soviets with the invasion of Norway. The Soviets apparently believed that the likelihood of their getting into war with the Western powers had been much reduced.[74] This reduced the operational need for Basis Nord with all its attendant diplomatic and military-political baggage.[75]

When *Jan Wellem* arrived in Narvik it carried 5,000 tons of fuel oil, 5,000 tons of diesel fuel, 700 tons of fresh water, 170 cubic meters of lubrication oil, and 500 tons of other supplies. Although capable of supporting operations by a pocket battleship for three months and of conducting at least four submarine replenishments, the *Jan Wellem* ended up refueling destroyers sent to Narvik to support the landing of German ground forces. It was present in Narvik when British destroyers carried out a surprise attack on 10 April. Between the 10 April attack and a second carried out by the battleship *Warspite*, it had to be sunk by its own crew. After almost all provisions had been unloaded, the *Jan Wellem* was scuttled at pier side on 13 April. It was later reported burned to make salvage by the British impossible, but whatever damage had been done was later made good: the ship survived the war to be scuttled in Kiel Bay in 1946.[76]

Despite *Jan Wellem*'s transfer to Norway and subsequent crippling, Basis Nord continued to function. The Soviets even provided a better anchorage, transferring the base from Zapadnaya Litza to Iokanga Bay on 1 May 1940. Little of operational value was accomplished there. In fact, the naval high command ordered all correspondence relating to Basis Nord destroyed—although this order was not completely carried out.

On 11 April 1940 the Soviet government declared itself "disinterested in the German action in Norway" and "understanding of the defensive measures taken by Germany." By mid-May, when a German victory in

Norway appeared certain, the Soviet press waxed strong in its support of German operations there. Basis Nord's military rationale had by now disappeared, and, shortly after France sued for armistice on 17 June 1940, operations at Basis Nord virtually ceased. Communications became more strained, even between Murmansk and Moscow, as the Soviet Union was now concerned that Hitler was planning war with Russia. The naval high command described the situation as one in which "German military successes have aroused great recognition in Moscow, but they are being followed with certain misgivings, since, if Germany's victory is decisive, a German advance against Russia later on is feared."[77] Indeed, the critical point is that, up to the German victory over France, the alliance was to Stalin's advantage. With Hitler astride all of Continental Europe and positioned on the Atlantic, Soviet resources and territory were considerably less important; although still needed to advance the German war effort, they were no longer critical.

A second possible resupply of the heavy cruiser *Hipper* was contemplated in August of 1940 and is the last mention of the base in the German archives. Between 2 and 8 August 1940 the heavy cruiser was headed east into the Barents Sea, and on the morning of 3 August it was fifty to sixty nautical miles northeast of the entrance to Motovskiy Gulf. Steaming on various courses, *Hipper* searched for targets of opportunity but found none.[78] On 10 August *B Dienst*, the German wireless intercept service, informed the navy that *Hipper* was the target of a British naval operation by the Home Fleet. The fleet command ordered *Hipper* to return to Germany "at once." German intelligence believed that an aircraft carrier, several heavy cruisers, and a "pack" of destroyers were between *Hipper* and home. It was the crew of *Hipper* itself that suggested the "possible withdrawal to Basis Nord or even to the White Sea or Kara Sea."

Hipper had sent so much radio traffic that it seemed certain to the Germans that the ship had been located by the British, even though the strength and disposition of the forces against it were unknown. It was ordered to break off operations and head home by 0700 on 8 August. The *Hipper* was to conduct a replenishment at sea using the oiler *Dithmarschen* without calling at either Trondheim or Basis Nord, as the latter might have led to possible internment or other complications. The Germans were aware that the Soviet Union desired to obtain *Lützow* and *Seydlitz*. The refueling took place, and *Hipper* made for home. The British did not engage *Hipper*, and the ship returned safely to Germany.[79]

A few days later Hitler's true anti-Soviet attitude surfaced once again. This time he was apparently concerned that the northern Norwegian fjords be defended "so that Russian attacks there would have no chance of success, and the foundation for occupying Petsamo would be laid." Given

Hitler's strategic outlook, it is hardly surprising that the order was given to close Basis Nord on 23 August 1940.[80] The German naval high command thanked the Soviet naval high command for use of the base in a very formal, almost unctuous, manner. The letter of thanks went through several revisions in Berlin and Moscow, with both the German naval high command and the Foreign Ministry providing input. The final letter was delivered to Fleet Admiral Kuznetzov at the Soviet naval commissariat by the German embassy in Moscow on 16 September 1940. The letter, which included a notification to Molotov, said in part:[81] "Since November 1939 the government of the Union of Soviet Socialist Republics has placed a bay on the Arctic coast at the disposal of the German navy as a supply base, port of refuge, and repair base. This bay has been of great value for German naval strategy. However, now that Norway is completely under German control, there is no longer any need to make use of a Soviet Russian [sic] bay for German naval purposes." When von Baumbach subsequently visited Kuznetzov he also thanked the Russian admiral for the assistance afforded the German navy by use of the Northern Sea Route (see chap 4). Kuznetzov responded to the attaché's thanks with several questions on the progress of the war, especially about the effects of the British bombing of Berlin, German operations in the southwest Pacific, and possible British knowledge of the return voyage of the German raider *Pinguin* via the Northern Sea Route. Von Baumbach reported that he volunteered little information, aside from denying that the British had any knowledge of *Pinguin*'s movements and pointing out that the British press had said that the German raiders had gained their position in the South Seas via the Atlantic route.[82]

Basis Nord as Operational Lynchpin

Basis Nord was a technical and political achievement limited by the larger canvas of Soviet-German relations. The communications difficulties that emerged during its existence were symptomatic of Soviet fear of foreigners on their soil. The concept of a foreign naval base operating and communicating securely with its home country without Soviet control was simply anathema to the control elements of the Soviet military bureaucracy. Moreover, real use of the base in any but the most clandestine of operations was not in Soviet interest. Given the technology the Soviets desired from the Germans, however, it is not surprising that the Soviets gave both the ill-fated *U-36* and the heavy cruiser *Admiral Hipper* clearance to use the base.

Basis Nord itself did represent something of a strategic capability; even with shoestring logistics and ramshackle floating depots, it was a physical base in the larger context of the German navy's dream to be astride the Atlantic. It was possible that the Arctic outpost could have been used with some effect to support both U-boats and heavy ship operations had either been available in significant numbers. That it was not used was the result of larger issues in the world war, the limits of the German navy to commit forces in the theater, the totally unanticipated Wehrmacht successes from Norway to France, and wise Soviet reticence at letting too much transpire at or originate from Basis Nord. Nord was ultimately much more significant as a political symbol of how far countries with divergent ideologies and objectives can come to work together. It was *not* a Subic Bay for the Germany navy. Operationally, little happened there because of the strategic success of Germany in the conquest of Norway, which gave Germany, by force of arms, a strategic position that the USSR was willing ad interim to provide by diplomacy.

Chapter Six

Cruiser "*L*"
From Germany with Reticence

A Clear Signal of Intent

The most tangible result the Soviet Union obtained from the Germans through naval negotiations was the uncompleted Cruiser "*L*," or *Lützow*. This ship was to have commemorated the battle cruiser that had been sunk as a result of leading the German attack on the British main body at Jutland.[1] It, in turn, had been named for a Colonel of Cavalry, who had served with distinction in the Russian army while it was engaged in freeing Prussia from Napoleon.[2]

Built at the *Deschimag Werke* shipyard in Bremen, Cruiser "*L*" was laid down in 1937, the fifth Admiral Hipper–class heavy cruiser built under a program created by Erich Raeder as part of his plan to rebuild the German navy after World War I. The program was supposed to produce only three ships displacing 10,000 tons each, but it was later increased to five ships of 18,000 tons displacement. Designed in the mid-1930s, the dimensions, displacement, and armament of Cruiser "*L*" anticipated a revision of the Versailles Treaty, under which such heavy cruisers were entirely prohibited to Germany. Cruiser "*L*" was christened the *Lützow* and was launched 1 July 1939. In fact, the new ships were to get 20.3-cm guns. The Germans dissembled about the size of the guns because Hitler did not want to alarm the British or adversely affect his rearmament of Germany.[3] According to Raeder, in his autobiography, Germany built ships like *Lützow* and *Seydlitz* "only under press of exceptional circumstances, which occurred when the Soviets began to build the *Kirov* class in the Baltic."[4]

The Soviet Union first asked for *Lützow* and *Seydlitz* on 4 November 1939. In December the Soviet government pressed its demands, adding another Hipper-class cruiser, the *Prinz Eugen*, to its request.

The führer decided that only *Lützow* could be used for the bargaining, along with plans for *Bismarck* and other "specimens of weapons for reproduction . . . and the like." Article 4 of the February 1940 economic agree-

Figure 8. Heavy cruiser *Admiral Hipper*. Like most of the inventory of German heavy ships assigned to operate against commerce, *Hipper* was to have been supplied out of Basis Nord. Such operations never came to pass because the Wehrmacht conquered better bases in Norway and France. (W. S. Bilddienst.)

ment struck between Germany and the Soviet Union included a general
schedule for delivery of war materiel, which included the cruiser. After
launching, the "hull and all equipment armament, spare parts, etc. [were]
to be delivered for completion in the USSR, with 80 percent of the total
to be delivered within 12 months of the signature of the economic agreement, the rest within 15 months. Complete plans, specifications, working
drawings and trial results of ex-*Lützow* [were to be provided to the Soviet
Union]."[5]

The cruiser was in Bremen fitting out when the agreement was concluded in February of 1940, so delivery was not difficult. Even though
Hitler had agreed to transfer of the ship, he was in no hurry to turn it over
to the Soviet Union. The 203-mm guns aboard the ship were very important to Stalin and had been one of his conditions for accepting *Lützow*. At
the time of the agreement, however, the guns for *Lützow* were in the hands
of the German army, which had to remove them from railroad mountings.
The army was directed to take Germany's military needs into account
before those of the Soviet Union, but in due course some of the weapons
(four of eight originally to be embarked) were sent to Bremen, and the ship
was made ready for transfer. Indeed, the Soviet reports and photographic
evidence indicate that the Soviets got a partially armed ship in very incomplete condition.[6]

Transfer of the cruiser was to be made through German coastal waters.
The objective was to use German ocean salvage tugs to tow the ship from
the yard in Bremen and turn it over to Soviet harbor tugs in the outer
roads of Leningrad. Even in the 1940s the German economy and its bureaucracy were intensely aware of every commercial opportunity to make
a Reichsmark. Because the winter of 1940 had been one of the worst in
history in the Baltic, the towing company was concerned about ice conditions.

The German Naval Weapons Office notified Vice Admiral Leopold
Bürkner, the head of the naval attaché section, that Cruiser "*L*" was considered sold to the Soviet Union on 11 February 1940. It was to be towed
from Bremen to Leningrad on 15 April 1940, considerably earlier than the
towing company wished.

The Soviet general staff and the German naval high command now had
to decide at what point the towed cruiser was to be protected by Soviet
naval escort. The demarcation line was agreed upon after a meeting between the German chief of naval construction, and his Soviet counterpart,
Commissar Tevossian, was to be communicated to the Soviet navy
through the German naval attaché in Moscow. It was agreed that the German navy was to be responsible for all maritime aspects of the transfer and
that both countries were to be responsible for the military security of the

unfinished ship in a war zone. By the scheduled departure date in mid-April orders had gone out from the German naval high command to the Naval Group West, at Wilhelmshaven, and east, at Kiel, to support the transfer. Protection was to be provided by both naval groups and was to include small craft, destroyers, and other escort vessels. The escort had to be minimal, however, as the Norwegian campaign was underway and there was a shortage of ships.[7]

Two days after the ex-*Lützow* left Bremen Captain Second Rank Vorontsov, the Soviet naval attaché in Berlin, requested performance characteristics and data for the 20.3-cm guns aboard the cruiser. At the time of his visit to the German naval high command the Soviet officer was also apparently under orders to obtain any possible information about German losses in the Norwegian campaign. Vorontsov was told that the performance characteristics of the weapons had already been discussed with the Soviet naval commission but that additional data could be provided through Admiral Karl Witzell, who would "clear up the military channels." Vorontsov's request for information on the guns was eventually met; his indirect request for information on the campaign was not.[8] Vorontsov was not the only professional Soviet naval officer to express an interest in ex-*Lützow*. Soviet navy fleet commander in chief, Admiral Kuznetsov, said in his memoirs:

> In late 1939, the cruiser *Lützow* was bought in Germany. Here is how I learned about it: I had a phone call from I. F. Tevosyan, who said that it had been decided to buy a cruiser being built by the Germans. He went to Germany for negotiations—this was not the first time that naval matters were decided without the participation of the People's Commissar for the Navy, and I was not at all surprised; I was worried by something else. I realized from what Tevosyan had said that there was actually no cruiser at all, and that we were only going to get the ship's hull, without the mechanisms and armaments. The idea was to tow it to Leningrad and to complete it there. "What if we do not manage to get everything necessary, say, the munitions." I thought; after all, there was a war on, and anything could happen in Germany. However, the decision was there, and it was too late to argue. The cruiser was bought, and in the spring of 1940, a German tug towed it to Leningrad.[9]

When the ex-*Lützow* arrived in Leningrad it was far from ready for service. With only two of its four turrets mounted it had only a skeleton bridge and virtually no finished superstructure above the first deck level.

It was delivered with twelve 37-mm AA guns and had no secondary armament installed at all (its sisters carried twelve 10.5-cm heavy AA guns,
twelve 37-mm light AA guns, eight 20-mm guns, and twelve deck-
mounted torpedo tubes). Not only was the ship woefully incomplete, but,
from the Soviet point of view, its fitting out was progressing too slowly.
According to the German officer in charge of the operation, Admiral Otto
Feige, the Soviets had boasted that, "given spoken advice and directions
from the Germans," they could take over the ship and surely "make it all
right and operate it."[10]

The Soviet assertions were undoubtedly optimistic, considering that it
took ex-*Lützow*'s sister ships—*Blücher*, *Hipper*, and *Prinz Eugen*—twenty-
seven, twenty-six, and twenty-four months, respectively, in German yards
to proceed from launch to commissioning. *Seydlitz* was never completed
but was partially converted to an aircraft carrier after being almost completed after thirty months construction work in June 1942. Its incomplete
hulk was captured by the Russians at Königsberg on 10 April 1945. Nevertheless, in late November 1939, ex-*Lützow* had been seventeen months
from completion, and, despite the transfer, its estimated completion period seemed in line with that of the three earlier ships. Crew strength,
final instructions for construction, training of various Soviet technical personnel, and German sea trial arrangements were, however, still being discussed.[11]

Ex-*Lützow* Becomes *Petropavlovsk*

On 25 September 1940 the Russians renamed ex-*Lützow* the *Petropavlovsk*.
Training Soviet personnel to operate German high-technology boilers,
fire control equipment, engine controls, and communications equipment
was, however, proving to be considerably more difficult. The primary issue was whether the Germans would send technical instructors to the
Soviet Union or the Soviet navy would send its personnel to Germany
for instruction.

Several months after the arrival of the cruiser a series of exchanges were
held in Leningrad between Rear Admiral Otto Feige, the German senior
officer on the scene, and Soviet Baltic Works director Boschenko. The
military-technical discussion between Feige and Boschenko seem to have
been separate from the gradual deterioration of Soviet-German relations
between the delivery of the ship and the conference. In November 1940
the Soviets were asked precisely how many German military advisors they
wanted aboard the cruiser and in what capacity. The Germans also inquired about when it would be possible to send Soviet technical personnel
to Germany for training in the ship's engineering, artillery and torpedo

operations. Yet whenever the Germans pressed the Soviets to define exactly what specialists and categories of personnel they wanted trained, the Soviets complained of the great difficulties of bringing enlisted personnel out of the country. The unwillingness of the Soviet naval command to send its people out of the country was obvious. Although the Soviets did not want German instructors in the Soviet Union, they still insisted that training must start without delay. The Soviet solution was to propose sending all prospective officers of the *Petropavlovsk* to Germany for training.

Neither side was prepared to carry out what was needed in any detail. Should translators be arranged, or could the translations be provided in Germany? Who was going to pay for all this? Who would be trained? Who would carry out the training? What sites would be appropriate? These and other questions were not resolved, except to say that the Soviet navy "would assume as much as it could of the work on the ship and each question would be worked out as the problem presented itself." That this series of questions arose at all, after the transfer of the ship, indicates a number of difficulties inherent in the larger Soviet-German relationship. First of all, the August 1939 pact, with its associated Trade Agreement and Protocols, brought a shift in policy that was as swift as it was fundamental: it sent a German ship built to fight Russian cruisers to the Soviet Union as naval assistance. Second, the Germans and the Soviets had to deal with each other's language differing approaches to personnel and training policies. Finally, neither nation had run such a program before. There were no precedents for quick solutions and no planning to take care of practical problems on either side.[12]

The Soviets said they wanted answers to their questions as quickly as possible but were told that the answers might require a long time. Feige's behavior certainly suited the führer's intentions to delay as long as possible. In January 1941 the naval high command told Feige's umbrella organization, the German Ships Sales Company, Ltd., that the earliest the German navy could begin training Soviet technical personnel would be a month before the beginning of the sea trials of the *Petropavlovsk*. The trials were scheduled to begin sometime in the fall of 1941, by which time Hitler hoped to have more than an embassy in Moscow. The Soviet naval authorities began to realize that they were going to get the *Petropavlovsk* in service later than they had hoped. Attaché von Baumbach informed the naval high command from Moscow on 3 January 1941 that he had "finally seen" Feige's letter concerning German training for the crew of the *Petropavlovsk*. Von Baumbach reported that the Soviets did indeed want their personnel trained in Germany, but they asserted that the motives for this were duplicitous: "While they want to muck about as much as they can in

German naval installations, they want to keep their cards as close to their chests as possible." Von Baumbach recommended to the naval high command that, if any Soviet personnel came to Germany, they should be given incomplete information about the ship. The attaché believed that the Soviets would come out of the exchange with more information than the Germans. The view of von Baumbach's superior, the chief of the naval attaché section, was that the Germans should deny that the training was required by the treaty and that, if it had to be done at all, it should be accomplished in the Soviet Union.[13]

Soviet naval authorities made every effort to complete their new cruiser more quickly. Von Baumbach was, again, called to the Soviet naval commissariat, where he was confronted by the prospective commanding officer of the *Petropavlovsk*, a Captain Vanifatev. Referring to the discussions in Leningrad with Feige, the Soviets stated that an understanding in principle had been reached concerning the training of their personnel for the *Petropavlovsk*. The Soviets then presented the attaché with another list of wishes and inquiries based on the talks in Leningrad. The proposal outlined by the naval commissariat to von Baumbach included six major inquiries and requests. First, the Soviets wished to send small groups of specialist officers to German factories, where boilers, turbines, auxiliary machinery, gunnery systems, and antiaircraft electrical systems were being manufactured. These small groups were to be made up of two to five officers and senior petty officers each. Second, the commissariat inquired about which firms could be expected to provide training and what form of payment would be acceptable. Third, the Soviets requested that all training be provided in Russian. If no German interpreters were available, the Russians would provide their own. Fourth, the Soviets requested that the technical instructions and operating equipment for the ship be turned over as set forth in the treaty. Fifth, they wished to embark ten to twelve officers who would eventually command the *Petropavlovsk* for orientation and training aboard an active ship of the Hipper class in German service. The final Soviet question was extraordinary: the commissariat wanted to know the wartime mission contemplated for the as yet uncompleted *Seydlitz*. Although the Germans had already rejected an earlier Soviet request for *Seydlitz*, the Soviets probed nonetheless regarding the use intended for the *Seydlitz* in war. Their questions implied an interest in the disposition of the ship, possibly for the Soviet navy. It is difficult not to surmise that the Soviets still had hopes of acquiring a second, unfinished heavy cruiser from Germany. This does appear to be a bold attempt at information collection.

Von Baumbach recommended a negative response to the whole Soviet proposal to the naval high command, a recommendation countersigned by German ambassador to Moscow von der Schulenburg. The naval high command sent two messages in response to the negative assessments of the attaché and the ambassador. The first concurred that the Soviet requests were too far reaching and that crew training for the *Petropavlovsk* in Germany was out of the question. The attached document indicated somewhat sarcastically that von Baumbach was trying to justify another trip to Berlin to solve problems with the Soviets—a clever ruse to get out of the unpleasant surroundings of Stalinist Moscow. In short, the high command believed that the Soviets would try to get their way by creating diplomatic difficulties, with repercussions in Berlin.[14]

The naval high command bluntly rejected taking Soviet exchange officers aboard German ships in war service with the retort: "No way!" It was, after all, known to senior members of the *Wehrmacht* that *Barbarossa* would be under way by the time operational schedules of their ships would allow embarking Soviet officers for training. In spite of that, however, the naval high command did fully support the suggestion that the *Petropavlovsk* be run by German officers and personnel.[15]

Von Baumbach traveled to Berlin on 24 January 1941 for another conference concerning details of the *Petropavlovsk* transfer at the German SKL. While those at the highest levels in the admiralty knew of Hitler's plan to invade the Soviet Union, the participants involved in this meeting did not. Therefore, the Germans were successfully able to give the impression that they were willing to help and that the Soviet Union's wishes would be fulfilled. The help from Germany would, however, take time. Training in gunnery, electrical systems, and fire control could be provided in German fleet schools during the fall of 1941. Five Soviet officers could train on *Seydlitz* when the latter was ready for sea trials, but embarkation on a cruiser already in service was not possible. The table of organization and duties in battle of the crew of the *Petropavlovsk* could be provided in Leningrad through a Russian-speaking officer. The Germans also decided that instructors could be sent to Leningrad to provide training in boilers, turbines, auxiliary machinery, and electrical installations at the beginning of the summer.

After the commissioning of the cruiser the Germans intended to send the appropriate papers and technical manuals, but instruction for any subject could only be given in German. The results of the admiralty conference were approved at higher levels and were forwarded through the German naval chain of command to Raeder's staff. At that level the additional proviso was added that the naval attache would forward the information to the Soviet Union and that the responses and subsequent German actions would always be carried out with the overall war situation and interests of the German nation in mind. Nothing would be done which could ultimately injure the defense of the country or interfere with its armaments programs. Von Baumbach passed the results to his Soviet counterparts.[16]

The second Soviet-German economic agreement was being negotiated, and its work was under way, while the exchanges regarding *Petropavlovsk* were going on at a lower level. When the economic agreement was signed in February 1941, the Germans promised to deliver much additional war material, including heavy turrets, although Hitler had no intention of meeting the obligation.

By 21 May 1941 German reconnaissance planes were penetrating Soviet air space with great regularity, and various states of alert had been declared by Soviet military forces. Still, getting the *Petropavlovsk* in service was a live issue. The Soviets had gotten around to requesting some very specific help by some very specific dates. They wanted the following done, and quickly:[17]

> automated boiler-firing technicians from the ship's builder, Deschimag—by late August or September 1941;
> organization of damage control central and fire control central from the ship's builder—by June or July 1941;
> controls for the ship's engines and communications from the ship's builder—in September or October 1941;
> electrical power systems—in July or August 1941; and
> an advanced estimate based on known data of the ship evaluating safety in battle and likelihood of sinking in action for the cruiser's internal security service—as soon as possible.

Further, in response to the Soviet requests the Germans inquired about which subjects the Soviets wanted taught so that the correct specialists could be sent to the Soviet Union. Understanding was achieved on that point, but the Soviets raised new requests. They now wanted to be given the plans and practical working instruction on the German high-pressure steam plant. The Soviets wanted information about steam condensers and something that resembled a gas analysis system, but apparently the Germans genuinely did not know what the Soviets were asking for in the case of the gas analysis system.

Von Baumbach was carrying out the intentions of higher authority to "drag his feet" when he told the Russians he would send their requests by courier. This was purportedly because the month of May was nearly gone and the naval high command "could take too long to answer the Soviet request." In fact, this method was a good deal slower than the teletype transmission of messages usually used.

Von Baumbach had an interesting exchange with the Soviet officer who presented the requests. The German attaché reported that this Soviet officer, very likely a Soviet secret police operative in naval garb, asked several questions that betrayed a general lack of naval knowledge and a particular lack of knowledge concerning *Petropavlovsk*. For example, when von Baumbach inquired about the prospective captain of the heavy cruiser, the Soviet's response was, "Who is Captain Vanifatev? I have never heard of him." Von Baumbach had to reiterate that Vanifatev was the man in whose hands he had placed copies of *Petropavlovsk*'s plans.

Leningrad Access Denied

In the meantime the Soviets had forbidden the Germans access to Leningrad. Although the German SKL had indicated that crew organization and technical training would be provided for the *Petropavlovsk* in Leningrad, the Soviet authorities were well aware of a German buildup on their western borders in May of 1941. It was not by chance that von Baumbach proposed sending German officers to assist the Russians at Leningrad, which at the time was the largest Soviet naval complex. The attaché thought dispatching several German engineers for training was a good idea, to buy time, and considered getting a German officer into Leningrad as a matter of highest service priority. In any case, if the Russians agreed, the officer should be routed through Moscow and get a briefing from von Baumbach.

The Soviet navy gave numerous indications that it did not suspect that a German invasion was only weeks away. For example, on 12 June von Baumbach received an invitation to visit the Soviets' naval base at Kronstadt. The visit, which was prevented by the German invasion of 22 June, was to have taken place on 23 June and would have been the first time a German officer inspected the island facility at the head of the Gulf of Finland. The German naval and armed forces high commands were both immediately informed of the invitation by radio.[18]

The last German mention of the *Petropavlovsk* under the agreement with the Soviet Union is dated from Berlin on 18 June 1941. It concerns more Soviet requests for the heavy cruiser, most of which were ostensibly to be met. All this was rather moot, however, as the Germans rolled across the Soviet frontier at 0300 four days later.The *Petropavlovsk* was not complete enough to be used at sea, but at least four 203-mm guns were installed.

The Program Bites Back

From the beginning of the war *Petropavlovsk* appears to have been used as a floating battery, opening fire in August 1941 on the advancing Germans along with the Soviet heavy cruiser *Maksim Gorkiy*. Both ships were stationed at the coal wharves in Leningrad. *Petropavlovsk*'s fire had significant effect on Leningrad's besieger, as seen in the diary of a dead German corporal: "in the harbor there are a battleship and some cruisers. It is hard to describe the craters which their shells make. One burst 200 meters from me. . . ."

According to German accounts, the *Petropavlovsk* was sunk in shallow water in September 1941, after being hit by eight 150-mm shells. During the siege of Leningrad it was bombed heavily by the Luftwaffe and was severely damaged in April of 1942.

The Soviet account of the ship's participation in the defense of Leningrad indicates that, on 7 September 1941, *Petropavlovsk* opened fire on German troops for the first time as the latter were trying to close the ring around Leningrad. In the next several days the cruiser fired forty broadsides from its reduced armament, expending about seven hundred rounds in all. On the morning of 17 September German artillery hit the cruiser with fifty-three rounds of 210-mm artillery shells from a range of six thousand yards, sinking the ship bow first. The Soviets reportedly managed to raise the ship sufficiently to get it in action again, by 17 September 1942, a year after its sinking, and the Soviets had moved it further up the Neva River at Leningrad. The *Petropavlovsk* was not able to open fire again until the end of December 1942. In the meantime the cruiser was renamed *Tallin*, as the name *Petropavlovsk* had been returned to the czarist-era dreadnought *Marat*. The battleship had also been bottomed on 17 September but was intermittently in action as a stationary battery off Kronstadt. Renamed the *Tallin* on 1 September 1944, ex-*Lützow* is credited with doing further damage to German positions during the 1944 Leningrad breakout. The Germans thought it had ended its days as a barracks ship in Kronstadt, having been salvaged by German naval prisoners of war after 1945. The Soviets then report that, since their navy had acquired new, modern units, it did not make sense to keep the ship in service. In March 1953 the ship was again renamed, this time *Dniepr*, and was placed at the Lieutenant Schmidt Bridge in Leningrad, where it remained until it was broken up later that year.[19]

Chapter Seven

Submarines
and Merchant Cruisers

Soviet Submarines and German Support

For Germany one of the most ideologically difficult aspects of detente with the Soviet Union was the support of the Soviet Union's invasion of Finland. Shortly after the attack began on 30 November 1939, the Soviets requested assistance from the German navy. On 9 December Ambassador Count von der Schulenburg and Captain von Baumbach sent an urgent message to the German high commands of the navy and armed forces, as well as the German foreign secretary, stating that the Soviet navy had informed Germany on a top-secret basis that they intended to establish a submarine blockade of Finland in the Gulf of Bothnia. The Soviets wanted the Germans to supply Soviet submarines operating against the regular Finnish commercial traffic on the Swedish ore route within the next three to four days. The Soviets suggested that this was to be a quid pro quo arrangement: the Germans would eventually receive Soviet supplies for their submarines in the same amounts they were provided to the Russians, although neither the location nor the occasion were specified. Von der Schulenburg thought the request was reasonable. He predicted that it would not have much impact on the Russo-Finnish War and might well be beneficial for repayment in kind. That was especially so, according to the ambassador, "if repayment took place outside the European theater." Most important, the Germans could ask for the same kind of thing from the Soviets in the future.[1]

The responses from the armed forces and naval high commands were immediate and superficially positive. On 10 December 1939 the naval high command told the naval attaché in Moscow to inform the Soviet commissariat for naval affairs that the German navy would lend immediate support. The Soviet suggestion of using merchant ships on the Swedish ore run, however, was not felt to be practical because the ships were not equipped for refueling at sea. The German high command reasoned that the best solution was to have a small diesel-powered ship accomplish the task, although it would require several days to find, outfit, and bring such a small ship into the navy.[2]

German naval logistics at this time was not on the scale of that later achieved by the British or American navies, although the World War II *Etappe* organization was global and designed to be in place shortly after hostilities began.[3] Early in the conflict, the German naval lines of supply consisted mainly of the *Etappe* organization as well as designated oilers, which were deployed for support of pocket battleship and armed merchant cruiser operations overseas. Several transport ships and other requisitioned vessels, usually taken up for a specific purpose and then returned to their owners after use, accounted for the rest of Germany's naval logistic forces. Indeed, the Soviets seem to have noticed German wartime control of merchant shipping and perhaps implied from this control greater resources or capabilities on the part of Germany.[4] The German navy was critically short of maritime and military assets and did not achieve full mobilization until 1942. So, when the Soviets asked for something not in the German program, the Germans had to scramble. In a very real sense both partners in the relationship were bound by their own rigid systems.[5] The German navy, as noted in chapter 1, was the priority investment for Hitler only in 1938–39. After that priority shifted to the ground forces. The Germans were limited in their operations by availability of fuel. They were limited in what they could build by the amount of iron ore that they could turn into steel. Private economic empires set up by Nazi potentates inside the Third Reich for their own profit wrought havoc with the allocation of resources.[6]

Given this strategic background, attendant disorganization and other difficulties, Naval Attaché von Baumbach was asked to obtain more details, while the Germans "looked" for the required Baltic submarine support ship. In order to outfit the ship the naval high command needed to know from the Soviets the precise amount and type of fuel required, the kinds of provisions desired, and a description of the oil intake fittings used on the Soviet submarines operating in the Gulf of Bothnia. The Soviet objective was to be able to deny entrance to the Gulf of Finland to anybody, British or German.[7] Despite the transparency of Soviet motives in this whole matter, von Baumbach sent the Soviet answers regarding fuel, provisions, and fittings back to Berlin on 11 December.

In their normal obtuse fashion the Soviets suggested that a German merchant vessel be provided to accomplish the task with three undercover Soviet naval officers as crew members. The Soviets even wanted a hidden chart house built below decks to assist navigation of the Swedish mine barrages (indicating that they had good knowledge of the mines and intended to violate Swedish territorial waters, a habit they would find hard to break).

The Germans agreed, and by noon on 12 December arrangements had nearly been completed. The undercover Soviet officers were ready, and the merchant vessel *Utlandsshoern* could leave as soon as its cargo was unloaded and replaced with U-boat supplies from Germany, or within three days. But later that afternoon the Soviets called the operation off. Von Baumbach telephoned the naval high command from Moscow to inform them that the Soviets had decided to abandon the plan.[8]

The German assessment of this sudden change in attitude was that the Russians probably had realized they had asked for something for which a quid pro quo could later be extracted. Moreover, because of Finnish resistance, they might not have been able to use it anyway. The Soviets also probably realized that the return would not be as important as what they would have to provide the Germans, and, of course, they may have had word about what the Finns were doing to the Soviet army. Nevertheless, the speed of the German response and their willingness to work with the Russians were designed to show that naval cooperation was available and that the relationship between the two services had been enhanced.

There was at least one other occasion of the German navy assisting Soviet operations—the escort of the Soviet steamer *Stalin*, carried out by German light forces on its return from Holland near Borkum. This positive action took place, however, in close propinquity to another that did not bode well at all for Soviet-German naval relations: the sinking of the German steamer *Bolheim*.

The *Bolheim* was attacked by a Soviet submarine enforcing the blockade of Finnish ports on the night of 10 December 1939. Although the German ship was proceeding with lights on and an illuminated German flag, a Soviet submarine attacked with gunfire on the surface, sank the ship, and made no attempt to rescue survivors. The captain of the *Bolheim* was killed; twenty-seven members of the crew made it safely to the Finnish coast in lifeboats. If this were but one incident, it could be forgiven as the baggage of war; after all, the German ship was in the blockade zone, and Germany had been informed of Soviet intentions the day before. The *Bolheim* incident was, however, only one of several such occurrences during the Soviet-German pact. Four other steamers—the *Oliva*, *Helga Boege*, *Pinnau*, and *Alwine Rub*—were fired on at various times by Soviet forces during the Russo-Finnish conflict, all without loss. Another German ship was fired on by Finnish coastal batteries because it was flying the Soviet merchant marine flag on 16 December 1939.[9]

The German embassy in Moscow brought these incidents to the attention of the Soviet foreign commissariat. The commissariat warned German crews to beware of the "difficulties" in Soviet waters and purportedly demanded better coordination among Soviet authorities in the identification and control of merchant traffic—or so a German Foreign Office memorandum reassured the armed forces and naval high commands in late April of 1940. Even so, in August of 1940 the German embassy in Moscow had to deliver a *note verbale* relating to another instance of overzealousness on the part of the Soviet border guard authorities. This time it was the steamer *Salzburg* in the Black Sea, on a voyage from Braila in Romania to Odessa in the Ukraine. Shots were fired at the ship by a Soviet border patrol unit off the Black Sea coast. The ship immediately stopped and anchored. The ship had its davits, compass light, and hull shot up, sustaining eight hits in all. The diplomatic note read in part that "the embassy would be very grateful to the Foreign Commissariat in the matter if they could prevent such occurrences in the future!" This particular incident was probably a result of the overly narrow interpretation of border lanes and rights of a riparian state which characterized Stalin's USSR.[10]

Soviet Support to Armed Merchant Raiders

The Germans had plans in place regarding commerce warfare for some years before World War II. Their experience in World War I, when some fifteen German merchant ships had been sent out to prey on Allied shipping, stood them in good stead. The armed merchant raider required a major force to deal with it, thus reducing the ships available to engage regular German war ships when they sortied.[11]

The Soviets, of course, were probably not surprised at the German raider strategy due to their assiduous appreciation of German World War I experience. Nevertheless, that the Soviets should play a role in the success of one of the more innovative German naval strategies is a matter of record. Perhaps the most interesting operational aspect of Soviet-German naval relations during the detente period was the agreement by the Soviets to let the Germans use their Arctic Ocean passage to the Far East. German use of the passage was to include both warships and mercantile vessels, primarily to assist the Germans in their circumvention of the British blockade. The subject arose in the fall of 1939 and was one of the major German requests to be actually realized. Both the Soviets and the Germans recognized the importance of having such a "continental" route allowing commerce and warships to transfer from the Soviet Union industrial heartland to the new lands in the Far East. German intelligence reports from Moscow recognized the value of such a route as early as the mid-1930s. In November of 1939 the German embassy in Moscow was requested to discuss the utility of the Northern Sea Route for warships with the Soviet naval commissariat. The Soviets were not forthcoming at first, although they acknowledged that destroyers had been sent to the Pacific by the route in the 1930s.

The discussion of Germany's use of the Northern Sea Route took place in January 1940, when the Soviet navy was requesting German help against Finland in the Gulf of Bothnia. Von Schulenburg raised the issue of possible German use of the Northern Sea Route with Molotov. Indeed, the winter of 1940 was to prove to be one of the worst on record, freezing even in the Baltic, a normally ice-free sea. Agreement in principle was reached, and the Germans were told to apply to civil authorities through the foreign commissariat for use of the passage. The Soviets said that, because of weather conditions, the passage could only be used during some six months of the year, and they had convoys already scheduled according to a five-year plan. But after intervention by higher authorities German ships would be added to Soviet convoys. By 10 January 1940 a list of potential German users, along with their displacement, dimensions, cargo, type of bows, and ice reinforcement, had been provided to the Soviet Foreign Ministry.

Because Soviet civil authorities had charge of the Northern Sea Route, a minor complication arose concerning warships using the route. Purportedly, this was a problem in principle only, as the Soviet navy supported the German naval application. According to German records, Rear Admiral Otto Schniewind of the German naval staff informed the embassy in Moscow that the Kriegsmarine's primary interest in the Northern Sea Route was threefold: use by commerce raiders, to provide imports for Germany, and as a means for "the return of German vessels from East Asia." The naval high command also observed that the strategic value of the route was that it allowed Germany "to maintain [raiding] operations . . . in order to keep enemy naval forces constantly tied down in remote sea areas," thereby supporting German naval operations in home waters.[12]

Beyond the strategic naval advantages the economic implication was that German shipping would not accrue to the enemy by default, or to neutrals or capture, as it could safely return to Germany. The Northern Sea Route meant safe access to the world's oceans. The naval high command also brought up the point that Soviet raw materials from the Far East provided as part of the German-Soviet economic agreement could be transshipped in German vessels, thus relieving the railroads, which were needed for other purposes by both countries.[13] In the mid-winter of 1939–40 there is no question that the Germans were very concerned about the state and future of their economy. Hitler was running a semi-mobilized economy, which was nominally following a four-year plan (1936–40). Hitler saw the primary purpose of the plan as securing self-

Figure 9. Armed merchant raider *Komet*. This ship conducted the only east-to-west ice passage of the Northern Sea Route by a German warship in World War II. Soviet support, however unenthusiastic, aided *Komet* in what was to be a very successful voyage of destruction of Allied shipping. (W. S. Bilddienst.)

sufficiency in a number of raw materials of major strategic importance until a new *Lebensraum* could be obtained by conquest.[14] Most of the German effort was focused on the building up of artificial fuel and rubber industries. The Office of the Plenipotentiary General for War Economy (GBK) and the OKW had not completed their plan for joint wartime economic mobilization when war began. By December 1939 the GBK was abolished. Private capital and banking largely supported and supplied German conquest up to the winter of 1942. Thus, the economics of the Northern Sea Route were largely unplanned, a fortuitous side benefit of the Russo-German Treaty of 1939. Getting ships from Germany that far north was difficult, but plans were set in motion anyway.

Events moved quickly. The German Foreign Office provided a list of some twenty-six ships in the Pacific, East Indies, and South America which could make use of the passage. Six whale factory ships and two merchant raiders were selected for the first German West-to-East convoy from the European to Pacific Arctic as the northern Pacific whale fishing grounds were less likely to contain allied warships than the Atlantic. Although no

Soviet ship of more than 4,000 tons displacement had ever used the seaway, the list of factory ships and one of the raiders the German navy sent to the Soviets included several ships well in excess of 4,000 tons. The Germans sent the data on the whalers with dispatch, although it took a month longer to provide details of the merchant raiders they wanted to use the route. There was to be one ship of 3,287 tons in July and one of 8,736 tons in August, according to two messages sent by the naval high command to the naval attaché in Moscow in mid-February 1940.

Again, as with the use of Basis Nord, difficulties with Soviet authorities arose in matters of detail: "In both cases there was a pronounced German desire to use the facilities as independently as possible . . . and there was strong Russian insistence upon keeping a close watch on every detail proposed or worked out by the Germans."[15] Initially, the Germans wished to send a team of shipping specialists to the Soviet Union for extensive discussions about the sea route. The specialists would be sent to Moscow to gather as much technical information about the route as possible. In particular, the naval high command wanted precise organizational knowledge of the Soviet Ice Reporting Service and Arctic Meteorological Service, in exchange for which they would offer the Soviets a complete set of the latest German meteorological gear to "pave the way for a good outcome of the talks."[16] The objective of the German negotiating team sent to Moscow was "to gain free and independent passage of ships through the Kara Sea up to Vilkitski Sound, with Russian icebreakers controlling passage from there to the Pacific."[17] The German negotiating strategy was to inform the Soviets openly about which of their ships were naval raiders and which were honest merchant ships, if the Soviets were, in turn, forthcoming.

The talks opened on 21 March 1940, before the successful German invasion of Norway, with Karl Hecking, an employee of the Hapag-Lloyd Shipping Line, representing the Germans, and B. Borissov, transportation chief of the Foreign Trade Commissariat, on the Soviet side. The Soviets were not forthcoming with giving permission to transit unescorted to the degree the Germans desired. Nevertheless, in the opening round the Germans caved in on one of their earlier points and submitted details of the German raiders to be sent over the Arctic route. As a matter of record, the Soviet delegates did not agree to any of the details of the German proposals. Instead, it was agreed that "the Soviet government intends to have warships escort the expedition through the Bering Strait." The Northern Sea Route negotiations occurred against the backdrop of the Norwegian campaign and its uncertain outcome; the Germans had not yet defeated France. Even so, the Soviets did provide the Germans with a complete set of their charts for transit over the whole of the Northern Sea

Route. Apparently, von Baumbach thought it prudent to stop at this point and established Soviet willingness to include the Germans in convoys with icebreaker escort. In any case, it is hard to disagree with the assessment that the Soviets "kept complete control over the conduct of the passage."[18] Allowing German merchant ships, or even worse, armed merchant raiders, to wander about unescorted in Soviet waters was simply unacceptable to the elements of control within the Soviet bureaucracy.[19]

The Soviets, however, were persuaded to accept a schedule of no less than four auxiliary cruisers and one deep-draft whale factory ship. The ships were to assemble in the bay at the southern end of Vaygach Island on 15 July 1940. Despite difficulties in scheduling and secrecy, two ships of this West-to-East convoy were to take on Soviet cargo bound for Tiksi in Murmansk. Perhaps the fact that the ships the Soviets requested to carry their cargo were the armed merchant raiders was coincidental; the selection, however, provided them with an excellent opportunity to examine the German raiders firsthand.

Since the Soviets were still technically a "neutral" power, there was the possibility of British ships being in the convoys using the Northern Sea Route, a difficulty the Soviets gleefully pointed out they would avoid for the Germans. During the course of the negotiations the Germans had pressed their request for information on the Soviet ice reporting and weather services. When the Soviets hesitated, von Baumbach advised that this specific request be abandoned, fearing greater damage to detente: "Russians must not be frightened or made distrustful through insistence on specific requests."[20]

The Germans ran into logistics problems that caused their cancellation of the East-to-West passage of ships from the Dutch East Indies. The ships were reduced from a total of twenty-six to four auxiliary cruisers and two whaling ships. The Soviets were not pleased. They may have been intending the Germans to carry cargo in significant quantity, and the reduction in the number of German ships upset their planning and cast doubt on German intentions. Even so, negotiations on the details of German use of the passage continued in late April and May of 1940.

By 30 April the naval high command in Berlin began to express reservations regarding the four auxiliary cruisers and the whalers, mentioning something about a British threat from Norwegian waters. Von Baumbach wisely cabled his superiors requesting permission to refrain from informing the Soviet authorities of the German misgivings: "We are unanimous here in fearing that the Russians may use the information that the dispatch of the auxiliary cruisers, etc., has become dubious as an excuse to cancel the whole project."[21]

For some months arrangements proceeded on the basis of four cruisers and two whaling ships. The Germans, however, may not have been totally disposed to deceive the Soviets when they planned to send four armed merchant cruisers across the Northern Sea Route. Their planning was based on the necessity of slipping through the British blockade and did not take into account subsequent military victories in Europe which resulted in German control of the coasts of France and Norway. Moreover, several German armed merchant cruisers did sortie during the first half of 1940. These included the *Widder*, which departed for overseas on 6 May; the *Thor*, which departed on 11 June; the *Pinguin*, which departed on 22 June; and the *Komet*, which departed on 3 July. Three of the four ships used the Denmark Straits for access to the open Atlantic.[22]

On 4 July 1940 German negotiator Hecking reported the final round of talks with the Soviets had been testy. Hecking had informed the Soviets that two ships had finally left port bound for the Northern Sea Route. The vessels were the armed merchant cruiser *Komet* and the tanker *Esso*. The *Esso* ran aground and had to abandon the voyage, but the *Komet* was still on its way.[23]

The Ice Passage

Komet was commanded by Rear Admiral Robert Eyssen, the most senior of the raider captains during World War II. Built in 1937 as a freight motorship *Donau* by Deutschewerft Hamburg, it belonged to North German Lloyd Steamship Company before being taken over by the German navy. Armed with six World War I–era 15-cm (5.9-in.) guns, six antiaircraft guns of various calibers, torpedoes, and thirty mines, it also carried two aircraft. *Komet* displaced about 7,500 tons and was capable of 16 knots on its diesel engine. Its range was fifty thousand nautical miles at 9 knots. Prior to being sent to the Northern Sea Route, it was equipped with a special strengthened bow and a special propeller suitable for ice navigation.[24]

The *Komet*'s voyage through the Northern Passage is described in considerable detail in the records of the German naval high command and, fortunately, also in the Soviet *Military History Journal*. Two aspects of it are of particular interest here: the navy-to-navy relations, as reflected in the use of the Northern Sea Route by a German raider, and the strategic results obtained by the raider itself.

The Soviet account notes that the German raider left Götenhafen (today's Gdynia) in the Baltic Sea, where it had been outfitting for a year on 3 June 1940. The Soviets focused on the raider's thorough equipage for operations in all climates and also noted that it "carried the most modern radio intercept, radio transmission detection and location equipment."

The Soviets state that the *Komet* made its voyage north along the Norwegian coast disguised as the Soviet icebreaker *Semyon Dezhnev*. *Komet*'s captain received his first Soviet sailing orders from the Glavsevmorputi (Soviet Main Northern Sea Route Administration). These included an offer to put into Murmansk. The Soviets (in 1990) noted that the offer was refused "for security reasons," and the raider put into Pechora Gulf, where it remained for nearly a month.[25]

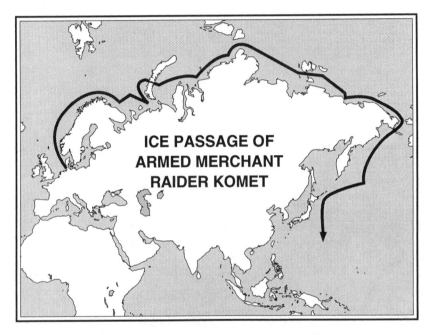

Map 3. Ice passage of the armed merchant raider *Komet*. This ship's operations were the most successful of those undertaken jointly by the Soviet and German naval authorities. Even this operation was fraught with political difficulties and mistrust.

The German account states *Komet* left Götenhafen on 3 July 1940, called at Bergen in Norway on 9 July, and proceeded into Soviet waters. Soviet authorities had wanted the ship to enter Murmansk, it was thought to pick up cargo for the Far East, but the German naval high command rejected the request and told von Baumbach so in a message dated 10 August 1940. The Germans asserted that it took two days for the German attaché to convince the Russians that the raider should not enter Murmansk for security reasons.[26] At the same time, the Soviets must have known that the longer the raider was forced to wait, the less likely weather would remain favorable for the long passage though northern waters. From mid-July to mid-August the auxiliary cruiser shifted from one open-ocean anchorage to another, waiting to be given directions from the Soviets about where to effect rendezvous with its convoy. While in Teriberka Bay, the ship carried the German cover name of *Donau*. Carrying a false name was as much a result of political exchanges between Moscow and Berlin as any problems with ice.[27]

Further, the Soviets asserted that the Germans used this time "for hydrological and meteorological surveys, photographing of the coast and military training of the crew. The ship picked up a lot of timber to be used in strengthening of the hull in case of great pressure from the ice."[28]

When the raider finally received orders at 0300 on 13 August to make a rendezvous with the Soviet icebreaker *Lenin*, it had to steam 330 miles at top speed because it was expected the following morning. Its instructions from the German naval high command were to proceed toward the Matochkin Shar Straits to meet the *Lenin*, which was to provide it with instructions and needed navigational equipment. The Soviets were to provide weather reports and all other information. *Komet* was under strict orders not to transmit during the voyage.

Komet arrived in the Matochkin Shar Straits in the Kara Sea on 14 August 1940. Taking aboard two ice pilots, the German raider steamed south to Teriberka Bay accompanied by the dispatch boat *Shtorm*. *Komet* proceeded through the straits, hoping to enter the western part of the Kara Sea. But an ice bar blocked its progress the following day. Eyssen and the two Russian pilots agreed that further progress was impossible without an icebreaker. The Soviet account says Eyssen could not find an icebreaker in the prearranged location and risked entry into the straits. The ship turned back for the entrance of Matochkin Straits and waited for three days in a cove until receiving orders from the *Lenin* to proceed. Because Eyssen knew he was to face a long voyage, he decided to allow some of his crew a brief shore leave on the island of Novaya Zemla. The Soviet pilots were none too happy about the cooperation with the Germans: "One can guess what these Soviet polar captains felt and experienced as they came in contact, on the bridge and in the officers cabins, with the officers and the crew of the fascist vessel which was carrying the Nazi flag in the Soviet Arctic." The pilots discovered a German radio intercept operation aboard the *Komet* and reported it at the earliest opportunity to the Soviet expedition commander, M. I. Shevelev. Although the Soviets had to carry out orders to get *Komet* through the ice passage, they used "any and all measures to delay *Komet*'s progress to the east, and by pointing out the heavy ice conditions, attempt to turn her back."[29] These attitudes, which were probably reflected by the German crew as well, albeit from a German perspective, reflect the difficulties in establishing positive relations at the working level when there was little trust on either side of the Russo-German relationship.

Komet had to weather a storm that passed through the Matochkin Strait on 19 August. Once the weather cleared the Soviets told the *Komet* to proceed east and use the icebreaker *Lenin* to get through the ice. The Germans were told where the ice was and were given a detailed course to pursue to the east. *Komet* was advised to follow only specific instructions from *Lenin* and to ignore local ice reports available on radio.

The exchange between *Lenin* and *Komet* was a professional high point in Soviet-German naval cooperation at the operational level. Two navies were pitted against a natural enemy—and succeeded in their collective objective, despite the lack of trust of the pilots on the Soviet side.

The German ship proceeded east, picking up further transmissions from a second icebreaker, *Stalin*, which was further to the East and provided clear updates to the three charts given to the raider. By 24 August (the Soviet account says 25 August) *Lenin* led the raider through Vilkitskiy Strait. When the two ships reached the Laptev Strait the Soviet icebreaker *Stalin* took over from the *Lenin*. Two days later *Komet* steamed past Cape Chelyuskin abaft to starboard. Admiral Eyssen had an opportunity to confer with the Soviets aboard *Stalin*. Captain M. P. Belonsov hosted the meeting, and, except for the chief of the Northern Sea Route, who declined to attend at the last moment for political reasons, all significant Soviet officials were present. The Soviets showed Eyssen the latest navigational corrections to charts provided to the *Komet*, the ice forecast, and, "in conclusion the culinary ability of the cook."[30] Icebreaker *Stalin* was to get the *Komet* through the ice, according to the German account.

The Soviets concluded that *Komet*'s mission was as stated but that the Germans had decided to take full advantage of the intelligence opportunities provided by the passage. The Soviets reported this assessment to Moscow and requested additional instructions, which were not forthcoming.[31]

Subsequently, a difficult passage in heavy ice and fog followed with *Komet* astern of the icebreaker *Stalin* navigating by a trail of oil the Soviets left on the water. Eyssen was impressed with the Soviet ice navigation and escort through the Laptev Sea. The German captain was given permission to proceed without escort into the Laptev Sea to the Sannikov Strait. By 30 August heavy ice conditions had been encountered south and east of the Bear Islands. Moscow finally responded to the concerns of *Komet's* pilots and ordered the Soviet escorts to break off the voyage and escort the German ship back to the west. Captain Melekhov told Eyssen that American destroyers and submarines had been sighted in the Bering Strait and that it was not safe to continue. Eyssen, however, told the Soviets he was determined to continue—with or without Soviet help.

Moreover, the *Komet* had suffered a steering failure. The icebreaker had escorted the cruiser to Aion-Schelkagsi, where both ships anchored and awaited new instructions from Moscow. Moscow wanted *Komet* to turn around.

In an attempt to get Captain A. P. Melekhov, the officer in charge of the eastern ice route, relieved of responsibility in this matter, Eyssen wrote a letter acknowledging the orders from Moscow and stating that he was proceeding on his own authority. The *Komet* had, according to the Soviet account, done the Northern Sea Route in twenty-three days—a record passage. The bill presented to Berlin for Soviet icebreaking, reconnaissance, and escort services was 950,000 Reichsmarks.

Eyssen successfully navigated the Chuckchi Sea. In early September he crossed into the Bering Sea and headed for the South Pacific and the British sea lanes to Australia and the East Indies. His voyage there was marked by the destruction of ten ships, seven of them in cooperation with the armed merchant raider *Pinguin*. The *Komet* sank 42,959 tons of shipping on the voyage. (The Soviets say it was nine allied ships with a total tonnage of 65,000 tons in cooperation with *Pinguin*). The most important lessons are drawn for the reader by post-Soviet Russians. The military historian A. V. Beznozov tells us:[32]

1. The operation took place during the height of the naval war.
2. Important weather intelligence was garnered of use to belligerents in violation of the 1920 Paris treaty.
3. Important intelligence of later use to the Germans in operations in the Arctic was gathered. (It surfaced in Arctic sailing instructions of 1941.)
4. The voyage of the *Komet* as well as the other Soviet basing deals for the Nazis became a sore point between the Soviets and the West and "to this day remain topics for criticism."

More than any other element of Soviet-German naval cooperation, the *Komet's* Northern Sea Route operation represented a true exchange of strategic position for diplomatic advantage. It was one of the best diplomatic tools the Soviet Union possessed, and they appear to have used it without serious damage to Soviet interests. Because the Germans had an alternative route for their raiders in 1940, and even 1941, it is clear this Soviet action in support of German naval operations added to the cost of the conflict to Britain and additionally to the Soviet Union. The availability of this route meant that the British navy, deprived of French support after May 1940, had to protect sea lanes in the Atlantic and Pacific and keep the Germans from crossing the channel as well. Indeed, the Soviets, until their recent collapse, were sensitive about such issues, because these issues undermined Soviet legitimacy. The political and military baggage of their relationship with Nazi Germany was part of the diplomatic underpinning for keeping Eastern Europe subservient, especially the Baltics. The "glorious" historical legacy of the "Great Patriotic War" was another pillar of intellectual justification for Soviet foreign policies, which the events just related severely undermined.

Conclusion

We have examined aspects of the military-political-naval relations between two great Continental powers, both of whom we now know had dreams of world maritime dominion. We have focused on the interplay of their navies during a turbulent time. Each power drew specific naval lessons from World War I. The substance of those lessons metamorphosed along different domestic military-political lines in Germany and the Soviet Union. Moreover, as the respective dictators tried to apply those naval lessons to their individual circumstances, the naval leadership, who nonetheless shared the objectives of their masters, were prisoners of the political and military policies of their leaders. When the two navies came into relatively intimate and prolonged contact, in 1939–41, the purely "naval" aspects of the relationship could not be expected to overcome the whims of their political masters, national character, ideology, or special interests.

The Soviets, initially, found themselves with the truncated physical remains of the Imperial Russian Navy's order of battle. They were left with an officer corps whose leadership and institutional outlook had been at least intellectually suspended, if not physically obliterated in Lenin's and Stalin's purges. The national leadership distrusted its naval professionals. The new Red Navy was more disposed to learn those lessons required of a lesser power, deprived as it was of the means of *guerre de main* (German *Grosskrieg*). The surviving cadre of naval theorists serving at the naval academy, led by Professor Petrov, wrote extensively of the need to resurrect a battle fleet in the 1920s. This was the same lesson that the German establishment drew from its World War I loss. The Soviets believed German submarine warfare had been successful, but the German successes did not merit a shift from traditional doctrine. By the early 1930s, however, the joint doctrine of combined land, air and sea defense driven by the Red Army's military reformer, Mikhail Frunze, forced the Red Navy's theorists to accept the reality of resource constraints imposed by a ruined economy and a military threat that demanded large ground forces. The Soviets recognized that they had limited resources, and the political agenda included the need to reconstruct Russia on a "totally new Socialist basis." The Russians did not labor under any treaty like the Germans, although they preferred to be perceived as generally abiding by major international agreements; the Soviets, like the Germans, were not above deceit if it suited their purposes. In fact, the Soviets subscribed to the 1922 Washington Naval Treaty and its 1930 follow-on. They also signed a secret agreement with England as a corollary to the 1935 Anglo-German naval agreement.

The Soviets, interestingly enough, profited by the German debates over *Kleinkrieg (guerre de course)* and *Grosskrieg.* They combined elements of both into their own naval doctrine, which Robert W. Herrick aptly named the "Soviet School." Soviet naval theorists and planners outdid the Germans regarding a truly balanced navy, with more emphasis on aircraft carriers, U-boats, and yet a full core of capital ships. The nearest physical expression of such a fleet was the three-million-person U.S. navy of 1945. Soviet experts' plans of a balanced fleet were overwhelmed by Stalin's capital ship obsession.

No military policy can be conducted in a vacuum. The Soviet-German military relationship and its naval components were driven by domestic and international policy concerns on the part of both powers. For the Soviets the requirements for a first-class naval military industrial base were an integral part of party policy. Stalin and the party saw the navy as a necessary instrument of defense but later as a means of projecting power. Soviet military-political policy was one of extreme distrust of German naval interests and intentions from the mid-1920s throughout the period of Russo-German detente in 1939–41. The obverse of this policy was to secure high quality German technology and to hobble German war production by deliberately excessive demands for hard-to-produce critical items. Like Hitler, Stalin intended to obtain a modern navy at any price. Many Soviet facilities and some of the ships were built by slave labor, as were some later German ships and facilities. The new Soviet navy had to be constructed under circumstances that, above all else, insured its loyalty to the party and its leader.

The German navy, on the other hand, was severely constrained by the Versailles Treaty. It was in need of money, resources, and facilities in which it could pursue developments in submarine, aviation, and mine warfare without legal or operational constraints, even from its own government. From 1919 to 1933 the German navy made very sparing use of Russian territory compared to the Reichswehr, primarily because of ideological and fiscal reasons. The German navy's covert programs were found not in Russia but, instead, in Spain, Finland, Turkey, and Holland. German lessons regarding World War I were at least as carefully manipulated by the leaders of the German navy, who were as schooled in the Tirpitz tradition as were any of Stalin's naval theorists. After the war began the German embrace of *Kleinkrieg* was driven by resource constraints and lack of time to build the Weltflotte.

The German navy was expected to be no less politically loyal than Stalin's fleet. Raeder had a highly trained cadre of military professionals, who could be rapidly expanded to meet Germany's national needs, as defined by the navy, as soon as Versailles was repudiated. There was no injury done to the core of the German navy by its political masters which could ever approach that done to the Russian services. The German naval leadership proceeded with both legal and illegal "end runs" well before the Anglo-German naval agreement lifted the Versailles strictures in June 1935.

The pre-Nazi German navy was, however, not politically popular; it was blamed by the Right for its role in the outbreak of revolution and the poor showing of its surface fleet. The German navy was despised by the Left because of its leadership's active support of the Kapp Putsch of 1920. In 1928 it had suffered a scandal over extraterritorial illegal weapons acquisitions schemes. In the first series of postwar apologist histories Erich Raeder's Reichsmarine was painted as more professional than Nazi. It is now clear that because of the navy's "affinity" for Nazism and because the dreams and objectives of its leadership were so convergent with the führer's, the navy became Hitler's most reliable instrument of state power. Although the navy had been given national industrial priority for a period late in the first decade of the Third Reich, the need of ground and air warfare soon overcame its Hitler-driven pride of place in German resource management. Ultimately, the goal of the German naval leadership since the 1918 defeat was to keep alive the best elements of imperial spirit and its attendant *Grossmacht/Seemacht* core beliefs and ideology.

Gargantuan dreams were something the dictators had in common. Hitler's orders were to concentrate on big ships in the immediate prewar period. Stalin, however, went far beyond Hitler, and the former's dreams included fifteen battleships and fifteen battle cruisers, which far exceeded Raeder's Z Plan of 1939 for twelve fast capital ships. In 1945 the Soviets destroyed German dreams, with help from some friends. By the 1960s the Soviets were able to build their version of Stalin's Weltflotte, including the modern technological equivalents of super battleships (whose actual military utility was never tested) and all the other elements of a balanced fleet. Ultimately, even this Weltflotte foundered on the shoals of resource constraints evaporating national will and the absence of a worthy successor to the *Vozhd* (Stalin).

Of necessity, both the Russian and German navies existed within the national military doctrine and planning efforts of their respective countries. During the period 1919–41 many changes occurred in the German and Soviet defense establishments and military commands which affected the role as played by both services. Perhaps the fundamental lesson is that both services were distinctly junior and subordinate to ground and air forces. Unity of command and objective were problems for the German services, especially at the national command authority level. That was not the case for the Soviets: they had other problems, not the least of which was personal survival.

National survival itself may not have been the immediate goal of the Soviet officers dealing with the Germans, but personal survival in Stalin's xenophobic Soviet Union was never far beneath the surface of any dealings with foreigners. Basis Nord, and to a lesser extent the northern sea ice passage of the raider *Komet* reflected the endemic Soviet distrust of foreigners as much as it reflected the German national strengths and weaknesses of bureaucracy and organization. The German officers involved in most of the dealings did not seem preoccupied with the Gestapo or *Reichsicherheitsdienst* looking over their shoulders, but the NKVD's presence was faced by both sides. Soviet national interests were never congruent with the German navy in the Baltic, as the difficulties during the Finnish war proved. Basis Nord and German use of the ice passage were both more politically symbolic than operationally useful. On the surface Stalin's actions do not appear to have been in Russia's interest. Yet Stalin was an accomplished player of international power politics. The Soviet policy of detente with Nazi Germany traded raw materials, a minimally useful base, and some grudgingly given operational-technical assistance on the Northern Sea Route for time, technology, and an unfinished cruiser. The unfinished cruiser contributed to the effective defense of Leningrad. The technology and weaponry went into the Soviet military-industrial complex and coastal defenses. It was intended by Stalin to provide Russia with a full spectrum of military-technical knowledge of German capabilities. It also strained German military production. Stalin no doubt was also pleased with the side effects of additional injury to Britain's interests and forces, which his actions made possible. But Stalin's actions ultimately did not buy him the time he sought, and, when evidence of German complicity began to mount, he could not accept the fact that he had been duped. His nearly fatal mistake was to believe that Hitler would keep his word until Stalin was ready to make his move.

Notes

PREFACE

1. Sergey Gorlov, "Soviet-German Military Cooperation, 1920–1930," *International Affairs* (Moscow: USSR Ministry of Foreign Affairs, 1990), 95–112. These documents are prefaced by a lucid introduction by the author, who is an attaché in the Department of Diplomatic History, USSR Ministry of Foreign Affairs.
2. Jost Dülffer, *Weimar, Hitler und die Marine. Reichspolitik und Flottenbau, 1920–1939* (Düsseldorf: Droste Verlag, 1973); Michael Salewski, *Die deutsche Seekriegsleitung, 1939–1945,* 2 vols. (Frankfurt am Main: Bernard und Graefe, 1970); Gerhard Schreiber, *Revisionismus und Weltmachtstreben. Marine Führung und deutsch italienische Beziehungen, 1919–1944* (Stuttgart: DVA, 1978). These works are placed in historiographical context in Keith W. Bird, *German Naval History: A Guide to the Literature* (London and New York: Garland, 1985), 580ff.; John Erickson, *The Soviet High Command: A Military-Political History, 1918–1941* (Boulder: Westview, 1984); Robert Waring Herrick, *Soviet Naval Theory and Practice: Gorshkov's Inheritance* (Annapolis, Md.: U.S. Naval Institute, 1989).
3. Adolf Hitler, *Mein Kampf* (Boston: Houghton-Mifflin, 1971), 660–61. See also Adolf Hitler, *Hitler's Secret Book*, ed. Gerhard L. Weinberg (New York: Grove Press, 1961), for consistency of his views on the Soviet Union.
4. For Stalin's early reticence in dealing with German military collaborations with the Soviets, see Gorlov, "Soviet-German Military Cooperation," 96. Alex de Jonge, *Stalin and the Shaping of the Soviet Union* (New York: William Morrow, 1986), 366.
5. Captain A. Golovko, "Interview" of Admiral A. Sarkisov, head of Naval Editorial Commission, "Sovetskaya voyennaya entsiklopediya," *Morskoy sbornik* (Naval Digest [Moscow]), no. 9 (September 1988): 88–89.
6. Andreas Hillgruber, *Probleme des Zweiten Weltkrieges* (Berlin: Köhler Verlag, 1967).
7. Schreiber, *Revisionismus*, 27ff; Schreiber, "Zur Kontinuität des Gross- und Weltmachtstrebens des deutsche Marineführung," *Militärgeschichtliche Mitteilungen* 26, no. 2 (1979), 101–71.
8. Erickson, *The Soviet High Command*, 476, 512.
9. The latest scholarship on the German side is provided by Charles S. Thomas, *The German Navy in the Nazi Era* (Annapolis, Md.: Naval Institute Press, 1990). See especially chap. 4, pp. 78–108, and chap. 6, pp. 141ff. Thomas chronicles Erich Raeder's efforts to convince Hitler of the need for a navy and then goes on to document the German navy's accommodation with the National Socialists, who wanted to build another Weltflotte.

10. Hitler, *Mein Kampf*, 273ff.
11. Hitler, 643ff. Hitler frequently meant what he said, and acted on what he wrote.
12. Thomas, *German Navy*, intro., xii–xiii, see nn. 6, 7, p. xvi. The line of scholarship supporting this assertion includes Michael Salewski, Keith Bird, and Jost Dülffer.
13. S. G. Gorshkov, *Sea Power of the State* (Moscow: Military Publishing House, 1976; Annapolis: Naval Institute Press, 1979). See also N. G. Kuznetsov, *Nakanune* (On the Ocean) (Moscow: Voyenizdat, 1965); and "Before the War," *International Affairs* (1965–66) (Moscow: Ministry of Foreign Affairs, 1966–67). *Nakanune* was a two-volume record of Kuznetsov's life of which "Before the War" was a limited serialized English version in the Soviet English-language foreign affairs journal. The Russian-language version was all too factual for the Brezhnev era, and so it was suppressed in the Soviet Union until the late Gorbachev era; the other work is N. P. V'Yunenko, B. N. Makayev, and V. D. Skugarev, *Voyenno-Morskoy Flot. Rol', Perspektivy Razitiya, Ispol' Zovaniye* (The Navy: Its Role, Prospects for Development and Employment) (Moscow: Voyennoye iz datel' stvo, 1988). Admiral Gorshkov did not physically write this book, but he guided the collective of authors in a function roughly equivalent to a senior substantive expert. This work can be considered something of a last will and testament for the Soviet/Russian navy by a man whose achievements eclipsed his German counterparts by an order of magnitude.
14. For suspicions of Kuznetzov, see Kuznetzov, "Before the War," *International Affairs* (November 1966): 98. For the Soviet suspicions dating back to the 1920s, see Gorlov, "Soviet-German Military Cooperation," particularly "Memorandum" from Soviet embassy, Berlin, 27 January 1928, 104. This policy probably applied to Stalin's approach to the U.S. navy in 1937 on battleships, but we do not yet have a definitive post-glasnost statement on it. The entire correspondence is included in *Foreign Relations of the United States: The Soviet Union, 1937–39* (Washington, D.C.: USGPO, 1952), 461ff.
15. U.S. Department of State, Washington, D.C., *Nazi-Soviet Relations, 1939–1941, Documents from the Archives of the German Foreign Office* (Washington, D.C.: USGPO, 1949).
16. *Das Deutsche Reich und der Zweite Weltkrieg*, vol. 5, pt. 1.

CHAPTER 1: THE NATIONAL CANVAS FOR NAVAL ISSUES

1. Ronald Hingley, *The Russian Mind* (New York: Charles Scribner's Sons, 1977), 148–49. The Curzon quote is from p. 154.
2. Walter Laqueur, *Russia and Germany: A Century of Conflict* (Boston and Toronto: Little, Brown, 1965), 13.
3. Office of Naval Intelligence, *Russo-German Naval Relations, 1926–1941* (Washington, D.C.: ONI, unpub. MS, 1945). (Hereinafter *RGNR*.) This is a descriptive chronology with references to German World War II records, including those of the naval high command (Seekriegsleitung) and the Ger-

man naval attaché in Moscow. The Soviet documents cited in the foreword come from the Soviet military attaché in Berlin as well as the Soviet high command and address, thus far, only the period to 1933.

4. Laqueur, *Russia and Germany*, 12.
5. John Erickson, *The Soviet High Command: Military-Political History, 1918–1941* (London: Macmillan, 1962), 144. For the Soviet view, see Gorlov, "Soviet-German Military Cooperation," 95. See also Kuznetzov, *Nakanune*.
6. Fred T. Jane, *Jane's Fighting Ships* (London: Sampson, Low, Marsden, 1920), 199.
7. Erickson, *Soviet High Command*, 9.
8. For the role in the revolution, see Evan Mawdsley, *The Russian Revolution and the Baltic Fleet* (New York: Macmillan, 1978). For technical difficulties, see Harriet Fast Scott and William F. Scott, *Armed Forces of the USSR* (Boulder, Colo.: Westview Press, 1984), 13; Paul Avrich, *Kronstadt 1921* (New York: W. W. Norton, 1970). This describes the entire rebellion and its subsequent bloody repression by Bolshevik authority.
9. For the latest on Kapp, see Thomas, *German Navy*, 29–38. For the authoritative work on Kronstadt, see Avrich, *Kronstadt 1921*.
10. Erickson, *Soviet High Command*, 92.
11. Erickson, *Soviet High Command*, 92. See also Jan Karski, *The Great Powers and Poland, 1919–1945: From Versailles to Yalta* (New York: New York University Press, 1985). See also Keith M. Bird, *Weimar the German Naval Officer Corps and the Rise of National Socialism* (Amsterdam: B. R. Grüner, 1977), 67–83.
12. See Gorlov, "Soviet-German Military Cooperation," 95.
13. Erickson. *Soviet High Command*, 84. There is an extensive body of literature concerning this issue, including R. H. Haigh, D. S. Morris, and A. R. Peters, *German-Soviet Relations in the Weimar Era Friendship from Necessity* (Totowa, N.J.: Barnes and Noble, 1985); for an assessment of the naval role, the Soviet navy, and the Kronstadt rising, see Jacobsen, *Locarno Diplomacy, Germany, and the West: 1925–1929* (Princeton N.J.: Princeton University Press, 1972); for a description of how the German socialist government played the Russian card, see Harvey Leonard Dyck, *Weimar Germany and Soviet Russia, 1926–1933* (New York: Columbia University Press); for a very broad treatment of Russo-German collaboration in context, see Cecil F. Melville, *The Russian Face of Germany* (London: Wishart and Co., 1932). This book assembles all the *Manchester Guardian* stories that revealed the cooperation.
14. Wallace L. Lewis, *The Survival of the German Navy, 1917–1920: Officers, Sailors and Politics* (Ph.D. diss., University of Iowa, 1969), 323. He cites F. L. Carsten, *Reichswehr und Politik, 1918–1922* (Cologne: Kiepenheurer and Witsch, 1964), 94. Lewis's entire story is in chap. 10, pp. 312–23. A shorter version of the Kapp Putsch is contained in Walther Görlitz, *The German General Staff, 1697–1945* (New York: Praeger, 1953), 220–22. See also James M. Diehl, *Paramilitary Politics in Weimar Germany* (Bloomington and London: Indiana University Press, 1977), 50ff. See also Bird, *Weimar*, 67–125.

15. Bird, *Weimar*, 309. Raeder was subsequently moved to a position as chief of the naval archives.
16. Erickson, *Soviet High Command*, 110, citing V. I. Lenin, *Collected Works*, 4th ed., 31:445.
17. Haigh, Morris, and Peters, *German-Soviet Relations*, 74ff.
18. Haigh, Morris, and Peters, *German-Soviet Relations*, 73 n. 80.
19. Haigh, Morris, and Peters, *German-Soviet Relations*, 78.
20. Heinz Höhne, *Canaris*, trans. J. Maxwell Brownjohn (New York: Doubleday, 1979), 130–31. For the ideological enemy, see Bird, *Weimar*, 8.
21. The phrase "virulently reactionary Navy" is from the Gerald O. Feldman review of F. L. Carsden, *Reichswehr and Politics in the American Historical Review* 72 (July 1967): 1424.

CHAPTER 2: NAVY TO NAVY
COEXISTENCE AND INTERFACE, 1920–1933

1. Robert Waring Herrick, *The Sea in Soviet Strategy* (Annapolis, Md.: Naval Institute Press, 1965), 7.
2. Herrick, *Sea in Soviet Strategy*, 7ff.
3. Herrick, *Sea in Soviet Strategy*, 11.
4. Erich Raeder, *My Life* (Annapolis, Md.: Naval Institute Press, 1960), 122ff.; see also Thomas, *The German Navy in the Nazi Era*, 34ff., for a much more balanced treatment.
5. *RGNR*, 3.
6. For Bauer's activities in the OHL et seq. see Wilhelm Deist, *Militär und Innenpolitik im Weltkrieg 1914–1918 Zweiter Teil* (Düsseldorf: Dröste Verlag, 1970), 1421–22.
7. For an early advocacy of unrestricted U-boat warfare, cogently argued, see A. von Tirpitz, *Deutsche Ohnmachtspolitik im Weltkriege* (Hamburg and Berlin: Hanseatische Verlagsanstalt, 1926), 369ff.; Position Paper of the U-Boat Officers Bauer, Bartenbach and Hansen concerning the tactical aspects of the [German] Diplomatic Note to America. Erickson, *Soviet High Command*, 147.
8. William Manchester, *The Arms of Krupp, 1587–1968* (New York: Little, Brown, 1970), 334.
9. Manchester, *Arms of Krupp*, 331.
10. The involvement of German specialists in the production of new Soviet 12.4-inch heavy guns is murky to say the least. Recently released documents edited by Sergey Gorlov note, "The Soviet proposal for a joint venture to produce heavy artillery was put off for the time being." (Contained in memorandum on the Results of Negotiations between the Soviet Military Delegation led by Iosif Unschlikht and the leadership of the *Reichswehr* [23–26 March], 100). For the "start from scratch" approach, see A. V. Platonov, "Artillery Armament for Battleships Laid Down during the Pre-war Years," *Sudostroyeniye* (Shipbuilding [Moscow: Ministry of Shipbuilding]), no. 7 (1990): 60–64.

11. Platanov, "Artillery Armament," 332. Putilov was then and remains a shipyard. It was later named Zhdanovsky and finally Northern Shipyard.

12. *RGNR*, 6ff; see also Erickson, *Soviet High Command*, 252; for a Soviet record of this conference, see Gorlov, "Soviet-German Military Cooperation."

13. Gorlov, "Soviet-German Military Cooperation," 101. See also intro.

14. Manchester, *Arms of Krupp*, 323–33. For the treaty violation, see Ministry of Defense, Navy (MOD [Navy]), German Naval History, *The U-Boat War in the Atlantic* (London: HMSO, 1989), 1:105ff., app. 1, "German U-Boat Building Policy, 1922–1945." Spindler was the author of many works on U-boat warfare. See Keith W. Bird, *German Naval History: A Guide to the Literature* (New York: Garland, 1985), 1069–70.

15. Erickson, *Soviet High Command*, 170. For more about Unschlikht, see Christopher Andrew and Oleg Gordievsky, *KGB: The Inside Story* (New York: Harper, 1990), 68, 74, 83, 884. In April 1922 Unschlikht was the Cheka chief's deputy. The political officer was a creation of Soviet totalitarianism whose principal claim to authority was political loyalty, not competence in the naval art. Such political officers had life and death authority over professional naval officers whose party loyalty was in question, especially in the early years of the Soviet Union. The Spindler mission/exchange took place in the context of a larger German effort to circumvent the naval provisions of Versailles. Unschlikht was also assigned to head up the communist secret police in Germany *after* the planned communist takeover of that country. (See pp. 82ff.)

16. *RGNR*.

17. *RGNR*, 12.

18. A. Chernyshev, "The First-Born of a Great Fleet," *Morskoy sbornik* (Naval Digest), no. 9 (1989): 76. Despite the apparent dead end of the 1926 Soviet-German naval activity, some lessons of German warship design were doubtless included in design of the heavy cruiser *Kirov*, which was accomplished in the later 1920.

19. *RGNR*, 13–14.

20. *RGNR*, 15.

21. Walter Hubatsch, *Der Admiralstab und die obersten Marinebehörden in Deutschland, 1848–1945* (Frankfurt: Bernard and Graefe, 1958), 192ff. See also Höhne, *Canaris*, 130–31. For intelligence control, see Gorlov, "Soviet-German Military Cooperation," 110 n. 2.

22. Gorlov, "Soviet-German Military Cooperation," 103; for the friendly reception of the Red Fleet, see 112.

23. For the Lohman affair, see Jost Dülffer, *Weimar, Hitler und die Marine. Reichspolitik und Flottenbau, 1920–1939* (Düsseldorf: Dröste Verlag), 90ff.; and Bird, *Weimar*, 180ff.

24. Gorlov, "Soviet-German Military Cooperation"; see also MOD (Navy), *German Naval History*, 105ff.

25. Gorlov, "Soviet-German Military Cooperation," 97.

26. It is noteworthy that the navy did not wish to raise the issue of potential

Western enemies with the Soviets. For the German side of this 1929 discussions, see *RGNR*, 18ff. See also Bird, *Weimar*, 198 n. 155. Bird documents the instructions to the German side as follows: (1) when German officers entertained their Soviet counterparts, no Russian officers could be allowed to bring enlisted personnel with them; (2) no German crew members could be invited to Russian ships at the same time as their officers; and (3) the Russians must give assurances that they would not meet with any German communists.

27. *RGNR*, 10.

28. P. S. Smirnov, was the army commissar assigned as naval minister at that stage of Stalin's rule. Smirnov portrayed potential construction of aircraft carriers as the definitive indication of aggressive intentions by Germany against the USSR. See Herrick, *Soviet Naval Theory*, 92.

29. The foregoing and succeeding chronology and record of conversation is based on *RGNR*. For a Soviet assessment of the German naval failure, see S. G. Gorshkov, *Sea Power of the State*, 2d rev. ed. (Moscow: Voyenizdat, 1976), 96–100.

30. See Walter Görlitz, ed., *The Kaiser and His Court: The Diaries, Notebooks and Letters of Admiral Georg von Müller, Chief of the Kaiser's Naval Cabinet, 1914–1918* (London: Macdonald, 1961). For additional criticism of the German command structure, see Hubatsch, *Der Admiralstab*, 178ff.

31. There is an extensive literature about this, the latest distillation of which appears in Thomas, *The German Navy in the Nazi Era*, 1–18. See also Bird, *German Naval History*, 515ff.

32. Carl-Axel Gemzell, *Organization, Conflict and Innovation: A Study of German Naval Strategic Planning, 1888–1940* (Stockholm: Esselte Studium, 1973), 300ff.

33. Raeder, *My Life*, 192–93.

34. The active order of battle of the German navy in 1930 included only four old Deutschland class pre-Dreadnought battleships, with another four in reserve. The new pocket battleship *Deutschland* would not be commissioned until 1933, though the Soviets were allowed to visit it on the stocks.

35. Herrick, *Soviet Naval Theory and Policy*, 21.

36. These destroyers were the core of the small postwar fleet Lenin had approved. They were laid down in Leningrad during World War I. *Uritskiy* was launched in 1915 as *Zabiyaka* and completed the same year; *Karl Liebknecht* was launched in 1915 as *Kapitan Belli* but not completed until 1928.

37. Erickson, *Soviet High Command*, 841.

38. Erickson, *Soviet High Command*, 953.

39. Oscar Parkes and Frances E. McMurtrie, eds., *Jane's Fighting Ships, 1926* (London: Sampson Low, 1926), 339. For a description of the cruiser by its first chief officer (C.O.), see N. G. Kuznetzov, "Before the War," 91–93ff. He describes his ship in the context of a conversation with Sergei Ordzhonikidze. Kuznetzov makes no mention of such a visit by German officers in his memoirs.

40. This discussion is taken from the German account of the visit contained in *RGNR*, 26–27.

41. For a discussion of this policy and its historical context, see MOD (Navy), *The U-Boat War in the Atlantic*, 1:105ff., app. 1, "German U-Boat Building Policy." In fact, the front firms set up by the Germans are even alleged to have sold plans to the Soviets.

42. For the alleged sale of plans, see Jan Breemer, *Soviet Submarine Design Development and Tactics* (London: Jane's Information Group, 1989), 53; for more from Brutzer, see *RGNR*, 27ff., memorandum to *Heeresleitung* dated 2 May 1931; for the Soviet view, see Gorlov, "Soviet-German Military Cooperation," 110ff., Nikolay Krestinskiy to Kliment Voroshilov, 21 July 1929. Pointedly, Krestinskiy notes the letter did not go to Stalin.

43. *Fuehrer Conferences on Naval Affairs: Brassey's Naval Annual 1948* (New York: Macmillan, 1948), 58 (entry for 22 November 1939 meeting of Raeder with Hitler and General Keitel). (Hereinafter *FCNA*.)

44. (Captain) Stephen W. Roskill, *White Ensign the British Navy at War, 1939–1945* (Annapolis, Md.: Naval Institute Press, 1966), 37.

45. *RGNR*, 30.

46. See U.S. National Archives, File T-1022, T-175-D, PG48801, "Diesel Engines for Russia," 31.12.36.

CHAPTER 3: NAVY TO NAVY: COMPETITION, 1933–1939

1. For "items," see Breemer, *Soviet Submarine Design*, 52; for Soviet investment, see (Captain First Rank) V. Krasnov, "Battleships of the *Sovetskiy Soyuz* Class," *Morskoy sbornik* (Naval Digest), no. 6 (1990): 63. *Morskoy sbornik* is an official publication that in 1990 was still functional under the direction of GLAVLIT, the main Soviet administration for publications. Every article was scrupulously cleared by censors. The money refers to the entire program, not just the ships that made it to construction. There were fifteen battleships and fifteen battle cruisers in the program. The equivalent U.S. cost was $100 million per ship (Iowa class). The figure is not unreasonable, according to discussions with other Soviet scholars.

2. Gorshkov, *Sea Power of the State*, 136–37.

3. (Admiral) S. E. Zakharov, *Istoriya voyenno-morskogo iskusstva* (History of the Art of Naval Warfare) (Moscow: Voyenizdat, 1969), 168.

4. Harriet Fast Scott and William F. Scott, *The Armed Forces of the USSR*, 16, see n. 32; Roy Medveydev, *Let History Judge: The Origins and Consequences of Stalinism* (New York: Alfred A. Knopf, 1972), 104–9. There is, of course, more: both V. M. Molotov and A. A. Zhdanov were heavily involved in the industrialization program, which had as one of its objectives a modern navy and detente with Germany as well. Ironically, both were seriously at fault when the German attack came, with Molotov telling Admiral Kuznetsov, less than a week before Operation *Barbarossa* fell on the Soviets, that "only a fool would attack us." See also Gavriel D. Ra'anan, *International Policy Formation*

in the USSR: Factional Debates in the Zhdanovsychina (Hamden, Conn.: Archon
Books, 1983), 8.

5. Gorshkovl, *Sea Power of the State*, 136.

6. Sergei Zonin, "An Unjust Trial," *Morskoy sbornik*, no. 2 (1989): 79. The key
statistics concerning the class were:

> standard displacement: 59,150 tons (this may have been light, standard, or
> empty; at full load such ships could approach 65,000 tons, which puts Zon-
> in's estimate at the high end of the spectrum)
> dimensions (meters): 260 × 36.9 × 9.2
> propulsion: 3 steam turbines—201,000-shaft horsepower developing 28
> knots; range at 14 knots, 5580 miles
> armaments:
> 9 × 406 mm (100 rounds per gun, 3 × triple turrets)
> 12 × 152 mm (170 rounds per gun, 6 twin turrets)
> 40 × 37 mm (10 × 4 barrel AA)
> aircraft: 4
> armor:
> 420 375-mm main belt / 365 230-mm bulkheads
> 155 100-mm armored deck
> 495 425-mm turrets

The standard of protection was designed to survive two twenty-one-inch
torpedo hits simultaneously, or three torpedoes and a mine.

7. War experience indicated that the 37-mm AA guns were found to be a superior weapon. In fact, no quadruple 37-mm was built during World War II,
although twin and single 37-mm were constructed.

8. If several hundred tons of rivets were not needed, then the weight saved by
welding could be put into improving combat capabilities such as speed, weapons, or protection. This applied to any design, not just a treaty-limited one.
The ships begun were:

> (hull #S239) *Sovetskiy Soyuz* (Leningrad Baltic 15 July 1938)
> (hull #S352) *Sovetskaya Ukraina*
> (hull #S101) *Sovetskaya Rossiya*
> (hull #S102) *Sovetskaya Belorossiya*

9. The foregoing section on the design and construction of the Sovetskiy
Soyuz–class battleship by (Captain First Rank, ret.) V. Krasnov, "Battleships
of *Sovetskiy Soyuz* Class," *Morskoy sbornik* (Naval Digest) (May 1990): 59–63.
William C. Green of Boston University kindly provided the author with
translations of this and the article on Kronshtadt class battle cruisers. For the
armament issues, see Platonov, "Artillery Armament," 62ff.

10. The Soviet details included:

> The details for this agreement were settled during the visit
> to Germany by I. F. Tevosyan, the first Peoples' Commis-
> sar for Shipbuilding industry. The mass of the projectile

fired by the German 380 mm gun with a length of 52 calibers consisted of 800 kilograms (the Soviet 305 mm gun fired a 470 kilogram projectile). The rate of fire was 2.3 rounds per minute, the combat reserve was 95 rounds per barrel (in the initial design the corresponding figures were 3 and 100). The range was lowered from 48,000 to 37,400 yards. The package offered by the firm included also two fire directors with one ten meter distance meter in each and six military search lights with a reflector diameter of 150 centimeters.

11. (Captain First Rank), V. Krasnov (ret.), (Candidate of Naval Science), "*Kronshtadt* Class Battle Cruisers," *Morskoy sbornik* (August 1990): 54–56. See Yu. M. Stvolinskiy, *Konstruktory nadvodnykh korabley* (Designers of Surface Ships) (Leningrad: Lenizdat, 1987); and V. Yu Vsov, "Tyazhelyye kreysery tipa Kronshadt" (Heavy Cruisers of the Kronshtadt Class), *Sudostroyeniye* (Shipbuilding), no. 11 (1989): 57–58. The main armament of the first two units was to consist of six 38.1-cm guns in Krupp mountings.
12. Gorshkov, *Sea Power of the State*, 137.
13. Zakharov, *Istoriya*, 169.
14. V. I. Achkasov and N. B. Pavlovich, *Soviet Naval Operations in the Great Patriotic War, 1941–1945* (Annapolis, Md.: Naval Institute Press, 1981), 5; see also Scott and Scott, *Armed Forces of the USSR*, 16; S. A. Tyushkevich, *The Soviet Armed Forces: A History of Their Organizational Development* (Moscow and Washington, D.C.: USGPO, 1978), 181ff.
15. Tyushkevich, *Soviet Armed Forces*, 185.
16. Erickson, *Soviet High Command*, 353. Erickson also notes that the Northern Fleet was "to provide cover for Murmansk with headquarters at Polyarniy." See also A. Golovko, *With the Fleet* (Moscow: Progress Publishers, 1988), 607ff.
17. The attempts by Stalin and his subordinates to acquire large-caliber naval guns from the United States is documented in *Foreign Relations of the United States, Diplomatic Papers: The Soviet Union, 1933–1939* (Washington, D.C.: USGPO, 1952), 459ff. See also Robert W. Herrick, *Soviet Naval Strategy: Fifty Years of Theory and Practice* (Annapolis, Md.: Naval Institute Press, 1968). See (Captain First Rank, ret. commander of Naval Sciences) V. N. Krasnovl, "Stalinism in the Navy and in Shipbuilding," *Sudostroyeniye* (Shipbuilding), no. 7 (1990): 64–69; see 64.
18. See Herrick, *Gorshkov's Inheritance*, 83. See Sergey Zonin, "An Unjust Trial," *Morskoy sbornik*, no. 2 (1989): 78–84.
19. Herrick, *Gorshkov's Inheritance*, 101; from Kuznetsov's memoirs, 478–79.
20. The hybrid is described in several published sources, and a copy of the proposed plan appears in Siegfried Breyer, *Battleships of the World, 1905–1970* (New York: Mayflower Books, 1980), 376.
21. V. Yu. Gribovskiy, "*Sovetskiy Soyuz*–Class Battleships," *Sudostroyeniye* (Shipbuilding), no. 7 (1990): 57.

22. Eva H. Harastzi, *Treaty-Breakers or Realpolitiker? The Anglo-German Naval Agreement of June 1935* (Boppard am Rhein: Harald Boldt Verlag, 1974), 157ff.

23. Harastzi, *Treaty-Breakers*, 233–34.

24. See Stephen W. Roskill, *Naval Policy between the Wars: The Period of Reluctant Rearmament, 1930–1939* (Annapolis, Md.: Naval Institute Press, 1976), 318–19. For the documents, see 319 note f.

25. Herrick, *Soviet Naval Theory and Policy*, 141–232.

26. Kuznetzov, "Before the War," 91–93.

27. Kuznetzov, "Before the War," 92–93.

28. Kuznetzov, "Before the War," 94.

29. Kuznetzov, "Before the War," no. 9, 1966.

30. (Captain Second Rank) M. Golovko, "Interview with the Chief of the Editorial Commission of the Soviet Military Encyclopedia," *Morskoy sbornik*, no. 9 (1988): 88–89.

31. See Kuznetzov, "Before the War," as cited in Herrick, *Soviet Naval Theory and Policy*, 287. The actual stenographic record exists. Some more insight is provided in both (Captain First Rank) V. Kraskov, "Battleships of the *Sovetskiy Soyuz* Class," *Morskoy sbornik* (May 1990): 59–63. Stalin shot many key designers, including the head of the design bureau; see 60–61.

32. This data comes from yet another glasnost-era revelation, this one in the Soviet foreign ministry journal *International Affairs*, no. 5 (1988). Professor Aleksander Roschichin, Soviet Ministry of Foreign Affairs (MFA) ambassador, who worked in the Third Western Department of the MFA (which dealt with USA, France, and England) is the article's author; it is entitled: "People's Commissariat for Foreign Affairs before World War," 113ff.

33. Valentin Berezhkov, "Stalin's Error of Judgment," *International Affairs* (September 1989): 13ff. The author was one of Stalin's personal interpreters and an eyewitness to the dictator's activities during the 1939–41 period.

34. K. M. Simonov, "Notes on the Biography of G. K. Zhukov, *Voyenno-istoricheskiy zhurnal*, no. 6–7 (1987): 48–56.

35. Simonov, "Notes," 56.

36. Khalkin-Gol is the Russian name for the locus of a major Soviet-Japanese land battle that occurred in the Far East in the summer of 1939. It is often considered both a political and military watershed for Stalin. Politically, it removed the prospect of a two-front war. Militarily, it validated armored warfare theories and brought Georgy Zhukov forward as a military commander.

37. Siminov, "Notes," 56. See also Erickson, *Soviet High Command*, 532–37.

38. Cruisers that displaced 10,000 tons and were armed with eight-inch guns. *Handbuch zür deutschen Militärgeschichte, 1648–1939*, pt. 7, vol. 8: *Deutsche Marinegeschichte der Neuzeit* (Munich: Bernard und Graefe, 1977), 444. (Hereinafter *DIMHNZ*.)

39. *DIMHNZ*, 445. See also Wilhelm Deist, *The Wehrmacht and German Rearmament*.

40. *DIMHNZ*, 447.
41. *DIMHNZ*, 468.
42. *DIMHNZ*, 449. See also Haraszti, *Treaty-Breakers*. For a British view, see Roskill, *Naval Policy*, chaps. 5 and 10. For Hitler on naval policies and their bankruptcy, see *Mein Kampf*, 140, 247, 273–75.
43. *DIMHNZ*, 459. See also Michael Salewski, *Die deutsche Seekriegsleitung, 1935–1945*, vol 1. *1935–1939* (Frankfurt am Main: Bernard ind Graefe, 1970), 57ff. There was, of course, a broader issue facing the British. They had to decide if they were going to declare war on the Soviet Union because of the latter's attack on Poland. The secret protocol to the Polish treaty with England only applied in the case of aggression by Germany. The British equivocated and rejected the Soviet-German partition of Poland, but they could not affect the outcome of the Soviet action. The British decided that their treaty only mandated going to war with Germany.
44. *DIMHNZ*, 470. See also Militärgeschichtliches Forschungsamt, ed., *Germany and the Second World War*, vol. 1: *The Buildup of German Aggression* (Oxford: Clarendon Press, 1990), "Naval Rearmament," 456–80.
45. Bird, *German Naval History*, 557–58.
46. *DIMHNZ*, 475. Dülffer.
47. Bird, *German Naval History*, 557.

CHAPTER 4: THE NAVAL DIMENSIONS OF THE
HITLER-STALIN PACT

1. Alex de Jonge, *Stalin and the Shaping of the Soviet Union* (New York: William Morrow, 1986), 358ff. For attitude, see 359; for more recent evidence that Stalin had attitudes in common with Hitler, see Christopher Andrew and Oleg Gordievsky, *KGB: The Inside Story of Its Foreign Operations from Lenin to Gorbachev* (New York: HarperCollins, 1990), 234. Gordievsky cites Valentin Berezhkov, Stalin's personal interpreter as the source for this. He was told it by A. A. Mikoyan who attended the politburo meeting. Mikoyan was Stalin's minister of foreign trade.
2. de Jonge, *Stalin*, 359. See also Erickson, *The Soviet High Command*, for Stalin's later concern about Allied will, on 513ff.
3. de Jonge, *Stalin*, 11, 361; Gustav Hilger and Alfred G. Meyer, *The Incompatible Allies: A Memoir History of German-Soviet Relations, 1918–1941* (New York: Macmillan, 1953), 98 n. 21, 314.
4. Erich Raeder, "Sind Kriegserklärung von Beginn der Feindseligkeiten in heutiger Zeit notwendig?" *Marine Rundschau* 15 (1904): 291–311; for evidence of early interest in Russia, see *My Life*, 30. He translated half of the Russian epic *Rasplata* (The Recoming), 31.
5. See (Admiral) Arseniy A. Golovko, *With the Fleet*, 8; and (Admiral of the fleet of the Soviet Union) N. G. Kuznetzov, "Before the War"; for Raeder's views, see Michael Salewski, *Die deutsche Seekriegsleitung, 1935–1945*, book 1. *1935–1941* (Frankfurt am Main: Bernard und Graefe, 1970), 356. He cites Raeder's memoirs, 2:244. See also Kurt Assmann, *Deutsche Schicksalsjahre: Historische Bilder aus dem zweiten Weltkrieg und seiner Vorgeschichte* (Wiesba-

den: Eberhard Brockhaus, 1950), 198. Kurt Assmann was a confidant of Er- ich Raeder and the German official naval historian from 1930 up to 1945. He was actually present in the führer headquarters in East Prussia in July 1944 and was wounded in the bomb explosion that unfortunately did not take Hitler's life.

6. Adolf Hitler, *Mein Kampf* (Boston: Houghton Mifflin, 1971), 326–27. See also 659–62ff.

7. See Hilger and Meyer, *Incompatible Allies*, 65, n. See also *Nazi-Soviet Relations*. The basic agreement was accomplished between 14 and 23 August 1939. See also Anthony Read and David Fisher, *The Deadly Embrace: Hitler, Stalin, and the Nazi-Soviet Pact, 1939–1941* (New York: W. W. Norton, 1988), 156–258, which takes the reader from the failure of the allied mission to Moscow to Stalin's toast to Hitler upon conclusion of the basic nonaggression pact.

8. The commercial agreement was achieved in principle on 19 August and spelled out in a German Foreign Office memorandum of 29 August. Four other documents including the German-Soviet Boundary and Friendship Treaty, three supplementary protocols, and a joint Soviet-German declaration were produced during the negotiations.

9. The protocols are at appendix D and dealt with the exchange of nationals in new conquered territories and a division of Soviet and German spheres of influence.

10. *Nazi-Soviet Relations*, 80–82. Exchange of letters between Hitler and Mussolini, 25 August 1939.

11. *Nazi-Soviet Relations*, 131–32.

12. Berezhkov's assessment applies to September 1939, because Stalin never really ruled out volte-face if the circumstances merited or *real* advantage could be gained. The Germans made a peace offer after their victory in Poland and were surprised to have it rejected. The constellation of events that led to a long war was not in place immediately. See, for example, *Germany and the Second World War*, 1:676–717.

13. Valentin Berezhkov, "Stalin's Error of Judgement," *International Affairs* (September 1989): 13ff.

14. Aleksei Roshchin, "The People's Commissariat for Foreign Affairs before World War II" *International Affairs* (May 1989): 108–14. For paragraph cited, see 113. For other reasons, 113–14ff. See also Gordievsky's comments in Andrew and Gordievsky, *KGB*, 244. Citing D. C. Watt, Gordievsky notes that: "The opening of the negotiations that led eventually to the Nazi-Soviet appears to have been conducted through NKVD rather than diplomatic channels."

15. Berezhkov, "Stalin's Error," 13.

16. Berezhkov, "Stalin's Error," 14. Reichminister Joachim von Ribbentrop to Ambassador Werner von der Schulenburg regarding conversation with Georgiy Astakhov, Soviet chargé d'affaires in Berlin, 2 August 1939.

17. Berezhkov, "Stalin's Error," 15.

18. Berezhkov, "Stalin's Error," 15.
19. Berezhkov, "Stalin's Error," 17, 20.
20. U.S. Department of State, *Documents on German Foreign Policy, 1918–1945,* ser. D, vol. 8: *The War Years (4 September 1939–18 March 1940)* (Washington, D.C.: USGPO, 1954), Memorandum of Conversation by Ambassador Ritter 2 January 1940, 588. (Hereinafter *DGFP.*) Stalin's behavior and the fallout were certainly true to course. For a description of Stalin's role in the negotiations, see Hilger and Meyer, *Incompatible Allies,* 301.
21. See Hilger and Meyer, *Incompatible Allies,* 302. Cf. *FCNA* for Hitler's discussion on technical details with Raeder.
22. *DGFP,* 8:752–54. See also *RGNR,* 78–79.
23. See Raeder, *My Life,* 282–83. Michael Salewski analyzes this decision at some length (132ff).
24. See USNA, PG32633, *Die Seekriegsleitung und die Vorgeschichte,* pt. 2, for a summary of the Soviet position.
25. For Ritter's role, see *KTB der SKI,* 5:43.
26. This policy was enunciated in the war diary of the German naval attaché, Moscow, 17 October 1939; see also *RGNR,* 119. Full texts of the agreements discussed appear in *DGFP,* 8:588–98. Memorandum by Ambassador Ritter; memorandum by an official of the Soviet Union, Moscow, 10 January 1940, 641–43; and memorandum by Ambassador Ritter, Berlin, 16 January 1940, 672–73. Ritter's final memorandum gave the schedule of German deliveries as approved by the führer. The second conference in the Kremlin, on 29 January 1940, is recorded on 718–22; on 8 February a final conference was held in the Kremlin, and the German memorandum of conversation for this is at 752–54.
27. These issues constitute some of the strategic underpinnings of Soviet-German naval relations. For the discussion of the nature of the 1940 economic agreement, see *Nazi-Soviet Relations,* 119; for Soviet offer, see 133 and discussion that follows. For a discussion of Russian oil, see *RGNR,* 78–79; for trade deficit problems and subsequent course of relations, see *Nazi-Soviet Relations,* 199ff. For Hitler's inclinations, see *FCNA,* 126. Ritter's problems getting German firms to deliver show up in *DGFP,* 8:923, memorandum for record by Ritter.
28. Bernard R. Kroener, Rolf-Dieter Müller, and Hans Umbreit, *Organization und Mobilizierung des deutschen Machtbereichs, Erster Halbband, 1939–1941, Das deutsche Reich und der zweite Weltkneg,* vol. 5 (Stuttgart: Deutsche Verlags-Anstalt, 1988), 434ff.; see graph on 435.
29. *RGNA,* 80–81.
30. *FCNA,* 119. Conference on 21 July 1940.
31. *Nazi-Soviet Relations,* Dr. Karl Schnurre to Ribbentrop, Foreign Office memorandum, W4520/40gRs, 28 September 1940. Schnurre was the head economic negotiator of the German Foreign Office at the time on commercial issues, although only counselor of legation, later minister, head of the Eastern European Section of the Political Division of the German Foreign Office (199ff.).

32. *Nazi-Soviet Relations*, Ribbentrop to Stalin, 13 October 1940, 207ff. Stalin's reply is at 216ff. For further information on Stalin on the relationship with Germany, see de Jonge, *Stalin*, 361; and for extension into the Baltic, see 365.

33. *FCNA*, 14 November 1940, 153.

34. *FCNA*, 79ff. The ultimate disposition of German naval artillery is chronicled in *Warship International* (1982): 95–97.

35. The Krupp correspondence is found in United States National Archives T-1022, reel 2000/PG33741. The German reference is Amt Gruppe Wehrwirtschaft Kriegsmarine den 21 April 1941. NR1108/4. The description of the effort is from *Warship International* (1982): 95–97.

36. *Warship International* (1982): 95–97.

37. Raeder, *My Life*, 332ff; also see 335; and *FCNA*, 134. See Bird, *German Naval History*, 586ff.

38. For Erich Raeder's assertion, see *My Life*, 334. In this context the word *sedulous* means impeccabably correct behavior.

39. E. L. Woodward, *British Foreign Policy in the Second World War* (London: HMSO, 1970), 1:13.

40. Woodward, *British Foreign Policy*, 13. See *DGFP*, 8:213 n. 1.

41. S. W. Roskill, *History of the Second World War, The War at Sea*, volume 1: *The Defensive* (London: HMSO, 1976), 1:41ff.

42. Roskill, *War at Sea*, 44.

43. Woodward, *British Foreign Policy*, 47–50.

44. Woodward, *British Foreign Policy*, 53. See also Klaus A. Maier, Horst Rhode, Berndt Stegemann, and Hans Umbreit, *Germany and the Second World War: Germany's Initial Conquests in Europe* (Oxford: Clarendon Press, 1991), 13–17.

45. For a record of the trip, see USNA, PG33740/reel 2006. For comment on the political commissar system, see narrative on 2.

46. Thomas, *German Navy*, 61ff.

47. Thomas, *German Navy*, Vorontsov trip.

48. Ruge, *Der Seekrieg*, 89.

49. Ruge, *Der Seekrieg*, 391. The *Lützow* referred to here is the pocket battleship ex-*Deutschland*, not the Cruiser "*L*" of the previous chapter.

50. For British version of the action, see Roskill, *White Ensign*, 62–63; for detailed discussion of this action, see William H. Garzke and Robert O. Dulin, Jr., *Battleships: Axis and Neutral Battleships of World War II* (Annapolis, Md.: Naval Institute Press, 1985), 135–36.

51. For additional data and quote on Norwegian campaign, see Roskill, *History*, 1:62ff. For the exchange between Vorontsov and his German hosts, see USNA, PG33740/reel 2006, Berlin, 19 April 1940, No. 6182/40.

52. See Herrick. The Soviets had a penchant for programming and systematizing their naval thought and then applying those lessons to naval policy and doctrine in ways that the Germans would have done well to imitate. The "brain trust" that resided in research and teaching positions in the Soviet naval academy, and to a lesser extent the general staff, was not synonymous with the Soviet naval command as such, although the naval command frequently accepted its judgments.

53. Herrick, *Soviet Naval Theory*, 126ff. The author stands deeply in Herrick's debt here. There is even more: the Soviets clearly appreciated for a long time the fact that the Germans had learned significant lessons from World War I, wherein they failed to grasp the strategic significance of Scandinavian bases. Herrick notes (140 n. 57) that Admiral Otto Groos's seminal work *Seekriegsleitung im Lichte des Weltkrieges* (Naval Lessons in the Light of the World War) and Vice Admiral Wolfgang Wegener's *Sea Strategy of the World War* were translated into Russian in 1928 and 1941, respectively. The Soviet brain trust studied both Groos and Wegener as background to their analysis. The former was the "accepted" official German navy view; Wegener represented the "new school." Wegener's book became the bulk of a standard Soviet text: *Operativno-takticheskiy vzglyady Germanskogo flota; Sbornik statei* (Operational-Tactical Views of the German Navy: A Collection of Articles). For a development of the Soviet argument, see n. 58.

54. USNA, PG33740/reel 12006, Moscow *Volkskommissariat für Auswartige Angelegenheiten*, 17 April 1940, naval attaché, Moscow, to Naval Attaché Division, German Naval High Command, Berlin (Matt [naval attaché division, naval staff]), translation No. A/1940/40, 17 April 1940, No. 6182/40.

55. For numbers of Germans in the Soviet Union versus numbers of Russians in Germany, see Ismail Akhmedov, *In and Out of Stalin's GRU: A Tartar's Escape from Red Army Intelligence* (Frederick, Md.: University Publications of America, 1985), 150. For an assessment of Captain Norbert von Baumbach, see N. G. Kuznetsov, *Before the War*, no. 12 (1966): 97: "[von] Baumbach left the Soviet Union shortly before the German army attacked. He never became an admiral. I saw an item in the press during the war saying that on Hitler's orders, Kapitän [zur see] von Baumbach had been shot for misinformation about the true strength of the Soviet navy. I do not know how reliable the report was, but I never heard anything more of von Baumbach." This is self-serving and is only included here because it does represent a clear Soviet view of one of the major German players.

56. For a text of von Baumbach's letter, see *RGNR*, 45–47. Captain First Rank Morov was the head of the office with whom von Baumbach regularly corresponded.

57. Von Baumbach's interlocutor was Gustav Hilger, a noted German diplomat, who was legation counselor from 1923 to 1939 and embassy counselor from 1939 to 1941, German embassy in the Soviet Union. See Hilger and Meyer, *Incompatible Allies*. Hilger knew von Baumbach for a number of years and worked with him, yet the Foreign Office/military chasm seems to have been in place. Another German staff member in Moscow at the time, Hans von Herwarth, also wrote a memoir, *Against Two Evils* (New York: Ranson Wade, 1981). Von Baumbach appears in an aside in the description of how to get a seat on the train: "ask the NKVD for it!" Herwarth said (39): "Another feature of Russian train travel in the 1930s was the legions of insects of every type, particularly bed-bugs. DDT had not yet been invented. In its absence, one particularly ingenious member of our Embassy had a tailor make him a

pair of pajamas which completely covered his hands and feet, leaving only his head out. This absurd but eminently practical outfit was the invention of our naval attaché, Commander Norbert von Baumbach."

58. Hilger and Meyer, *Incompatible Allies*, 319ff.

59. For more on the German Foreign Office memo, see the German document, Berlin Auswärtiges Amt (*A.A.*), 24 April 1940, USNA, PG33743/reel 2006, to naval high command and armed forces high command; for German treatment of Russian ships, see *KTB der SKL* copy of SIRS Nr5800/40gii PG33740/reel 2006, 8 August 1940; and *KTB der SKL*, 8 August 1940, 12:65; for interception of the merchant cruisers by Russian warships, see *KTB der SKL*, 12:65, for possible engagement of Russian destroyers, see *KTB der SKL*, 28 July 1940, entry for *Hipper*, vol. 12; see also 8 August 1940, 12:65, for entry on Russian destroyers. For Roskill, see *History*, 260.

60. *Nazi-Soviet Relations*, chronology, analytical list of documents, 24–25.

61. Roskill, *History*, 250–53ff. See also MOD (Navy), *U-Boat War*, 48–59.

62. *Nazi-Soviet Relations*, 24.

63. *Nazi-Soviet Relations*, analytical list of documents, xxvii–xxix.

64. Tukhachevskiy visited Germany and attended maneuvers in 1932. He was murdered on 12 June 1939 by the *Narodnyi Komissariat Vnutrennikh* (NKVD) on the grounds that he spied for the Germans. The most recent description of Tukhachevskiy's demise and its circumstances is Gordievsky, *KGB*, 139. See also Thomas G. Butson, *The Tsar's Lieutenant: The Soviet Marshal* (New York: Praeger, 1984), 162, 169, 187, discuss Tukhachevskiy's actual dealings with the Germans.

65. See Erickson, *Soviet High Command*, 845.

66. For the Galler dinner, see USNA, PG33740/reel 2006, von Baumbach to SKL/MarAtt OKM 1m/2 and 3, 16 December 1940.

67. In 1937–38 he was a Soviet "volunteer" in Spain. From 1938 Alafuzov served as deputy chief of the main naval staff, from 1943 as chief of staff of the Pacific Fleet, then chief of the main naval staff. In 1945–48 he served as chief and 1953–58 deputy chief of the Naval Academy. Professor Alafuzov wrote an objective study of *German Naval Doctrines* in 1956, and his early presence in Soviet-German naval relations is testimony to his long tenure in Soviet naval relations with the Germans. In 1963 he wrote the sole unfavorable review of Sokolovskiy's *Military Strategy*, attacking its description of the Soviet navy's role. The second edition incorporated all of his suggested changes. Professor William C. Green to author, 23 August 1989. For the German connection, see Herrick, *Soviet Naval Theory*, 140; see 293 for a list of other citations regarding Admiral V. A. Alafuzov. Headquarters of the Naval High Command to Naval Attaché division, Berlin, 2 January 1941.

68. Roskill, *History*, 165–66.

69. Roskill, *History*, 259.

70. Roskill, *History*, 292.

71. Roskill, *History*, 157–60.

72. Roskill, *History*, 175–76. The facts were *Hipper* and four destroyers had been

the object of a British attack from the carrier *Furious* on 12 November 1939. The attack missed the cruiser and four destroyers because they had left port. They had left to return to Germany on 10 November. Ironically, *Hipper* barely missed the British main fleet on the night of 10 November.

73. Roskill, *History*, 195. The *Scharnhorst* was damaged by a torpedo that was launched by destroyer *Acasta* in the final melee after carrier *Glorious* and destroyer *Ardent* had been sunk. The torpedo hit *Scharnhorst* abreast after the turret, causing severe damage.

74. USN Operational Archives, Navy Yard Washington, D.C., Office of Naval Intelligence, United States Navy, English translation of *War Diary*, Operations Division, German Naval Staff, *KTB der SKL*, pt. A, entry for Russia, 14 September 1939, 1:57. For the definitive exegesis on the *KTB der SKL*, see Michael Salewski, *"Das Kriegstagebuch der deutschen Seekriegsleitung im Zweitien Weltkrieg," Marine Rundschau* 3 (1964): 137–145. For the historical imbroglio on the Soviet side concerning the German attack on Russia and prior Soviet-German relationship, see Vladimir Petrov, *22 June 1941—Soviet Historians and the German Invasion* (Columbia: University of South Carolina Press, 1968). This recounts the ideological "trial" conducted against Aleksandr M. Nekrich, the author of *June 22, 1941*. Nekrich subsequently left the Soviet Union and took up his position in the West. Because of glasnost, he has been able to return to his homeland for visits, but he has no intention of giving up his faculty job at Harvard. He is also a well-known lecturer, and his works again are being read. For Golovko, *With the Fleet;* and Kuznetzov, "Before the War."

75. *KTB der SKL*, 23 September 1939, 1:113, conference of Raeder with Hitler; see also *FCNA*, 43; for von Baumbach, see *KTB der SKL*, 27 September 1939, 1:141.

76. *KTB der SKL*, 1:151, for agreements (full texts appear *DGFP*, 8:164–75). Included here is an agreement "affirming that Peace should be restored in Europe now that the Polish problem is definitively settled." For the discussion with the flag officer for U-boats (hereinafter B.d.U.), see *KTB der SKL*, 1:19.

77. For the naval strategic impact, see Roskill, *History*, 53–54. For the British view that war on Russia would not help defeat Germany, see Woodward, *British Foreign Policy*, 1:11–13. For the authoritative Polish assessment of the situation, see Jan Karski, *The Great Powers and Poland, 1919–1945: From Versailles to Yalta* (London: University Press of America, 1985), 329ff., chap. 19, "Anglo-French-Polish Military and Economic Agreements: Commitments in Bad Faith, 1939." See also 365–71.

78. USNA, 1820/PG32633, 32625/reel 1820. *Die Seekriegsleitung und die Vorgeschichte des Feldzüges gegen Russland*, September 1939, July 1941. This is a two-part compendium of background to the Russian campaign which pulls together most mentions of relevant subjects in summary form. It was assembled by Rear Admiral Kurt Assmann, official German naval historian. See pt. 2, p. 4, for führer decision; for von Baumbach's earlier reports, see

PG48800–48801/reels 2911–12. See also Frances E. McMurtrie, ed., *Jane's Fighting Ships 1939* (London: Samson Low, Marston, 1939), 422ff.

79. Roskill, *History*, 37. The British action, vis-à-vis the German supply ship *Altmark* in early 1940 in Norwegian waters, stands as an illustration of probable Allied reaction. This ship was, in fact, a German naval auxiliary that sought shelter in neutral Norwegian waters. The British pursued it to free the prisoners transferred from *Graf Spee*, which they had earlier destroyed in the South Atlantic.

80. *RGNR*, 39–41. See USNA, PG33740/reel 2006, for original correspondence. For development of wish lists, see *KTB der SKL*, 23 September 1939, 1:113; for conference of Rader with Hitler, see *KTB der SKL*, 1:151 and 2:19. For U-boat war expansion, see USNA, T–1022 series, Records of the German Navy, PG33640/reel 2006, information copy of Oberkommando der Marine, 3 October 1939.

81. Woodward, *British Foreign Policy*, 32.

82. Woodward, *British Foreign Policy*, 38.

83. Woodward, *British Foreign Policy*, 32.

84. Hinsley et al., *British Intelligence*, 1:115. See also Gemzell, *Organization*, 370ff. See also Gemzell, *Raeder, Hitler und Skandinavien, Der Kampf für einen Maritimen Operationsplan* (Lund, Sweden: CWK Gleevup, 1965), 273ff. See also *Germany and the Second World War*, volume 2: *Germany's Initial Conquests in Europe* (New York: Clarendon Press, 1991), 16.

85. Roskill, *History*, 41. For von Baumbach's memorandum, see USNA, T–1022, PG32825/reel 1915, naval attaché, German embassy, Moscow, to naval high command, attaché division, 19 October 1939 transmittal, memorandum dated 13 October 1939.

86. *KTB der SKL*, 2:107–8.

87. *RGNR*, 39–41.

88. USNA, PG33742/reel 2006, *Vortrag Chef M.Wa über Behandlung der russischen Bestellungen* (Report of the Chief of Naval Weapons Department Naval High Command Concerning the Negotiations over the Russian Requests). This was a true manifestation of Stalin's intent to gather as much information as possible about German naval technology, and it included a very detailed list, including three thousand to five thousand Zeiss field glasses.

89. *Foreign Relations of the United States Diplomatic Papers: The Soviet Union, 1933–1939* (Washington, D.C.: USGPO, 1952), 670ff.

90. Prior to the conclusion of the Nazi-Soviet pact the Soviets were negotiating with the United States for the 16-inch weapon; negotiations broke off when the Soviets invaded eastern Poland. See Breyer, *Battleships of the World*, 377.

91. USNA, PG33742/reel 2006, "Report of the Chief of Naval Weapons Department to the Naval High Command," attachment 1. This contains the eighty-nine classes of items from which these principal items are taken. The Soviets also wanted the main fire-control systems for the German weapons as well as assurances on barrel life; the same was desired for 15-cm (5.9-in.)

and 13-cm (4.1-in.) guns. They wanted 10.5-cm antiaircraft guns with attendant installations; 20 to 50 range finders; 3,000 to 5,000 sets of binoculars; 200 long-range ships' binoculars; 14 small and 10 medium-sized seagoing tugs; 2 75-ton floating cranes; 2 cable-laying ships; sail and diesel-powered ships for training; minesweepers; armored plate for ships of all sizes; electrical welding apparatus for armor plating; marine cable of several varieties; 100 watertight ammeters; asbestos lagging; portable and stationary pumps for ships; air-launched training torpedoes for ships; a complete air-launched torpedo release mechanism; 100 to 150 marine chronometers; underwater listening devices for coastal defense, and large and medium ships; photo equipment for use with submarine peri-scopes; long-range naval transmitters and receivers; and ships' combined com-munications stations with a high-speed capacity.

92. The source is USN Operational Archives, Navy Yard, Washington, D.C., N.I.D., 24/T36/45, *Russian German Cooperation from August 1939 to June 1941*, item 4, "Naval Requirements," 7.

93. Irina Morozova and Galinav Takhnenko, "The Winter War—Documents on Soviet-Finnish Relations in 1939–1940," *International Affairs*, no. 5 (1989), 49–71. This visit to German naval facilities took place at a time when the Soviet Union was preparing to go to war against Finland, basically to improve its naval position in the Baltic. The German Foreign Office, al-though it avoided a policy that would contravene the pact, on October 7 and by October 9, signaled the Finns that Germany's hands were tied and Ger-many could not intervene on Finland's behalf. On 2 December German dip-lomats around the world were ordered to support the Russian side in the conflict with Finland. The Soviets offered to lease the Finnish island of Hanko as well as other territory. Final Finnish refusal was received on 10 November, and the talks were broken off on 13 November. War commenced on 30 November 1939 and lasted until 12 March 1940. See Hinsley et al., *British Intelligence*, 1:113–14. For the German foreign policy course, see *DGFP*, 8:106ff.; for naval support, see 507ff.; for the granting of request, see 511; for the prospect of intervention, see 802. The Soviet navy, including the Red Banner Baltic Fleet, the Northern Fleet, and the Lake Ladoga Flotilla, were all engaged in active combat operations against Finland. The Soviets requested aid from Germany on 9 December, specifically asking for support to be given, via supply ships, to Soviet submarines operating in the Gulf of Bothnia. On 10 December the request was granted. By 22 February the Ger-mans were well aware of the prospect of United Kingdom and French troops intervening and correctly determined iron ore to be the target. Finland re-quested aid from England and France. Subsequently, Finland sided with Ger-many in 1941. Meanwhile, the Germans were reportedly poised to attack the West as early as 12 November, though the attack was not launched for other reasons until the spring of 1940.

94. Naval Intelligence Division (United Kingdom), file 24T/T36/45, item 1, "Visit of Russian Delegation to German Shipyards in November 1939," 1–3. For the source of delegation membership speculation, see Gordievsky, *KGB*, 403, 508, 621.

95. See USNA, T–1022/reels 2917, 2918, for post-*Barbarossa* files on inspection of Soviet installations.
96. *KTB der SKL,* 3:15.
97. *FCNA,* 56.
98. *FCNA,* 60–61. For "free hand," see *DGFP,* 8:650.
99. USNA, *Die Seekriegsleitung und die Vorgeschichte,* pt. 2, p. 6, refers to *KTB der SKL,* sec. C VII/39, 8 December 1939.
100. *FCNA,* 12 December 1939, 67.
101. *KTB der SKL,* 4:34, 8 December 1939.
102. *FCNA,* 63.
103. *KTB der SKL,* 27 December 1939, 4:150.
104. For a summary of the Soviet position, see USNA, PG32633/reel 1820, *Die Seekriegsleitung und die Vorgeschichte,* pt. 2, 11 January 1940, 7. For Stalin conducting the negotiations, see *RGNR,* 78. The *KTB der SKL* is cited as the source for this; see *KTB der SKL,* 5:43, for Ritter as the German plenipotentiary.
105. For arrangements being made, see *FCNA,* 30 December 1939, 70; see also *KTB der SKL,* 5 January 1940, 5:18, and 13 January 1940, 5:62ff.
106. *Die Seekriegsleitung und die Vorgeschichte,* pt. 1, 26 January 1940, 4; for naval attaché activity, see *FCNA,* 76; for Ship 45 clearance and also Soviet sphere of influence, see *Vorgeschichte,* pt. 2, p. 7.
107. This policy was enunciated in the war diary of the German naval attaché, Moscow, 17 October 1939; see also *RGNR,* 119. For the anti-Comintern pact in content, see William L. Shirer, *The Rise and Fall of the Third Reich: A History of Nazi Germany* (New York: Simon and Schuster, 1960),
108. For an intercept of the secret protocol, see U.S. Department of Defense, *The Magic Background of Pearl Harbor* (Washington, D.C.: USGPO, 1977), 1:A126.
109. USNA, PG32825/reel 1914; cf. also in PG33740/reel 2006, naval attaché, German embassy, Moscow, at the time in Berlin, to Naval Attaché Division, German naval high command, Berlin, 15 February 1940, "Wishes of the German Naval High Command vis-à-vis Soviet Russia." For a review of these items, see *RGNR,* 51.
110. For Stalin's attitude toward the Germans in October 1939, see Schulenburg to Ribbentrop, Moscow 19 October 1939, *Nazi-Soviet Relations,* 126–27; for German pleadings, see Ribbentrop memorandum of conversation, 11 December 1939, 130–31, *Nazi-Soviet Relations.*
111. *DGFP,* 8:369, for Göring et al.; for bottlenecks remark, see *Nazi-Soviet Relations,* 134. For access, see *DGFP,* 8:422; for evidence of serious trouble, see 502ff. and 558ff., covering the rejection of Stalin's demands for German war material.
112. See *DGFP,* 8:558ff., for rejection of Soviet demands; see 570ff. for Schulenburg-Molotov exchange.

CHAPTER 5: BASIS NORD

1. Herrick, *Soviet Naval Theory,* 122ff. The Germans do not seem to have appreciated that they had been very carefully studied and that the Soviets were not "continental minded . . . simple stoic creatures," as the first German

postwar conference on the Russian navy characterized them. Hans Joachim von der Osten, "Die Sowjetische Marine im Deutschen Urteil, 1917–1940," *Marine Rundschau* (7–8 September 1962), 81ff.

2. The World War I *Etappe* included *Etappe Tsingtau* (twelve ships), *Etappe China* (two ships), *Etappe Japan* (four ships), *Etappe Manila* (twelve ships), *Etappe Batavia* ([South *etappe*] eight ships), *Etappe San Francisco* ([Northwest America] three ships), *Etappe Peru* (two ships), *Etappe Valparaiso* ([Southwest America] ten ships), *Etappe La Plata* (nine ships), *Etappe Brazilien* ([Rio de Janerio] twelve ships), *Etappe Westindien* (six ships), *Nordamerika* ([New York] twenty-one ships), *Etappe Westafrika* (thirteen ships), *Etappe Ostafrica* (three ships), *Etappe Mittelmeer* (six ships).

3. Erich Gröner, *Die deutschen Kriegeschiffe 1815–1945*. Vol. 4. *Hilfschiffe 1: Werkstattschiffe Tender und Begleitschiffe, Tanker und Versorger* (Koblenz: Bernard and Graefe, 1986), 204–30, for World War I; 230–48, for World War II. See also Paul Schmalenbach, *German Raiders: A History of Auxiliary Cruisers in the German Navy, 1895–1945* (Cambridge: Patrick Stephens, 1979). For the need for supplies and fuel, see 105ff. In World War II the *Etappe* included: *Nord; Spanien* ([Spain] fourteen ships); *Afrika* (thirteen ships); *Niederländisch-Indien* ([Netherlands Indies] three ships); *Japan* (fifteen ships); and Helmat ([Homeland] forty-one ships). The *Etappen* included all ships capable of meeting basic requirements to become armed merchant raiders or armed naval support ships. Finally, there was *Etappe Mittelmeer* ([Mediterranean] three ships).

4. *FCNA*, 46.

5. Hinsley et al., *British Intelligence*, 1:115, 117. See also Woodward, *British Foreign Policy*, 1:50ff.

6. *KTB der SKL*, 7 October 1939, 2:52. See also A. V. Beznozov, "The Secret of Basis Nord," *Voyenno-istoricheskiy Zhurnal* (Military History Journal [Moscow]) (July 1990): 115–19.

7. SKL Operations Division (1) to SKL Naval Attaché Division, Berlin, 11 October 1939, USNA, PG33741/reel 2006.

8. See also Beznozov, "Secret of Basis Nord."

9. Von Baumbach discussion with the naval high command is recorded in the *KTB der SKL*, 17 October 1939, 2:108.

10. Beznozov, "Secret of Basis Nord," 53–57. This account, published in an official Soviet/Russian journal, holds that the reason the Soviets rationalized for such a base was to allow the Germans to support their blockade of the British Isles. *KTB der SKL*, 2:109.

11. Naval attaché, Moscow, to group leader, Naval Attaché Division, Naval High Command, 28 October 1939, 3, USNA, PG33740/reel 2006.

12. For the capture of *City of Flint*, see *FCNA*, 9 October 1939, 44.

13. Patrick Abbazia, *Mr. Roosevelt's Navy, The Private War of the U.S. Atlantic Fleet, 1939–1942* (Annapolis, Md.: Naval Institute Press, 1975), 71–74.

14. For German diplomatic background, see *DGFP*, 8:342ff., no. 2.

15. For a U.S.-Soviet exchange on the matter, see U.S. Department of State,

Foreign Relations of the United States: The Soviet Union, 1933–1939 (Washington, D.C.: USGPO, 1952), 984ff.

16. U.S. Department of State, *Foreign Relations*, 984ff.
17. U.S. Department of State, *Foreign Relations*, 984ff.
18. For German war diary entry, see *KTB der SKL*, 24 October 1939, 3:158; for von Baumbach's instructions for Soviets sending out ships, see 164; for release of ship, see 190; for orders to pocket battleships, see *KTB der SKL*, 30 October 1939, 196.
19. Roskill, *History*, 70.
20. For U.S. first knowledge of the *City of Flint* problem, see U.S. Department of State, *Soviet Union, 1933–1939*, especially on Soviet neutrality, 986ff.; for State Department's "recognition of the obvious," see 1001. Chip Bohlen, counselor to the U.S. embassy in Moscow, was sent to investigate and got nowhere; parenthetically, Averell W. Harriman, U.S. minister to Norway, later ambassador to Russia, made representations when the ship put into Tromso, and it was subsequently released; for the report of the U.S. master, see 1013; for German assessment, see *FCNA*, 10 November 1939, 560.
21. Roskill, *History*, 61.
22. For the U.S. attitude toward the *Bremen* episode, see Abbazia, *Mr. Roosevelt's Navy*, 70.
23. For HMS *Salmon* intercept, see Roskill, *White Ensign*, 44–45; Cajus Bekker, *Hitler's Naval War* (New York: Kensington, 1977), 74; Raeder's account is in *My Life*, 333–34; Friedrich Ruge's, in *Der Seekrieg: The German Navy's Story 1939–1945* (Annapolis, Md.: Naval Institute Press, 1957), 72.
24. Bekker, *Hitler's Naval War*, 74; Raeder's account is in *My Life*, 333–34; Ruge's is in *Der Seekrieg*, 72.
25. Roskill, *History*, 82–87. For the return of the ship and its political impact, see *The Goebbels Diaries: 1939–1941*, ed. and trans. Fred Taylor (New York: Penguin Books, 1982), 64. For the thanks to the Russians, see Matt (naval attaché division/naval high command) to von Baumbach, Berlin, 10 January 1940, N.Nr., 36/40g, USNA, PG33740/reel 2006.
26. Beznezov, "Secret of Basis Nord," 115–16.
27. For Soviet concerns regarding British intelligence, see Beznozov, "Secret of Basis Nord." Appendix 1 describes in depth the more significant ships assigned to Basis Nord. It is composed of data from the *SGNR* document, German archives and Erich Gröner, *Die deutschen Kriegeschiffe, 1815–1945*, vol. 4, *Hilfschifffe 1: Werkstattschiffe/Tender und Begleitschiffe, Tanker und Versorger* (Koblenz: Bernard und Graefe Verlag, 1986), 230–31; for *Jan Wellem*, see 33–34.
28. *KTB der SKL*, 30 October 1939, 2:196.
29. Golovko, *With the Fleet*, see 6–48. See also Beznozov, "Secret of Basis Nord." As noted above, it took until 1990 for the existence of the German base to be openly discussed in the Soviet literature. Not surprisingly, Admiral A. G. Golovko, commander of the Northern Fleet, published his memoirs in 1979 (before glasnost) and is completely silent about the issue. More signifi-

cantly, *Morskoy sbornik*, which has uncovered much Stalin-era skulduggery, remains silent on this episode. In mid–1990, however, A. V. Beznozov described "The Secret of Basis Nord."

30. Golovko, *With the Fleet*, 7.
31. The document establishing Basis Nord is from the naval high command and is found, among other places, in the papers of the naval attaché Moscow, 31 October 1939; it is addressed to various subordinate naval commands as well as the armed forces high command, the Oberkommando der Wehrmacht (hereinafter OKW); see USNA, PG33740/reel 2006. The pocket battleship messages are recorded in *KTB der SKL*, operations division, 30 October 1939, 2:197. The premature U-boat support orders were found in paper PG33740. For a discussion on the evolution of the "wet triangle," see Gemzell, *Raeder*, 368; and 264 ff. for "Lebensraum" connection. For Raeder's early ideas, see 278ff.
32. Peter Padfield, *Dönitz, The Last Führer: Portrait of a Nazi War Leader* (New York: Harper and Row, 1984), 158–59.
33. Padfield, *Dönitz*, 161.
34. Padfield, *Dönitz*. B.d.U. to Operations Division, naval high command, 5 November 1939, USNA, PG32825/reel 1914.
35. See attachments to B.d.U.: attachment 1, for role of Seventh Flotilla; attachment 2, for communications; for naval high command staff recommendations, see follow-up memo, 9 November 1939, SKL to B.d.U. See also Dönitz for knowledge of Soviet nets and procedures from wireless intercept, 9 November 1939.
36. For developments in Moscow concerning the base, see naval attaché Moscow to naval high command, Naval Attaché Division, 15 November 1939, "Final Arrangements by the Soviet Navy Concerning the Impending Use of Basis Nord for U-boat Support"; also for sailing directions and for Raeder.
37. For *U–36* directive, see USNA, PG32825/reel 1915, 17 November 1939; for loss of *U–36*, see *KTB der SKL*, 20 December 1939, entry for *B Dienst*. For details of ill-fated *U–36*, see Erich Gröner, *Die Deutschen Kriegschiffe 1815–1945* (Munich: J. F. Lehmanns Verlag, 1966), 382, 385. Gröner describes *U–36* as 745-tons surface displacement, an early type 7 standard German U-boat, designed for high-seas operations. It was capable of diving to depths up to two hundred meters. Its resting place is southwest of Kristiansand, Norway: latitude 57° north, longitude 5° 20′ east. *U–36* still holds forty dead.
38. Stephen W. Roskill, *Hankey Man of Secrets*, volume 8: *1936–1963* (London: St. Martin's Press, 1974), 427.
39. Roskill, *White Ensign*, 59ff.
40. Hinsley et al., *British Intelligence*, 1:111–12.
41. Hinsley et al., *British Intelligence*, 105, 107. HMS *Salmon* displaced 715 tons on the surface; had a crew of forty-four; its dimensions were: 217 feet x 23¾ × 10½; armament included one 3-inch and one 20 mm AA gun as well as thirteen torpedoes; diesels drove it at 14.5 knots on the surface. It was

launched in 1934 and lost off the Norwegian coast 17 July 1940. From *Jane's Fighting Ships, 1944–45* (London: Samson Low, 1945), 556 for loss, 69 for data.

42. For *U–38* operation, see USNA, PG30035/reel 3832, *KTB U–38*, November–December 1939; see B.d.U. order 0800, 29 November, in *KTB* cited.

43. Golovko, *With the Fleet*, 210.

44. Ross to SKL, information copy to von Baumbach, USNA T–1022, PG32825/reel 1014.

45. Ross to SKL.

46. Ross to SKL.

47. Ross to SKL.

48. Naval high command to naval attaché, Moscow, 29 November 1939, USNA, PG32825/reel 1915.

49. Von Baumbach to SKL, 9 December 1939, USNA, PG32825/reel 1914. File on communications with Basis Nord, USNA, PG32825/reel 1914. Von Baumbach to naval high command, Naval Operations Section, 16 December 1939.

50. File on communications with Basis Nord, USNA, PG32825/reel 1914.

51. See communications file, Auerbach to high command, USNA, PG32825/reel 1914; Ross to high command, enclosure 1 to report 483/39 from naval attaché, Berlin G/Kdos v. 16.12.39. Von Baumbach to high command, endorsement on Ross, 16 December 1939, 6. For leaks, see *Paris Soir* message, 29 December 1939, and Schulenburg/von Baumbach draft in von Baumbach to OKW/SKL, naval attaché sec., 5 January 1940, USNA, PG33740/reel 2006; for *Nationaltidende*, see USNA, PG33740/reel 2006, 28 December 1939; for *Sachsenwald* loadout, see USNA, PG32825/reel 1915.

52. Hinsley et al., *British Intelligence*, 1:105.

53. Von Baumbach to SKL, USNA, PG32825/reel 1914; for its operations, see Jockhen Brennecke, *Eismeer, Atlantik, Ostsee, die Einsatze des Schweren Kreuzers Admiral Hipper* (Munich: Wilhelm Hehne Verlag, 1975), 113ff. For security of German communications, see John Winton, *Ultra at Sea: How Breaking the Nazi Code Affected Allied Naval Strategy during World War II* (London: William Morrow, 1988), 6.

54. For a discussion of *Etappe Russland*, see Hecking to SKL information copy to von Baumbach, USNA, PG32251/reel 1914; for orders for *Jan Wellem*, see OKW to naval attaché, Moscow, B. No. 230/40gKdos *Ausland* IV, 26 January 1940, PG32825/reel 1914; for signal of arrival, see naval attaché, Moscow, to OKW, B. No. 80/40gKdos, 7 February 1940, naval attaché sec., SKL Moscow files, USNA, PG32825/reel 1914.

55. Von Baumbach to OKW and SKL, B. No. 50/40gKdos, 30 January 1940, for orders getting through; for *Wellem*'s outfit, see OKW to von Baumbach, 26 January 1940, USNA, PG32825/reel 1914.

56. *KTB der SKL*, 2 February 1949, 6:15.

57. Von Baumbach to naval attaché sec., SKL, 19–21 February 1940ff., USNA, PG32825/reel 1914.

58. Hinsley et al., *British Intelligence*, 1:430.
59. Hinsley et al., *British Intelligence*, 1:430.
60. *KTB der SKL*, 21 February 1940, 6:126.
61. *KTB der SKL*, 22 February 1940, 6:130–31.
62. For British forces operating off Norway, see *KTB der SKL*, 138; for deliveries to Finland, see *KTB der SKL*, 12 March 1940, 7:74. The Reuters note made the war diary.
63. Hinsley et al., *British Intelligence*, 1:111.
64. Stephen W. Roskill, *The British Navy at War 1939–1945* (Annapolis: Naval Institute Press, 1966), 40–170. For the Soviet side, see Beznozov, "Secret of Basis Nord," 54ff.
65. *RGNR*, 70.
66. See Ivanov briefing, which detailed the then current Soviet reaction to the German naval campaign in Norway, and the impressive nature of the German success there. See 78–84 and passim.
67. For the first Soviet analysis, see Beznozov, "Secret of Basis Nord"; see also Herrick, *Soviet Naval Theory*, 127 and 129–30.
68. Herrick, *Soviet Naval Theory*, 127.
69. For Soviet press attitude on Norwegian campaign, see *KTB der SKL*, 19 March 1940; for other later assurances from Soviets to Germans, see *KTB der SKL*, 28 April 1940, 7:170. For block on Soviet attitude, see also *KTB der SKL*, 19 March 1940.
70. *RGNR*, 70.
71. *RGNR*, 71.
72. *Nazi-Soviet Relations*, 13.
73. *Nazi-Soviet Relations*, 138.
74. *Nazi-Soviet Relations*, 138.
75. *Nazi-Soviet Relations*, 138.
76. *Nazi-Soviet Relations*, 142.
77. For the Soviet press's attitude toward the Norwegian Campaign see *KTB der SKL*, 19, March 1940.
78. For the "disinterest," see Rear Admiral Kurt Assmann, "Background to the Operation *Barbarossa*," USNA, PG32633/reel 1820, 8. This data is extracted from *KTB der SKL*, sec. C, 8:180, 10 April 1940; for more on Soviet press, see 8:9; for cooling concerning Basis Nord, see Assmann, "Background," 10, from *KTB der SKL*, sec. A., 10:83; for quotation from the naval high command, see Assmann, "Background," 10:38.
79. For the last mention of active use, see *KTB der SKL*, August 1940, 12:58.
80. Brennecke, *Eismeer*, 113ff.
81. For Hitler's fixation on Norway, see *FCNA*, 13 August 1940, 126; for the decision to close the base, see *RGNR*, 72. For Hitler's fixation on Norway as a possible Allied attack route, see Michael Salweski, *Die deutsche Seekriegsleitung, 1939–1945*, vol. 1: *1939–1941* (Frankfurt: Bernard und Graefe, 1970), 457–58ff.
82. For *Phoenicia*'s orders, see USNA, PG33740/reel 2006. SKL to OKW Aus-

land iv., and SKL to A.A. (Foreign Ministry), 29 August 1940, Subject bases on the Murman coast. For the von Baumbach/Kuznetzov discussion and the letter to Kuznetzov and its various drafts, see PG33740, SKL 16 September 1940, Zul.skl1c 13178/40gKdos and especially German naval attache Moscow, *Anlage zum Mantelbericht B*, Berlin 30 September 1940.

CHAPTER 6: CRUISER "*L*": FROM GERMANY WITH RETICENCE

1. The World War I battle cruiser was a much larger ship of 26,500 tons standard displacement. It accounted for at least one of its British enemies, HMS *Invincible*, before succumbing to twenty-four heavy shell hits and one torpedo. It lies in the center of the North Sea. See Siegfried Breyer, *Battleships and Battle Cruisers, 1905–1970* (Garden City, N.Y.: Doubleday, 1978), 277–78. See also John Campbell, *Jutland: An Analysis of the Fighting* (Annapolis, Md.: Naval Institute Press, 1986), 255ff., for the fate of this valiant ship.
2. For Colonel Lützow's origins, see Walter Görlitz, *The German General Staff, 1657–1945* (New York: Frederick Praeger, 1953), 41–42.
3. Regarding the size of the cruiser's guns, see E. H. Haraszti, *Treaty-Breakers or "Realpolitiker": The Anglo-German Naval Agreement of June 1935* (Boppard am Rhein: Harald Boldt, 1974), 229–30.
4. Raeder, *My Life*, 199ff. For the construction data, see Erich Gröner, *Die Deutschen Kriegschiffe, 1814–1945* (Munich: J. F. Lehmann's Verlag, 1970), 1:131–32; for the exchange between the British and Germans over the cruiser being built as counter to *Kirov*, see Public Record Office (hereinafter PRO), Admiralty files (hereinafter ADM) 116/3369, Ambassador (Herbert) von Dirksen to Viscount Halifax. Dirksen claimed the two ships were to have 15-cm, not 20.3-cm guns, in four triple turrets, which was not true. Stalin may have gotten wind of this assertion, as he brought up and rejected the concept that the ships could have 15-cm guns. For a further discussion, see Haraszti, *Treaty-Breakers*, 251–52. For a very truncated discussion, see Raeder, *My Life*, 192ff.
5. For the first demand, see Assmann, "Background," pt. 2, p. 4; for *Lützow* only, see pt. 2, p. 5; for plans, see *KTB der SKL*, 7 December 1939, 4:35; for the 20.3-cm (8-in.) gun holdup, see *FCNA*, 8 December 1939, 63.
6. For delivery of the cruiser *Lützow*, see *DGFP*, 8:563. For the state of the cruiser after launching and the desire to finish, see Assmann, "Background," 26 January 1940, pt. 2, p. 7. For Stalin on the guns, see chap. 1 of this work. See also *Sudostroyeniye* (May 1983): 58–61. The photographic evidence is the last German photo prior to delivery (58).
7. For the towing company memorandum, see USNA, PG33740/reel 2006, 21 March 1940; for naval high command guidance on who should do what during the tow, see *Hauptamt Kriegsschiffbau* (main naval construction office), Berlin, 4 April 1940; concerning the details of the turnover, see 5 April 1940, *Verkauf Kreuzer "L" an die Russen* (Sale of Cruiser "*L*" to the Russians), which orders the ship to be ready in ten days for transshipment; for additional guid-

ance on how the tow was to be accomplished, see B. No. M.Wa. Willa 75661/40g, Berlin, 6 April 1940. Finally, for the actual departure order, see B.Nr.1./SKL Iab 130757/40g (naval high command), Berlin, 15 April 1940; *Überführung des Kreuzers nach Russland* (Transfer of the Cruiser to Russia).

8. Memorandum of conversation with Captain Second Rank Vorontsov (German spelling, Woronzow) on 17 April 1940, naval attaché sec., to German naval high command, 19 April 1940, PG33740/reel 2006. This conversation was, of course, concerned with the larger issue of what had happened to the German navy in the Norwegian campaign and, even more important, in the context of other Soviet moves in the Balkans, which were to come shortly. See Assmann chronology *Die Seekriegsleitung und die Vorgeschichte des Feldzuges gegen Russland* (The Naval High Command and the Background to the Campaign against Russia), USNA, T1022/PG32663, 8–9.

9. Kuznetzov, *Before the War*, 96.

10. *RGNR.*

11. For details on the entire class of cruisers, see Gröner, *Die deutschen Kriegsschiffe*, 130–131; for *Seydlitz*'s conversion to a carrier, see 138. The following data (extracted from Gröner) are relevant: *Lützow* was laid down in 1937 and launched 1 July 1939. The ship cost 83,590,000 Reichsmarks, slightly less than its sister ships. Its designed displacement was 14,240 tons, full load about 18,200, had it been fitted out. It was 207.7 meters long, 21.9 meters in beam, and designed draft of 6.37 meters. Its oil-fired turbines gave it a top speed of 32 knots and a range of 6,800 sea miles at 20 knots. It had three screws. Its armament as designed consisted of 8-inch (20.3-cm) guns, 60 caliber, with a maximum range of 36,000 meters.

12. Feige to von Baumbach, 28 November 1940, for initial detailed Russian needs; von Baumbach endorsed this and sent it to the naval high command in Berlin. The conference with the Russians was held on 27 November with a follow-up on 28 November. PG33740/reel 2006. For dates and conditions of *Lützow* delivery, see *Shipbuilding*, 58ff.

13. For von Baumbach's comments and endorsement to the Feige letter and Russian requests, see von Baumbach to Naval Attaché Division, SKL, 3 January 1941, PG33740/reel 2006. See also von Baumbach, and the following, for chief of the Naval Attaché Division's opinion.

14. For the Russian proposal, see Baumbach to Naval Attaché Division; for the comment thereon, see Naval Attaché Division, naval high command to naval weapons department, Berlin, 15 January 1941, USNA, PG33740/reel 2006—SKL Att 11g Berlin 15.1.41 top M.Wa.Wi., 1&3SKL (First and Third Directorates of the German naval high command, the first dealing with operations, the third with intelligence and planning), "Training for Russian Personnel Cruiser L."

15. For SKL operations endorsement, see SKL to Naval Attaché Division, Stl an Matt11 Nr.439/411g, Berlin, 15 January 1941. PG33740/reel 2006.

16. For the record of the conference held in Berlin, 25 January 1942, see USNA, PG33740/reel 2006.

17. State of construction of "L" is reported in German Embassy Moscow to Naval High Command Berlin, Naval Attaché Division, 21 May 1941, USNA, PG33741/reel 2006; as well as the very specific Soviet requirements. This document was jointly prepared by Ambassador Count von der Schulenburg and von Baumbach.

18. For the record on invitations and subsequent information messages, see naval attaché, Moscow, to naval high command (hereinafter OKM) and OKW, German Embassy Berlin, 12 June 1941, PG337441/reel 2006.

19. The final item is naval high command (SKL) to German Embassy Moscow, "Russian Requests re-Cruiser *L*," Berlin, 18 June 1941, USNA, PG33741/reel 2006. For disposition and Soviet War History, see *Shipbuilding*, 61.

CHAPTER 7: SUBMARINES AND MERCHANT CRUISERS

1. For Soviet request for support, see PG33740/reel 2006, Ambassador Moscow and naval attaché, German Embassy Moscow, to operations division, naval high command and armed forces high command, personal for state secretary of foreign affairs, German Foreign Ministry, No. 905, 9.12.39, received on 12 September 1939.

2. For German response, see *RGNR*, 43; and PG33740/reel 2006; and 1SKL la 207 1Gkds to naval attaché, 10 December 1939.

3. See Gröner, *Die Deutschen Kriegschiffe*, 4:230ff.; and discussion in chapter 5 of this work.

4. V. I. Achkasov and N. B. Pavlovich, *Soviet Naval Operations in the Great Patriotic War, 1941–1945* (Annapolis, Md.: Naval Institute Press, 1973), 40.

5. The confusion, delays, and difficulties attendant to German mobilization surface in Hinsley et al., *British Intelligence*, 1:500–514, and are exhaustively covered in B. R. Kroener et al., *Organization und Mobilizierung des deutschen Machtbereichs: Das Deutsche Reich und der Zweite Weltkrieg*, 5:1 (Stuttgart: Deutsche Verlags–Anstalt, 1988). This is the fifth volume of the Federal German Military Archives history of World War II. Not surprisingly, Raeder, Ruge, and Salewski all point to logistics as a severe German problem.

6. See, for example, Albert Speer, *Infiltration: How Heinrich Himmler Schemed to Build an SS Industrial Empire* (New York: Macmillan, 1981). See also Kroener et al., *Organization und Mobilizierung*, 426–86.

7. For a summary of the reasons of these operations, see Erickson, *Soviet High Command*, 541–45.

8. For subsequent exchanges, including Soviet abandonment of the plan, see *KTB der SKL*, 12 December 1939, 4:67; for German assessment of result of exchanges, see *RGNR*, 45; for escort of the *Stalin* described below (later sunk by German bombers, according to Ruge in *The Soviets as Naval Opponents* [Annapolis, Md.: Naval Institute Press, 1973], 167); see *KTB der SKL*, 12 January 1940, 5:59.

9. For the attack on *Bolheim*, see *KTB der SKL*, 12 December 1939, 4:67; cf. Assmann, *Vorgeschichte*, pt. 2, p. 6, 12 December 1939, for lack of specific

mention; Assmann discusses a fire fight between Soviet warships and German steamers but does not mention the result.

10. William E. Butler, *The Law of Soviet Territorial Waters: A Case Study of Maritime Legislation and Practice* (New York: Praeger, 1967), 601, 105ff.

11. Paul Schmalenbach, *German Raiders: A History of Auxiliary Cruisers in the German Navy, 1895–1945* (Cambridge: Patrick Stephens, 1979), 132. See also *Handbuch zur deutschen Militärgeschichte, 1648–1939*, 7th ed., Wolfgang Petler, Roth Güth, Jost Dülffer, *Deutsche Marinegeschichte der Neuzeit* (Munich: Bernard and Graefe Verlag für Wehrwesen, 1977), 480–81.

12. For this exchange on use of the Northern Sea Route, see *RGNR*, 89, sources from OKW to German Embassy, Moscow, 12 January 1940.

13. *RGNR*, OKW memo, 12 January 1940.

14. Hinsley et al., *British Intelligence*, 1:501.

15. Hinsley et al., *British Intelligence*, 90–91.

16. Hinsley et al., *British Intelligence*, 90–91.

17. OKW memo. For an assessment of Russian control on details, see *RGNR*, 91.

18. For further assessments, see *RGNR*, 97.

19. For talks on the Northern Sea Route, see *RGNR*, 91ff.; for Soviet humor, see 93; for background on negotiation, see 94–95.

20. For von Baumbach's suggestion, see *RGNR*, 96.

21. *RGNR*, 96.

22. Fritz E. Giese, *Kleine Geschichte der deutschen Flotte*, 148–49.

23. *RGNR*, 98. See also von Baumbach to naval high command, Berlin, 30 April 1940. PG33740/reel 2006. For the identity of auxiliary cruiser, see Paul Schmalenbach, *German Raiders*, 49.

24. For technical data on *Komet*, see *Die Deutschen Kriegschiffe*, 6:109–10.

25. Beznozov, "Secret of Basis Nord," 53–57.

26. *RGNR*, 101–3. See also Beznozov, "Secret of Basis Nord," 55ff.

27. *RGNR*, 105.

28. Beznozov, "Secret of Basis Nord," 54ff.

29. Beznozov, "Secret of Basis Nord," 54ff.

30. Beznozov, "Secret of Basis Nord," 55.

31. This account is taken largely from *RGNR*, 100ff; for order to wait on 17 August 1940, see 103; for Soviet order on 15 August 1940, see 104; for account of visit aboard *Stalin*, see 105ff.; for results of voyage, see Schmalenbach, *German Raiders*, 138; and *RGNR*, 108.

32. Beznezov, "Secret of Basis Nord," 56.

Select Bibliography

I. ARCHIVAL SOURCES

A. U.S. Department of the Navy—Operational Archives Section of the Division of Naval History

Assmann, Kurt. *Report on the German Naval War Effort,* N.I.D., *24T, 65/45.* (Listed under author's name in Operational Archives.)

Assmann, Kurt, and Gladisch, Walther. *Aspects of the German Naval War,* N.I.D., *24T, 237/46.* This document is an account of the factors influencing German naval strategy between 1939 and 1945. This was completed without the aid of official documents by two authors who had direct access to the entire German naval planning process. (Listed under authors' names in Operational Archives.)

British Admiralty, Naval Intelligence Division. *24T, 178/45, Extracts from a File on Russo-German Relations Containing a Digest of War Diaries between August 1939 and the German Invasion of Russia.*

Office of Naval Intelligence, United States Navy. *Miscellaneous No. 28, Russo-German Naval Relations, 1926–1941.* This document is based on work done in 1943 by Kurt Assmann and others. It is a primary source guide as its analysis is based on massive citation of the German documentary sources and serves as a guide for research on the smaller period 1939–41.

Office of Naval Intelligence, United States Navy. *English Translations, War Diary, Operations Division, German Naval Staff* (Kriegstagebuch der Seekriegsleitung) (1939–45). Listed in notes as *KTB der SKL.* This massive work translated most, but not all, of the first part of the war diary of the German naval high command. It is an operational record, referred to by Assmann in the work mentioned above and, in fact, part of a larger war diary that includes two other parts dealing with background questions of a military nature and special questions not discussed below. Most of the Operations Division record is in translation for the period 1939–41. The record for September 1940 through June 1941 is not available in translation.

B.D.U. War Logs. An English translation of the cryptic but incisive record of U-boat operations kept by Grand Admiral Dönitz, flag officer commanding U-boats, 1939–45.

TR 15, Cruise of Armed Merchant Cruiser Komet, through the Northern Sea Route 1940. An English summary of the ship's voyage. Cross-indexed as *PG70961.*

B. U.S. National Archives, Washington, D.C. Captured Record Group 242. File T-1022. This microfilm publication consists of 4,183 rolls, containing records of the German navy from 1850 to 1945. These were selectively microfilmed by the United States navy and transferred by the Navy History Division (see A above) to the National Archives with related files and registers.

The U.S. National Archives record collections were most useful in preparing this study. Two methods of finding documents exist, one by microfilm reel number, the other by PG (standing for "Pinched German") number. Possession of either allows one to locate a document within the appropriate archival file. For the purposes of this study the following collections were the most important:

Reels 2911–14 / PG numbers 48800–48810. Papers of the German naval attaché to Moscow, Captain Norbert von Baumbach, 1936–41. These papers contain documents supporting every issue discussed in this work. Reel 2914 contains reports on the Russian navy, including some leading personalities. Other post-Barbarossa documents by von Baumbach may be found in reels 2917 and 2918.

Reel 1820 / PG32633 and 32625. *Rear Admiral Kurt Assmann, Die Seekriegsleitung und die Vorgeschichte des Feldzuges gegen Russland.* This document is the chronology of assembled German papers having anything to do with the background of the German invasion of Russia on the naval side. It appears in translation, in part, in *Russo-German Naval Relations*, cited above.

Reel 2006 / PG33740-41. *Papers on Relations with Friendly Powers.* These files contain much of the record of the Soviet-German naval institutional relationship and papers on the transfer of Cruiser *"L."*

Reel 1925/PG32883, *Records of Basis Nord.*

Reels 1914–15/PG32824–25, *Papers on Basis Nord and Inspections and Courier Run.* For more on Basis Nord, see PG32860-32903 *Etappendienst.* These latter documents are only partially legible records of the German naval intelligence service; entries under Russia should be viewed.

Reel 2598 / PG49186. *File on Finland and Russia: Cypher Reports on Russo-Finnish War.*

Reels 2959–60 / PG49188–96 and PG49197–99. *Intelligence on the USSR, 1930–November 1939.*

Reel 2970 / PG33033, *KTB U-36*, through October 1939. The last volume went down with the boat.

Reels 2832–33 / PG30035, *KTB U-38, 1939–1945.* This is the boat that scouted Basis Nord.

C. Federal German Military Archives, Freiburg im Breisgau
This entry is included so researchers who wish to find the original documents, rather than U.S. translations or microfilm archival copies, can source them in the German military archives.

Das Kriegstagebuch der deutschen Seekriegsleitung im Zweiten Weltkrieg.
Teil A. die "Zeitliche Zusammenstellung der Meldungen und Befehle die für operationen von Wichtigkeit sind" (The Daily Assemblage of Signals and Orders for Operations Conducted).

Teil B. Wochenlichter Lageüberblick und Überlegungen allgemeiner militärischer Art
(Weekly Review of the Situations and General Concerns Related to Military
Art).
Heft 2a. *Nordsee/Norwegen, Marinegruppenkommando Nord* (Volume 2a. Northsea/
Norwegian Waters, Naval Group Command North).
Heft 4. *Ubootskrieg* (Volume 4. Undersea Warfare).
Heft 7. *Wochenübersichten zu Politik, Völkerrecht und Propaganda* (Volume 7. Weekly
Overview Concerning Policy, Maritime Law, and Propaganda).
*Teil C. Besondere Überlegungen zu Einzelfragen und zu den Problemen der Seekriegfüh-
rung Weisungen, Operationsauswertungen* (Special Background to Particular
Questions and Problems of the Conduct of War at Sea).
Heft 1. *Kreuzerkrieg in ausserheimischen Gewässern* (Volume 1. Cruiser Warfare in
Foreign Waters).
Heft 2a. *Nordsee-Norwegen* (Volume 2a. North Sea Norway).
Heft 4. *Ubootskrieg* (Volume 4. Undersea Warfare).
Heft 7. *Niederschriften über die Lagevorträge des ObdM beim Führer* (Volume 7.
Memorandums of Conversations of the Navy Commander-in-Chief with the
Führer).

D. British Archival Sources

1. Public Record Office, Chancery Lane London (hereafter PRO), *Foreign Office
   Manuscripts, F.O.371/289, N 57764/97/38.* An appreciation of how little was
   known about the Molotov-Ribbentrop Pact.
2. PRO, *Foreign Office Manuscripts, F.O.837/439 MEW* (Ministry of Economic
   Warfare), Summary of Enemy Economic Developments No. 49 of 30 October
   1940. This and others of the series may throw additional light on Soviet-German merchant marine operations and maritime cooperation.

II. PUBLISHED DOCUMENTS

U.S. Department of State, Washington, D.C. *Nazi-Soviet Relations, 1939–1941,
Documents from the Archives of the German Foreign Office.* Washington, D.C.:
USGPO, 1949. This is a one-volume summary of all the most critical docu-
ments "essential to the understanding of the political relations between Nazi
Germany and the Soviet Union from the first efforts to reach an agreement in
the spring of 1939 to the outbreak of war in June 1941."

U.S. Department of State, Washington, D.C. *Documents on German Foreign Policy, Series D, 1918–1945.* This is a multivolume series that covers the same
ground as the reference immediately above but in much greater detail. It is
useful for a full understanding of the political and military background of Soviet-
German naval relations.

U.S. Department of Defense, Washington, D.C. *The "Magic" Background of*

Pearl Harbor. Volume 1. *(February 14, 1941– May 12, 1941).* Washington, D.C.: USGPO, 1977.

Petrov, Vladimir, and Nekrich, A. M., *June 22, 1941 Soviet Historians and the German Invasion.* Columbia: University of South Carolina Press, 1968. This work is unique. It is the most comprehensive examination ever done of the period of the Ribbentrop-Molotov Pact in the Soviet Union. Regarded as too objective for Stalin's successors, it was banned from Soviet bookshelves after its printing and distribution. Its author, A. M. Nekrich, was tried and stripped of his titles and membership in the Academy of Sciences. He is now a professor of history at Harvard University. Following the recent changes there, he has been able to return to Russia.

III. PUBLISHED WORKS AND MONOGRAPHS

Abbazia, Patrick. *Mr. Roosevelt's Navy, The Private War of the U.S. Atlantic Fleet, 1939–1942.* Annapolis, Md.: Naval Institute Press, 1975.

Achkasov, V. I., and Pavlovich, N. B. *Soviet Naval Operations in the Great Patriotic War 1941–1945.* U.S. Naval Intelligence Command translation. Annapolis, Md.: U.S. Naval Institute Press, 1981. First published in the Soviet Union in 1973, this work makes no mention of cooperation with the Germans prior to the outbreak of World War II.

Akhmedov, Ismail. *In and Out of Stalin's GRU—A Tartar's Escape from Red Army Intelligence.* Frederick, Md.: University Publications of America, 1984. Useful for insights of Soviets stationed in Germany in June 1941 as well as other elements of background to the Molotov-Ribbentrop Pact.

Andrew, Christopher, and Oleg Gordievsky. *KGB: The Inside Story of Its Foreign Operations from Lenin to Gorbachev.* New York: HarperCollins, 1990.

Antonov-Ovseyenko, Anton. *The Time of Stalin: A Portrait of Tyranny.* Translated by George Saundes. New York: Harper and Row, 1980. An inside analysis of Stalin's dealings with Hitler.

Bathurst, Robert B. *Understanding the Soviet Navy: A Handbook.* Newport, R.I.: Naval War College Press, 1979. Contains some limited data concerning the evolution of the Soviet navy, 1939–41.

Bekker, Cajus. *Verdammte See: Ein Kriegstagebuch der deutschen Marine.* Oldenburg and Hamburg: Gerhard Stalling Verlag, 1971.

———. *The German Navy, 1939–1945.* New York: Dial Press, 1974. An encapsulated, well-illustrated popular history derived from *Verdammte See.*

Bialer, Sewerin, ed., *Stalin's Successors—Leadership, Stability, and Change in the Soviet Union.* New York: Cambridge University Press, 1980. Of some utility in assessing the motivations behind Soviet naval activity, 1939–41.

Bird, Keith W. *German Naval History: A Guide to the Literature.* 2 vols. New York: Garland, 1984. This is the definitive historiography of German naval history.

———. *Weimar: The German Naval Officer Corps and the Rise of National Socialism.* Amsterdam: B. R. Grüner, 1977.

Brennecke, Jochen. *Eismeer Atlantik Ostsee. Die Einsätze des Schweren Kreuzers "Admiral Hipper."* Munich: Wilhelm Heyne Verlag, 1975.

Breyer, Siegfried. *Battleships and Battle Cruisers, 1905–1970.* Garden City, N.Y.: Doubleday, 1978. This is the authorized translation by Alfred Kurtis of *Schlachtschiffe und Schlachtkreuzer 1905–1970.* Munich: J. F. Lehmann's Verlag, 1970.

Butson, Thomas G. *The Tsar's Lieutenant: The Soviet Marshal.* New York: Praeger, 1984.

Campbell, John. *Jutland: An Analysis of the Fighting.* Annapolis, Md.: Naval Institute Press, 1986.

Carr, Edward H. *German-Soviet Relations between the Two World Wars.* Baltimore: Johns Hopkins Press, 1951.

Chen, Allen F. *Fighting the Russians in Winter: Three Case Studies.* Fort Leavenworth, Kans.: Combat Studies Institute, 1981.

de Jonge, Alex. *Stalin and the Shaping of the Soviet Union.* New York: William Morrow, 1986.

Deist, Wilhelm. *The Wehrmacht and German Rearmament.* Toronto: University of Toronto Press, 1981.

———. *Militär und Innenpolitik im Weltkrieg 1914–1918 Zweiter Teil.* Düsseldorf: Dröste Verlag, 1970.

Dönitz, Karl. *10 Jahre und 20 Tage.* Frankfurt am Main: Atheneum, 1958; English language ed., London: Wiedenfeld, 1963; for the Soviet edition, with an interesting introduction, Military Publishing House, 1968.

Drea, Edward J. *Nomonhan: Japanese-Soviet Tactical Combat, 1939.* Fort Leavenworth, Kans.: Combat Studies Institute, 1961.

Dülffer, Jost. *Weimar, Hitler und die Marine. Reichspolitik und Flottenbau, 1920–1939.* Düsseldorf: Droste Verlag, 1972. This basic interpretation of original source documents is the first serious attempt to collate and analyze German naval history of this period.

Erickson, John. *The Soviet High Command.* Boulder, Colo.: Westview Press, 1983.

———. *The Road to Stalingrad.* Boulder, Colo.: Westview Press, 1983.

Fleischhauer, Ingeborg. *Der Pakt Hitler, Stalin und die Initiative der deutschen Diplomatie, 1938–1939.* Berlin: Ullstein, 1990.

Garzke, William H., and Robert O. Dulin. *Battleships: Axis and Neutral Battleships in World War II.* Annapolis, Md.: Naval Institute Press, 1985.

Gemzell, Carl-Axel. *Organization, Conflict and Innovation: A Study of German Naval Strategic Planning, 1888–1940.* Lund, Sweden: Esselte Studium, 1973. This is an interesting study filled with important documents and sources useful to the present work.

Giese, Fritz E. *Kleine Geschichte der deutschen Flotte.* Berlin: Haude und Spenersche Verlag, 1971.

Golovko, A. *With the Fleet.* Moscow: Progress Publishers, 1988. Originally published in Russian in 1977.

Gorshkov, S. G. *The Sea Power of the State.* Annapolis, Md.: Naval Institute Press,

1979. This translation of the 1976 edition published by Voenizdat (Military Publishing House), in Moscow, is of great interest as the sanctioned version of Soviet naval history; the 1979 edition is as yet available only in official translation. Neither mentions Soviet-German naval relations during 1939–41.

Gröner, Erich. *Die Deutschen Kriegschiffe, 1815–1945.* Volume 1. Munich: J. F. Lehmann Verlag, 1966.

————, Dieter Jung, and Martin Maass. *Die deutschen Kreigschiffe 1815–1945.* Volume 4. *Hilfschiffe 1: Werkstattschiffe, Tender und Begleitschiffe, Tanker und Vensorger.* Munich: Bernard und Graefe, 1986.

Handbuch zur deutschen Militärgeschichte, 1648–1939. Part 7, volume 8. *Deutsche Marinegeschichte der Neuzeit.* Munich: Bernard und Graefe Verlag, 1977.

Haraszti, Eva H. *Treaty-Breakers or "Realpolitiker"? The Anglo-German Naval Agreement of June 1935.* Boppard am Rhein: Harald Boldt Verlag, 1974.

Herrick, Robert W. *Soviet Naval Strategy: Fifty Years of Theory and Practice.* Annapolis, Md.: Naval Institute Press, 1968.

————. *Soviet Naval Theory and Policy Gorshkov's Inheritance.* Annapolis, Md.: Naval Institute Press, 1989. This is a major work and almost belongs in the published documents section.

Hildebrand, Hans H., Albert Rohr, and Hans-Otto Steinmetz. *Die deutchen Kriegsschiffe, Biographien—Ein Spiegel der Marinegeschichte von 1815 bis zur Gegenwart.* 7 vols. Bonn: Herford, 1979.

Hilger, Gustav, and Alfred G. Meyer. *The Incompatible Allies German-Soviet Relations, 1918–1941.* New York: Macmillan, 1953.

Hinsley, F. H., E. E. Thomas, C. F. G. Ransom, and R. C. Knight, *British Intelligence in the Second World War.* 3 vols. London: Her Majesty's Stationary Office, 1979–84. Principal insights into how little was known by the West about Soviet-German relations in 1939–41. Source of PRO references earlier in bibliography.

Hingley, Ronald. *The Russian Mind.* New York: Charles Scribner and Sons, 1977.

Höhne, Heinz. *Canaris: Patriot im Zwielicht.* Munich: C. Bertelsmann, 1976.

Hubatsch, Walther. *Der Admiralstab und die obersten Marinebehörden in Deutschland, 1848–1945.* Frankfurt am Main: Bernard und Graefe Verlag, 1959.

Irving, David. *Hitler's War.* New York: Viking Press, 1977.

Kroener, B. R., Rolf Dieter Müller, and Hans Umbreit. *Organization und Mobilizierung des deutschen Machtbereichs. Erster halb band. Kriegsverwaltung, Wirtschaft und Personelle Ressourcen, 1939–1941. Das Deutsche Reich und der Zweite Weltkrieg.* Volume 5. Stuttgart: Deutsche Verlags-Anstalt, 1988.

Marine Rundschau, eds., *Das deutsche Bild der russischen und sowjetischen Marine.* Frankfurt am Main: E. S. Mittler and Son, 1962.

Mawdsley, Evan. *The Russian Revolution and the Baltic Fleet War and Politics, February 1917–April 1918.* New York: Barnes and Noble, 1978.

McMurtrie, Frances E., ed. *Jane's Fighting Ships 1939.* London: Samson Low, Marston, 1939–44. (Annual.)

Medvedev, Roy. *All Stalin's Men: Six Who Carried Out the Bloody Policies.* Garden City, N.Y.: Doubleday, 1984. This book can be considered published documents or memoirs because of the unique access the author probably had to both documents and people during its preparation.

Militärgeschichtliches Forschungsamst (Research Institute for Military History), ed. *Germany and the Second World War*. Volume 1. *The Build-up of German Aggression*. Oxford: Clarendon Press, 1990.

―――, ed. *Germany and the Second World War*. Volume 2. *Germany's Initial Conquests in Europe*. Oxford: Clarendon Press, 1991.

Ministry of Defense (Navy). *German Naval History: The U-Boat War in the Atlantic, 1939–1945*. London: HMSO, 1989.

Morris, Eric. *The Russian Navy: Myth and Reality*. New York: Stein and Day, 1977. This book makes no mention of Soviet-German naval cooperation.

Padfield, Peter. *Dönitz, The Last Führer: Portrait of a Nazi War Leader*. New York: Harper and Row, 1984. A very important book, the first scholarly portrait of a World War II German naval leader.

Ra'anan, Gavril D. *International Policy Formation in the USSR. Factional Debates during the Zhdanovschina*. Hamden, Conn.: Archon Books, 1983. This is a unique study based on Soviet sources which provides primary source material for an understanding of how Stalin operated during 1939–41.

Raeder, Erich. *My Life*. Annapolis, Md.: Naval Institute Press, 1960.

Read, Anthony, and David Fisher. *The Deadly Embrace: Hitler, Stalin, and the Nazi-Soviet Pact, 1939–1941*. New York: W. W. Norton, 1988.

Rohr, Albert. *Handbuch der deutschen Marinegeschichte*. Oldenburg and Hamburg: Gerhard Stalling Verlag, 1963.

Roskill, Stephen W., Captain. *History of the Second World War: The War at Sea*, Volume 1. *The Defensive*. London: HMSO, 1976.

―――. *Hankey Man of Secrets*, Volume 3. *1931–1963*. New York: St. Martin's Press, 1974.

―――. *Naval Policy between the Wars*, Volume 2. *The Period of Reluctant Rearmament, 1930–1939*. Annapolis, Md.: Naval Institute Press, 1976.

―――. *White Ensign the British Navy at War, 1939–1945*. Annapolis, Md.: Naval Institute Press, 1966.

Rossler, E. *Die Deutschen U-boote und ihre Werften*. 2 vols. Munich: Bernard und Graefe Verlag, 1979–80. An illustrated history, principally technical, with some operational analysis but no mention of Soviet-German cooperation.

Rössler, Eberhard. *Geschichte des deutschen Ubootbaus*. Munich: J. F. Lehmann's Verlag, 1975.

Ruge, Friedrich. *The Soviets as Naval Opponents, 1941–1945*. Annapolis, Md.: Naval Institute Press, 1979.

―――. *Der Seekrieg: The German Navy's Story, 1939–1945*. Translated by Commander M. G. Saunders, R.N. Annapolis, Md.: Naval Institute Press, 1957. The only mention of the Russians is a laconic telling of *Bremen*'s escape via Murmansk.

―――. *In vier Marinen*. Munich: Bernard und Graefe Verlag, 1981.

Salewski, Michael. *Die deutsche Seekriegsleitung, 1935–1945*. Volume 1. *1935–1941* Frankfurt am Main: Bernard und Graefe, 1970.

Sandhofer, Gert. *Das Panzerschiffe "A" und die Vorentwürfe von 1920 bis 1928*. Freiburg: Sonderansdruck, Mar 1968.

Saunders, M. G., ed. *The Soviet Navy*. New York: Praeger, 1958. Contains the essence of the Soviet-German naval relationship, albeit in cryptic form.

Schellenberg, Walter. *The Labyrinth: The Memoirs of Hitler's Secret Service Chief.* New York: Harper and Brothers, 1956.

Schmalenbach, Paul. *German Raiders: A History of Auxiliary Cruisers in German Navy, 1945–1945*. Cambridge: Patrick Stephens, 1979.

Schreiber, Gerhard. *Revisionismus und Weltmachtstreben. Marineführung und deutsche italienische Beziehungen, 1919–1944*. Stuttgart: Deutsche Verlags-Anstalt, 1978.

Scott, Harriet Fast, and William F. Scott. *The Soviet Art of War: Doctrine, Strategy and Tactics*. Boulder, Colo.: Westview Press, 1982.

———. *The Armed Forces of the USSR*. 2d ed. Boulder, Colo.: Westview Press, 1981.

Showell, Jak P. Mallmann. *The German Navy in World War II: A Reference Guide to the Kriegsmarine, 1939–1945*. Annapolis, Md.: Naval Institute Press, 1979.

Speer, Albert. *Infiltration: How Heinrich Himmler Schemed to Build an SS Industrial Empire*. New York: Macmillan, 1981.

Thomas, Charles S. *The German Navy in the Nazi Era*. Annapolis, Md.: Naval Institute Press, 1990.

Tuleja, Thaddeus V. *Twilight of the Sea Gods: The Men, Ships, and Battles of the German Navy in World War II*. New York: W. W. Norton, 1958.

Volker, Karl Heinz. *Dokuments und dokumentarfotos zur Geschichte der deutschen Luftwaffe*. Stuttgart: Deutsche Verlags-Anstalt, 1968.

Von Herwarth, Hans. *Against Two Evils*. New York: Rawson, Wade, 1981. The memoirs of a young German diplomat stationed in the German embassy in Moscow from 1939 to 1941.

Von der Porten, Edward P. *The German Navy in World War II*. New York: Thomas W. Crowell, 1969. An interesting work, also with mention of cooperation with the Soviets.

Walt, Donald Cameron. *How War Came: The Immediate Origins of the Second World War 1938–1939*. New York: Pantheon, 1989.

Wegener, Edward. *The Soviet Naval Offensive*. Annapolis, Md.: Naval Institute Press, 1975.

Weinberg, Gerhard. *Germany and the Soviet Union, 1939–1941*. Lieden: n.p., 1951.

Whaley, Barton. *Covert German Rearmament, 1919–1939: Deception and Misperception*. Frederick, Md.: University Publications of America, 1984.

Wheeler-Bennett, J. W. *The Nemesis of Power: The German Army in 1918–1945*. New York: Viking Press, 1967.

Winton, John. *Ultra at Sea: How Breaking the Nazi Code Affected Allied Naval Strategy during World War II*. New York: William Morrow, 1988.

Withoft, Hans-Jurgen. *Lexikon zur deutschen Marinegeschichte*. Herford: Koehlers Verlag, 1977–78.

Wolfe, Robert. *Captured German and Related Records: A National Archives Conference*. Athens: Ohio University Press, 1974.

Woodward, E. L., Sir. *British Foreign Policy in the Second World War*, volume 1. London: HMSO, 1970.

IV. ARTICLES

Berezhkov, Valentin. "Stalin's Error of Judgement," *International Affairs*, no. 9 (1990): 13–24.

Beznozov, A. V. "The Secret of Basis Nord," *Voyenno-istoricheskiy Zhurnal* (Military History Journal [Moscow]) (July 1990): 115–19.

Bogart, Charles, et al. Question 41/71 (concerning the disposition of surplus heavy guns from World War II navies), *Warships International*, no. 1 (1982): 95–97.

Editorial response, "Cruiser *Petropavlovsk*," *Sudostroyenie* (Shipbuilding) (May 1983): 58–61.

Golovko, M., Captain 2d Rank. "Interview with the Chief of the Editorial Commission of the Soviet Military Encyclopedia: *Morskoy sbornik* (Naval Digest), no. 9 (1988): 88–89.

Gorlov, Sergey. "Soviet-German Military Cooperation, 1920–1933. Documents published for the first time," *International Affairs*, no. 7 (July 1990): 95–113.

Kraskov, V., Captain First Rank, Candidate. "Heavy Cruiser *Kronshtadt*," *Morskoy sbornik*, no. 8 (August 1990): 54–57.

———. "Battleships of the *Sovetskiy Soyuz* Class" *Morskoy sbornik*, no. 5 (May 1990): 59–63.

Krasnovl, V. N. "Stalinism in the Navy and in Shipbuilding," *Sudostroyeniye* (Shipbuilding), no. 7 (1990): 64–69.

Kuznetzov, N. G. "Before the War," *International Affairs*, nos. 5–12 (1965).

Morozova, Irina, and Galina Takhnenko. Documents on Soviet-Finnish Relations in 1939–1940. "The Winter War," *International Affairs*, no. 9 (Sept. 1990): 49–71.

Pankrashkova, Margarita. "Talks between Great Britain, France and the USSR in 1939," *International Affairs*, no. 9 (September 1989): 25–35.

Roshchin, Aleksei. "People's Commissariat for Foreign Affairs before World War II," *International Affairs*, no. 5 (1988): 108–14.

Salewski, Michael. "*Das Kriegstagebuch der deutschen Seekreigsleitung im Zweiten Weltkreig*," *Marine Rundschau*, no. 3 (1967): 137–45.

Simonov, K. M. "Notes on the Biography of G. K. Zhukov," *Voyenno-istoricheskiy zhurnal* (Military-Historical Journal), nos. 6–7 (1987): 48–56.

Speijel, Helm. "Reichswehr und Rote Armee," *Viertelsahrshefte fur Zeitgeschichte* (January 1953): 9–45.

Yakoshevskiy, A. S., Colonel. "Truth and Fiction in the 1939 Soviet-German Nonaggression Pact," *Voyeuno-istoricheskiy zhurnal* (Military History Journal), no. 1 (January 1986). This is a classic defense of the righteousness of Stalin's actions and a classic example of "old thinking."

Index